Future of Business and Finance

The Future of Business and Finance book series features professional works aimed at defining, analyzing, and charting the future trends in these fields. The focus is mainly on strategic directions, technological advances, challenges and solutions which may affect the way we do business tomorrow, including the future of sustainability and governance practices. Mainly written by practitioners, consultants and academic thinkers, the books are intended to spark and inform further discussions and developments.

Khalil Dindarian

Embracing the Black Swan

How Resilient Organizations Survive and Thrive in the face of Geopolitical and Macroeconomic Risks

Springer

Khalil Dindarian
Berlin, Germany

ISSN 2662-2467 ISSN 2662-2475 (electronic)
Future of Business and Finance
ISBN 978-3-031-29343-6 ISBN 978-3-031-29344-3 (eBook)
https://doi.org/10.1007/978-3-031-29344-3

This Springer imprint is published by the registered company Springer Nature Switzerland AG
The registered company address is: Gewerbestrasse 11, 6330 Cham, Switzerland

To all who are walking or are planning to walk the same path as I, I say, go for it! You will never regret the efforts you make, but you will forever rue those you didn't. To anyone who has ever done anything to make our world a more peaceful and resilient place, I say, you are heroes, and the whole world thanks you.

Disclaimer

All views and opinions expressed herein are entirely my own as the author of this work, unless expressly stated to be otherwise, and they in no way represent any of the organisations, enterprises or publishers with which I am affiliated or with which I have any professional connection.

Parts I and II of this book are based on the research carried out by me as part of my PhD thesis, in which selected portions of two parts herein have appeared previously:

'Khalil Dindarian (2018), Exploring Enterprise Resilience through the Theoretical Lens of Complexity: a case study situated in the high value manufacturing sector', University of Manchester. This thesis can be found at the University of Manchester's official repository by following this link:

https://research.manchester.ac.uk/en/studentTheses/exploring-enterprise-resilience-through-the-theoretical-lens-of-c

Preface

Why do we need a new book about Resilience?

The idea of this book originated with the main research problem crystallised from my PhD research study (Dindarian, 2019), 'Exploring Enterprise Resilience through the Theoretical Lens of Complexity', and from my experience of more than 30 years of practice within a high-value engineering company operating in the global business environment.

The original plan was to publish the results of my PhD research in the form of papers in different academic journals, after duly consulting with some friends and colleagues on the matter. In the course of some fascinating discussions that I had with Prof. Dr. Jalid Sehouli[1] and Prof. Dr. Ulrich-Wilhelm Thomale [2], I learned much about the growing importance of Resilience in the medical field. Both Jalid and Ulrich gave me many ideas for further research following on from my PhD, in various knowledge domains such as medicine, politics, economics and engineering. Mike Waters[3], a communication specialist from Ireland, and one of my best friends, one day asked me, 'Why don't you do a book on Resilience? The current situation in the world demands such a book'. As a result, in addition to my original PhD themes, I consider two related topics, Geopolitics and Macroeconomics, both of which are responsible for the changes in the global system structure. Last but certainly not least, my dear wife Azadeh suggested doing a full book on the results of my PhD, rather than a series of academic papers. Thus, the journey of this book began.

Initially, I started writing an academic textbook with a focus on engineering and project management, which I envisaged would have academic relevance for students

[1] Prof. Dr. Jalid Sehouli, Medical Director of the Gynaecology Department, including the Centre of Oncological Surgery, at Berlin's Charité university hospital and author of multiple scientific articles as well as works of fiction.

[2] Prof. Dr. Ulrich-Wilhelm Thomale, Head of Paediatric Neurosurgery at the Department of Neurosurgery at Berlin's Charité university hospital and author of multiple scientific articles.

[3] Founder and Managing Director of *SkillsBar*, a communication training specialist based in Romania.

and lecturers. The different subject areas on which such a book would touch, however, led me to the realisation that it would be of considerable interest to other interest groups as well. The results of the research I carried out as part of my PhD are highly relevant in terms of today's global changes, given the ongoing global Covid epidemics and the Ukraine crisis, both of which have changed almost all areas of our lives, with a particularly strong impact on public health, the energy issue, political decision-making, economic development, social & family life, art & culture, sports & recreation, science, and education, among many other areas of knowledge that all have, in turn, a profound effect on human psychology, belief, nature and resources. As a result, I ended up writing for the worlds of geopolitics, macroeconomics, and other closely related topics such as healthcare, business, and finance, with the primary focus being on Enterprise[4] Resilience.

My contention in this book is that the areas of emergent strategy, resilience, complexity, and emerging risks all need to be opened up, not closed down. Now, more than ever, what is needed is a bridging between them and between their many different tendencies, not their isolation.

This book, aimed at both academics and practitioners, will show how a framework for resilience can be created, one that will help organizations in the twenty-first century not only to survive, but to thrive in the face of unexpected events and developments.

I want you, dear readers—both academics and practitioners, whatever your knowledge area—to join us in the developmental journey of this book, which I hope will also challenge you to revisit your thinking on dealing with adverse events. Hopefully, this book will strengthen you and inspire you in taking the necessary steps to make our world more resilient.

Berlin, Germany
January 2023

Khalil Dindarian

[4]The term 'enterprise' is used for all types of companies, communities, associations and unions of an economic, political or social nature.

Acknowledgments

No words could ever truly convey the enormous debt of appreciation I owe to those who motivated, helped, and encouraged me in the writing of this book, especially Mike Waters, who encouraged me to undertake the project in the first place, along with various other friends and family members.

Indeed, I would like to express my deepest gratitude and thanks to all my friends for their motivation and support. Special thanks are due to Guido Bosch, Dr. Wolfgang Kreischer, Prof. Dr. Jalid Sehouli, and Prof. Dr. Ulrich-Wilhelm Thomale, for their valuable discussion and feedback.

I am most grateful to my all supporters, to those who participated in my in-depth and semi-structured interviews, and to all the participants in my questionnaires, without whose support this work could not have happened. Thank you all for your time and effort from the bottom of my heart!

A debt of sincere gratitude is also due to the publishers of this book, Springer, especially to Executive Editor Dr. Prashanth Mahagaonkar and his team, for all their help, motivation, and guidance and for allowing me the benefit of their vast combined experience.

Last but most certainly not least, special thanks are due to my family, especially my dear, lovely wife for her endless support, encouragement, and motivation throughout this journey. Thank you, Azadeh, for all the discussions and for your valuable feedback, for your patience whenever I was preoccupied, and for always being there for me.

Finally, my darling child, you were, are and always will be my greatest inspiration. This work could never have been completed without your encouragement, kind words and, of course, constant smile. You wished me to dedicate this book to everyone else but you, but for this selflessness, you deserve even more credit and thanks.

Khalil Dindarian
Berlin, January 2023

Introduction

Why do we need to understand the concept of 'Enterprise Resilience'?

Our world is changing more dynamically and faster than ever before, becoming ever more complex in the process. Among the issues currently facing mankind, with serious ramifications for our future, are digitalization and the socio-technical system, climate change and new global competition, namely, geopolitics and macroeconomics. Political upheaval, military conflict, natural disasters and economic recessions have all had massive negative impacts on private lives, governments and organizations.

All of this happens because of the increasing complexity of the global network. How well we can deal, or at least cope, with this complexity is uncertain. One thing that is beyond question, however, is that how we handle all these challenges is critical. The dynamic changes resulting from this high degree of complexity in turn give rise to emergent risks that require an effective emergent strategy. All of this presents new—and monumental—tasks for business and political leaders, economists, the medical profession, virologists, sociologists, technology innovators, engineers, managers and other professional groups.

In 2020, the world was faced with one of the most adverse events in modern human history, the COVID-19 pandemic. It was not the first such event of its kind, but it was arguably the worst. We have had similar issues such as the SARS, Swine Flu and Ebola epidemics, the Lehmann Brothers crash, the 9/11 terrorist attacks in the USA and a plethora of terrorist attacks in Europe, Africa and the Middle East, to name but a few. As a result of geopolitical and macroeconomic changes, we have recently borne witness to the Ukraine conflict, which is drawing the world into further crisis, reminding us of the enormous importance of energy and food distribution in the global world. The ongoing global Covid-19 epidemic and Ukraine crisis have not only cost millions of lives but also have wrought havoc on our social, political, healthcare and economic systems. The new global competition operating under the umbrella of geopolitics and macroeconomics is of paramount importance. All these events were unexpected, so-called interrelated emerging risks, created by man or nature, or a combination of both. Such unexpected events can and do disrupt the global dynamic system and its behaviour. Therefore, a systemic-thinking approach is proposed as a way of seeing the behaviour of the entire system, rather than as just one part of it. It is in this light that the area of Resilience is considered.

The greatest emergent risks in today's troubled world are related to the Covid pandemic and Ukraine crises, with the massive economic fallout from both the pandemic and the West's sanctions on Russia having to be tackled. Organisations need even more support so they can cope with such emerging risks, improve strategic direction and ensure business continuity. Ultimately, only resilient companies will overcome the uncertainty of today's global business environment and survive events like epidemics and political crises, with relatively small losses; some will even benefit from them. It is, therefore, of critical importance to make Resilience a part of our strategic plan and incorporate consideration of the emerging risks in our strategic decision-making process. The first question on which we must focus, therefore, is how we can identify those emerging risks. From there, we need to ask ourselves how we can assess those risks and then embed the findings of our assessment in strategic management and decision-making processes.

Organisations are increasingly seeking to improve their resilience through a more sophisticated approach to the analysis of corporate intelligence. We may refer to this as 'the holistic approach' and address the question of how organisations may adopt a holistic approach to the execution of strategy through a nuanced understanding of 'complexity thinking'. I would argue that a significant knowledge-to-practice gap exists here, despite the existence of a rich landscape of theoretical literature embracing complexity theory, strategy, risk, uncertainty and enterprise risk management.

Today, more than ever, enterprises are facing emergent risks and uncertainties in a fast-changing world where complex environmental changes are constantly taking place. For this very reason, we will make the case for a greater emphasis on resilience within organisations; this is generally understood to be flexibility, adaptability and the ability to self-organise in response to constantly updated information gleaned from that organisation's interaction with the geopolitical and macroeconomic environments.

The current complexity of the global business environment and the high rate of change both create a potentially dangerous level of uncertainty, with a negative impact on business continuity. If an organisation is to stand a realistic chance of survival in the face of unexpected events, it will need to have prepared itself for such events taking into consideration what it knows is happening around it, both locally and globally, and to have made its preparations accordingly. As its environment changes, it must be able to change with it. Traditionally, risk processes and conventional enterprise risk management are designed in a static way, in readiness for foreseen and anticipated events. They cannot, however, be relied upon for dealing with an uncertain environment and for preparing one for unforeseen events and occurrences.

During the course of my PhD studies, a Process, Organisational, Environmental and Technological (POET) Complexity Framework emerged, which can be used to assess people's knowledge of complexity and its application in practice. Practitioners and academics can use this Complexity Framework to help them better understand the impact of risk and uncertainty on an operational level such as in a multi-project environment, thus enabling the formulation of an effective operational emergent strategy. It is an appropriate methodology that recognises the interconnectedness of risks, which can enable practitioners to interrelate emerging risks through robust analytical methods. The POET Framework also offers the ability to assess further aspects of an organisation, such as Enterprise Resilience or Organisational Resilience. This is argued as a bottom-up approach, with decision-making being at micro level.

Furthermore, in proposing an Organisational Resilience Framework for enterprise resilience, this book will outline a number of organisational resilience categories. From this, it is hoped that both academics and practitioners can benefit in terms of an assessment of Organisational Resilience in practice. On top of that, the application of the proposed frameworks can provide responses to unexpected incidents through the sharing of strategic thinking, thereby aligning the top-down and bottom-up approaches, and the sharing of decision-making authority throughout an organisation.

Finally, I want to highlight the fact that the provided Enterprise Resilience Framework (ERF), designed to make sense of Complexity Thinking, lies at the heart of 'holism', a key concept in Enterprise Risk Management (ERM) processes, and can be used to support the executive decision-making process in practice.

The modern business environment, characterised by unprecedented growth in the use of digital technologies, presents new challenges to organisations, particularly in the context of the management of risk and uncertainty. Capturing the necessary intelligence required to properly inform corporate decision-making lies at the heart of an organisation's capabilities for developing and deploying effective strategies.

An effective emergent strategy is characterised by Resilience, which refers to the characteristics of strategic management and their relationship to Resilience. It also concerns environmental changes, such as unexpected events that can have an impact on an organisation and the ways that corporate, business and operations units are adapting their strategy to cope with such changes. In this regard, I believe it would be useful to describe the characteristics of strategic management and the critical factors in strategic decision-making, the relationship between Strategy and Resilience, and finally, the relationship between Strategy and ERM.

Resilience is concerned with Emergence, which is in turn a characteristic of Complexity, an emergent property that concerns a system's ability to deal with high levels of uncertainty. Resilience can, in effect, be described as the ability of a system to adapt to a threat and can ultimately be seen as an emergent and adaptive process.

This book shows the application of what is referred to as Complexity Thinking (a holistic view) to enterprise risk-management processes, thus enabling a greater understanding of the concept of ERM processes and their application in practice. In addition, it offers a way of dealing with emerging risks, and this can change the strategic direction of companies.

There are differences, it can be strongly argued, between conventional ERM and Enterprise Resilience, an understanding of which differences is vital. It is this that provides a methodology for the integration of emergent risks with strategic risk, and for recognising their interconnectedness so that practitioners will be able to interrelate emerging risks through robust analytical methods.

In this light, one of our main objectives is to present an Enterprise Resilience Framework (ERF) suitable for the purposes of establishing Organisational Resilience, for countering those risks that can affect business activities to such an extent that a company suffers considerable damage or even faces an existential threat. The appropriate implementation of an ERF can ensure business continuity, improve company performance, and allow competitive advantage to be maintained, in turn protecting stakeholder interests and the corporate reputation and brand, and maintaining—or even increasing—share value.

Increased attention to business continuity and changes in times of uncertainty has highlighted several questions that have been of concern to both academia and practice: How can an organisation adapt its strategy in the face of changes in order to ensure business continuity? How can Complexity Theory support the concept of a Resilient Organisation? How can an organisation embed Complexity Thinking into its ERM processes, to enhance and strengthen Organisational Resilience? What tools may be used to assess the extent of Complexity that must be addressed, and to help determine how Complexity Thinking may be incorporated into ERM processes?

In this book, we will draw on information from my PhD study, including both the literature that formed the basis of the thesis and the findings of my research. Methods of building Enterprise Resilience through the theoretical lens of complexity will be presented. This will, hopefully, allow us to gain a better insight into the underlying theory and, in the process, explore a range of relevant topics. While considering what has already been done in the field, we will identify some of the information sources other researchers have used and discuss remaining gaps in the body of theoretical knowledge.

As a first step, we will look at Complexity Theory with the purpose of presenting to the reader various aspects of the knowledge area of Complexity, so that he may better understand both its theory and its practical application.

In this new and complex world, it is evident that governments and organizations—both public and private—must learn to anticipate emergent risks and deal with them. The integration of emergent risks with strategic risk as well as the management of ‘black swan’ events has assumed paramount importance. This is the huge challenge now facing senior managers, political leaders, economists, scientific and technical innovators, engineers, the medical profession, and other professional and management groups. The traditional ERM approach of dealing with risks in isolation is no longer valid in itself; the paradigms have now shifted, and a new all-encompassing, emergent strategy must be developed at operational as well as strategic level, that will cover all emerging risks under the umbrella of Complexity, thus creating the new level of protection that we call Resilience. This book, aimed at both academics and practitioners, will show how a framework for Resilience can be created, one that will help organizations in the twenty-first century not only to survive, but also to thrive.

This book is divided into three main parts. The first, from an academic viewpoint, considers the existing disciplines in the scientific field. Given its theoretical nature, it sets out to describe the pedigree of the topics presented. In essence, it offers evidence about how we can embed complexity thinking into our decision-making processes. Both natural and man-made disasters have had a major impact on complex environmental changes. Consequently, corporate, business, and operational units are adapting their strategy to those undesirable changes. The ability to make decisions for this strategy—which decisions are referred to as Effective Emergent Strategies—becomes paramount for business continuity both during and after negative complex environmental changes.

The second part is concerned with practical application of the theory through case studies. On the one hand, a bottom-up research study is presented. The complexity of delivering a portfolio is discussed, particularly how a high-value engineering portfolio design can meet the requirements of external stakeholders. The ability of an organisation to deal with complexity is researched, using this case study as an illustration. Furthermore, this part of the book outlines the application of ERM (enterprise risk management) in practice, with the focus being on (i) Strategic risk management, (ii) Decision-making processes, (iii) Dealing with unexpected changes, and the application of 'Emergent Strategy', and (iv) The selection of a project portfolio as well as the use of the concept of organisational resilience in practice.

The second part goes on to link the academic implications of the book with practical application and examines how the application of organisational resilience, both in general and in the industrial sphere specifically, is addressed. This chapter offers recommendations for the implementation of a conceptual organisational resilience framework in practice, and moreover, it offers ideas for future academic research and study.

In the third and final part, we will examine from a more practical perspective the everyday issues that seem to be never-ending: in essence, geopolitics and macroeconomics, and their attributes with which we are confronted every day, either directly or indirectly, in a positive or negative way. The primary focus is on uncertainty and change in the processes of both geopolitics and macroeconomics. Part three, in essence, takes a closer look at the complexity of both systems and the structural and behavioural changes affecting them. Such changes are the result of the dynamics and volatility of the elements of the two systems, such as political power and decision-making, increases in world population and demographics, the disproportionate use of natural resources (particularly water and food), increasing energy demand, the availability, use and distribution of other resources, and land use for agricultural production and its impact on health. Other factors include the unequal ratio of global agricultural labour force to total population, and disproportionate consumption of food, water, energy and other resources. These are the most important factors within the geopolitical and macroeconomic systems; however, there are further important factors, such as healthcare, education, industrial development, commerce, services, finance and global politics.

References

Dindarian, K. (2019). *Exploring enterprise resilience through the theoretical lens of complexity: a case study situated in the high value-manufacturing sector*. The University of Manchester.

Contents

Abbreviations

ANZUS	Australia, New Zealand, United States Security Treaty
BRICS	Five leading emerging economies: Brazil, Russia, India, China, and South Africa
BSI	British Standards Institute
CAD	Computer Aided Design
CAS	Complex Adaptive System
CCTV	Close Circuit Television
COSO	Committee of Sponsoring Organisations of the Treadway Commission
CPU	Central Processing Unit
DfT	Department for Transportation
DMU	Diesel Multiple Unit
EHS	Environment, Health & Safety
ENIAC	Electronic Numeric Integrator And Computer
EOB	Employee-owned Business
ERF	Enterprise Resilience Framework
ERM	Enterprise Risk Management
EVA	Economic Value Added
GDP	Gross Domestic Product
GNP	Gross National Product
GPS	The Global Positioning System
ICOR	International Consortium for Organisational Resilience
ICT	Information and Communications Technology
LCC	Life Cycle Cost
NATO	The North Atlantic Treaty Organization
NGO	Non-Governmental Organization
OPEC	The Organization of the Petroleum Exporting Countries
PPM	Project Portfolio Management
QFD	Quality Function Deployment
RAMS	Reliability, Accountability, Maintainability & Safety
RKI	Robert Koch Institute
SRA	Strategic Rail Authority
SRM	Strategic Risk Management

STIKO	Standing Committee on Vaccination
UNESCO	The United Nations Educational, Scientific and Cultural Organization
UNHCR	The UN Refugee Agency
UNICEF	The United Nations International Children's Emergency Fund
UNIVAC I	Universal Automatic Computer I
US GAAP	US Generally Accepted Accounting Principles

List of Figures

List of Tables

Part I

Embedding Complexity Thinking in the Decision-making Process

Prologue

1

1.1 The Following Questions Will Be Addressed in this Book

All unforeseen events can have unpredictable consequences for an organisation; such external forces make it volatile and render it subject to constant change due to its interconnectedness with the business environment in which it operates. Without preparation for such events, any help for that company after the event may be too late, and it is here that the limits of conventional silo risk management become clear. There are certain phenomena of which managers need to be aware and to understand to be able to avert such external forces and successfully lead the company out of the crisis.

Organisations need to be better able to foresee their future. For this to happen, they need to understand the notion of Resilience and its processes; the importance of Resilience must be impressed on them, as must an understanding of why it is nevertheless still greatly underestimated. The question of why there are so few truly resilient entities must be considered. The focus of Resilience, therefore, is on the processes that enable an organisation to address crises and adversity and allow it to deal—or at least cope—with such events.

We will consider some of the organizations, bodies and other entities that can be said to be highly resilient and examine how resilience-thinking affects different disciplines and environments, such as politics, economy, organisations, technology and processes. This will, in turn, help us to answer the question of how Resilience is understood to work, and how it is applied in both theory and practice. There will be some discussion of how problems are perceived and addressed in practice and of the relationship between Resilience and other knowledge areas such as Complexity Theory, Strategy and Risk Management from both the top-down and bottom-up perspectives. We will identify the sources of information and data that those other researchers have already used and look at where the concept of Resilience comes from. Moreover, we will show where is there a need for Resilience, and what environments are best suited to the implementation of a Resilience Process. Last

K. Dindarian, *Embracing the Black Swan*, Future of Business and Finance,
https://doi.org/10.1007/978-3-031-29344-3_1

but not least, we will present an overview of the best ways of implementing such a process.

The four knowledge areas of Strategy, Resilience, Complexity and Risk-&-Uncertainty—including Enterprise Risk Management—relate to practical experiences and daily events that organisations face, whether planned or unexpected. We will see how economic, commercial and financial organisations can prepare for unexpected events, protect against the negative aspects of the changes arising from such events, and even profit from them. Strategy and structure, strategy formulation and decision-making processes are all characterised by an appropriate balance between the need for protocols and procedures (sometimes known as the 'reductionist' approach) and 'heuristic' capability. Demands for strict governance, risk management and audit often lead organisations down a route that is dominated by procedure and protocol, which can often stifle innovation and risk-taking behaviour in a way that may ultimately lead to reduced value outcomes. The development of strategy within an organisation ought, therefore, to be holistic rather than reductionist.

Strategic thinking and strategy formulation, along with the process of strategic decision-making as well as, on an operational level, the characteristics of complex projects and organisational resilience, provide a deeper understanding of the relationship between the four abovementioned areas of knowledge. The implementation of an effective emergent strategy requires a mature knowledge-based organisational setting; this is a capability that should be understood and measured. Paradigms from organisational psychology are drawn upon in order to better understand how the body corporate can evolve into a knowledge-based Complex Adaptive System (CAS) which will be responsive to internal and external changes embedded with the capability of building business continuity. It is in this light that organisational resilience is considered.

Resilience can thus be summed up as the ability of an organisation to self-organise as a result of both negative and positive feedback generated by the interaction of that organisation with its macroeconomic environment. Self-organisation is a feature of a complex system, and there is a strong argument for a complexity-theory-based approach to an understanding of resilience in global organisations.

Both the current literature and practical experience provide us important descriptions of the methods available for improving upon the traditional reductionist paradigms prevalent in most corporate risk management processes. This enables practitioners to recognise the interconnectedness of risks and to link emerging risks with each other through sound analytical methods.

There exists a holistic view of decision-making for corporate strategic change, which formulates a framework for assessing corporate resilience that is defined by competitive advantage, business continuity, stakeholders and shareholder values.

On a tactical level, it is pointed out that conflicts and contradictions often emerge from marrying organisational goals with operational-level decision-making. Finally, it is indicated how organisations can apply complexity thinking (the holistic view) to enterprise risk-management processes. The challenges faced by organisations in communicating information, knowledge and developing a culture of risk management are considered.

It is noted in the literature that the difficulties encountered in aligning project portfolios with shifting corporate objectives may cause an organisation to lose market opportunities. Strategy theorist Michael Porter suggests that managers have a tendency to focus their attention on individual components of success such as core competencies or critical resources, although managing [strategic] fit across the entirety of the company's activities enhances both competitive advantage and sustainability. What all of this implies is that the development of strategy within an organisation should be holistic rather than reductionist. The domains of the holistic view are well known, but they have been researched only as a single domain. Additionally, in some cases, the single domains are integrated in combinations of two or more, for example uncertainty and risk management. It has been recognised, however, that the practice processes of the holistic view combined with the areas of Strategy, Resilience, Complexity, Risk-&-Uncertainty, and ERM still have not been discussed at length in the literature to date (Srivannaboon, 2006; Porter, 1996; Brauers, 1986; Dale, 1994; Chapman & Ward, 2004; Ross, 2004; Aaltonen, 2011; Samson et al., 2009; Thompson & Bank, 2010; Thompson & Calkin, 2011; Ward & Chapman, 2003, 2008, 1995; Xu et al., 2009).

The Complexity Theory provides a Complex Adaptive System for an assessment of the holistic view. Furthermore, multiple projects have an important role in aligning strategy with operation. As a basis for our discussion, we will use a high-technology manufacturing portfolio—in reality, part of a multi-project program—based on an experienced practitioner's application of the Complex Adaptive System. Over the last four decades, the decision-making strategy within the railway sector has had to deal with increased demand in terms of project portfolios, especially after privatisation of the British railway network between 1994 and 1997. Over recent decades, the worldwide railway industry has witnessed new opportunities emerging, and this set the strategy for entry into the UK Railway market; as previously mentioned, however, there are conflicts and contradictions that often emerge from marrying organisational goals with operational level decision-making. A need arose for a better understanding of strategic thinking and decision-making processes in order to identify suitable ways of managing this (Aritua et al., 2009).

To begin with, an in-depth literature review is presented so that we might better understand the theoretical landscape of strategic thinking and decision-making processes. It is extended to further relevant topics, including—but not limited to—Strategy, Resilience, Complexity, Risk-&-Uncertainty and ERM. This includes a literature review intended to help our understanding of how the body corporate can evolve into a knowledge-based Complex Adaptive System, embedded with the capability of building sustainable business continuity. Following on from the literature review, we discuss some in-depth interviews with senior managers that will hopefully give a better insight into Strategy and decision-making, with a particular focus on emergent strategy. Next, an in-depth case study is presented, which will aid our understanding of Complexity from the practitioner's point of view. The main focus here is on people's knowledge of complexity and its application in practice.

Indeed, it is interesting to see how individuals deal with complexity when it comes to the delivery of complex portfolios into the global market. This includes professionals who have worked in a range of engineering branches, on major projects across different business divisions, in a variety of countries such as the USA, Germany, India, Spain, Austria and the UK.

The terms and definitions below are designed to make reading easier for the layperson and to help them to follow the topics of this work in specific and specialized areas.

Strategy is based on definitions from arguably the best-known strategy theorist, Alfred D. Chandler, and two other leading strategy theorists, Henry Mintzberg and Michael Porter. Further definitions are used, such as Exploring Corporate Strategy, to extend our understanding of, and further explore, this knowledge domain (i.e. Strategy). Strategy and structure and strategy formulation both fall into the main area of strategy, and strategic thinking and strategic decision-making introduce other important aspects. Strategic thinking and decision-making promise the path to success for an organisation, but they can also lead to a negative outcome if the strategy does not fit the prevailing situation or cannot be implemented as planned. Strategic thinking and decision-making can and do face obstacles, often related to unexpected events, misplaced predictions and excessive trust in statistical guidelines. The existing theoretical perspective of strategy is highlighted so as to offer the theoretical landscape of strategic thinking and decision-making processes. The relevant strategy topics presented are based on existing literature, to enhance understanding and provide a clearer grasp of strategy. These topics are divided into two sections: Strategy-&-Structure and Strategy Formulation, which in turn lead us to the primary focus of this study: strategic thinking and decision-making. Strategy-&-Structure is considered in the light of Chandler and other relevant literature from recent decades, and the discussion of Strategy Formulation centres on the thinking of Mintzberg and Porter (Porter, 1979, 1996; Chandler, 1977; Mintzberg, 1972; Gerry Johnson & Scholes, 2011; Chandler, 1991).

The definition of the knowledge area, Resilience, has been used in various sciences, such as the study of physical, ecological and social systems, in different combinations and contexts. The application of a range of aspects of the definition of Resilience, such as David Chandler's, suited to this research study, has been considered. In addition, the British Standards Institute's (BSI) definition of Organisational Resilience is applied. The scope of the Resilience domain is researched in relation to the areas of complexity, risk-&-uncertainty, crises, governance and business continuity. The Organisational Resilience Framework is developed based both on theoretical knowledge and on information and insights obtained from interviews with experienced practitioners (CRRI, 2013; Chandler, 2014; BSI, 2014).

The knowledge area of Complexity, and Complex Adaptive Systems in particular, is researched based on the definition given by John H. Holland and John. H. Miller, while System Complexity is discussed around the definition given by John Mansfield and recent research studies, and the notion of Complexity Framework is developed from the definition offered by recent research study. The scope of the Complexity domain is researched from the broad knowledge area, Systems, such as Natural and Artificial Systems, Social Systems, Technical Systems, and Socio-Technical Systems. Moreover, the topic of 'Complicated Systems versus Complex Systems' is addressed. Complex Adaptive Systems are also extensively presented. The Application of Complexity Theory is, in practice, considered in terms of project complexity and stakeholder complexity in a multi-project environment. In general, complexity theory is considered to assist in understanding and exploring the theoretical landscape of strategic thinking and decision-making processes; the focus is, therefore, on exploring people's knowledge of complexity and its application in practice. The area of Complexity can, in turn, be divided into four categories: Process Complexity, Organisational Complexity, Environmental Complexity and Technological Complexity. Those categories help in building a Complexity Framework, which is discussed in a later section (Aritua et al., 2009; Dunović et al., 2014; Holland & Miller, 1991; Mansfield, 2010; Bosch-Rekveldt et al., 2010).

The knowledge area of Risk-&-Uncertainty has been broadly defined in the literature. However, it is important to recognize different aspects of Risk-&-Uncertainty, such as the definition from Chris Chapman and those emerging from recent research studies. The knowledge domain, Enterprise Risk Management (ERM), has been defined in different ways in the literature. The definition of ERM for our purposes in this book reflects the generally accepted one used, in practice, in the Enterprise Risk Management COSO[1] Framework. The scope of the ERM domain is described based on various risk processes, risk identification (particularly the top-down and bottom-up approaches) and the linking of identified risks. Lastly, the relationship between ERM and Organisational Resilience is considered (Chapman & Ward, 2004; Ward & Chapman, 1995, 2003; Chapman, 1990; Thomé et al., 2016; COSO and C.o.S.O.o.t.T, 2004).

The following sections present four main knowledge domains: Strategy, Resilience, Complexity and Risk-&-Uncertainty. This extends to several operational topics: portfolio management, program management, project management and risk management.

References

Aaltonen, K. (2011). Project stakeholder analysis as an environmental interpretation process. *International Journal of Project Management, 29*(2), 165–183.

Aritua, B., Smith, N. J., & Bower, D. (2009). Construction client multi-projects–a complex adaptive systems perspective. *International Journal of Project Management, 27*(1), 72–79.

Bosch-Rekveldt, M., et al. (2010). Grasping project complexity in large engineering projects: The TOE (technical, organizational and environmental) framework. *International Journal of Project Management*. In Press, Corrected Proof.

Brauers, W. K. (1986). Essay review article: Risk, uncertainty and risk analysis. *Long Range Planning, 19*(6), 139–143.

[1]The Committee of Sponsoring Organizations of the Treadway Commission (COSO)

BSI. (2014). *Guidance on organizational resilience, in BS 65000:2014* (p. 16). © The British Standards Institution.

Chandler, A. D. (1977). *Strategy and structure: The history of American industrial enterprise*. MIT Press. The visible hand, Harvard University Press, Cambridge, MA. (1980) the growth of the transnational industrial firm in the United States and the United Kingdom: A comparative analysis. Economic History Review, 1962. 33: pp. 396-410.

Chandler, A. D. (1991). The functions of the HQ unit in the multibusiness firm. *Strategic Management Journal, 12*(S2), 31–50.

Chandler, D. (2014). *Resilience: The governance of complexity*. Routledge.

Chapman, C. (1990). Introduction to new series on risk management. *International Journal of Project Management, 8*(1), 3–4.

Chapman, C., & Ward, S. (2004). Why risk efficiency is a key aspect of best practice projects. *International Journal of Project Management, 22*(8), 619–632.

COSO and C.o.S.O.o.t.T. (2004). *Commission, enterprise risk management framework*. American Institute of Certified Public Accountants.

CRRI. (2013). *Definition of community resilience: An Analysis*. Available from: http://www.resilientus.org/publications/carri-special-reports/

Dale, A. (1994). Scientific uncertainty in a world of risk–a review. *Futures, 26*(8), 862–867.

Dunović, I. B., Radujković, M., & Škreb, K. A. (2014). Towards a new model of complexity–the case of large infrastructure projects. *Procedia-Social and Behavioral Sciences, 119*, 730–738.

Gerry Johnson, R. W., & Scholes, K. (2011). *Exploring strategy* (9th ed.). Book.

Holland, J. H., & Miller, J. H. (1991). Artificial adaptive agents in economic theory. *The American Economic Review, 81*(2), 365–370.

Mansfield, J. (2010). *The nature of change or the law of unintended consequences: An introductory text to designing complex systems and managing change*. World Scientific.

Mintzberg, H. (1972). Research on strategy-making. In *Academy of management proceedings*. Academy of Management.

Porter, M. E. (1979). *How competitive forces shape strategy.*

Porter, M. E. (1996, Novemer). *What is strategy?*

Ross, J. G. (2004). Risk and uncertainty in portfolio characterisation. *Journal of Petroleum Science and Engineering, 44*(1–2), 41–53.

Samson, S., Reneke, J. A., & Wiecek, M. M. (2009). A review of different perspectives on uncertainty and risk and an alternative modeling paradigm. *Reliability Engineering & System Safety, 94*(2), 558–567.

Srivannaboon, S. (2006). *Linking project management with business strategy*. Project Management Institute.

Thomé, A. M. T., et al. (2016). Similarities and contrasts of complexity, uncertainty, risks, and resilience in supply chains and temporary multi-organization projects. *International Journal of Project Management, 34*(7), 1328–1346.

Thompson, B. P., & Bank, L. C. (2010). Use of system dynamics as a decision-making tool in building design and operation. *Building and Environment, 45*(4), 1006–1015.

Thompson, M. P., & Calkin, D. E. (2011). Uncertainty and risk in wildland fire management: A review. *Journal of Environmental Management, 92*(8), 1895–1909.

Ward, S. C., & Chapman, C. B. (1995). Risk-management perspective on the project lifecycle. *International Journal of Project Management, 13*(3), 145–149.

Ward, S., & Chapman, C. (2003). Transforming project risk management into project uncertainty management. *International Journal of Project Management, 21*(2), 97–105.

Ward, S., & Chapman, C. (2008). Stakeholders and uncertainty management in projects. *Construction Management and Economics, 26*(6), 563–577.

Xu, Y., et al. (2009). Alternative risk measure for decision-making under uncertainty in water management. *Progress in Natural Science, 19*(1), 115–119.

Strategy

2

It is worth noting from the beginning that the strategy domain is already well developed by such renowned strategy theorists as, among others, Alfred D. Chandler, Henry Mintzberg and Michael Porter and in other relevant literature from recent decades. Nevertheless, the science of strategy deserves some consideration here to enhance our understanding and to provide a clearer grasp of strategic thinking and decision-making processes (Chandler, 1977; Mintzberg, 1972; Porter & Millar, 1985).

In terms of the application of strategy theory in practice, it seems there is no single definition of strategy. Indeed, there are many definitions: some refer to the external environment, such as the number of competitors, the prevailing market conditions and the size of the market, while others are more concerned with the organization's internal environment. Strategy formulation helps us to understand the relationship between the strategic thinking and decision-making processes. Competitive advantage is another concept of strategy formulation we will use in this section to more closely consider how to deal effectively with competitors, including the sources of competitive advantage. In addition, we will describe and evaluate corporate behaviour and link it to strategy.

The logical conclusion is that strategic management is a framework for analysing the environment, integrating enterprise activities, learning and adapting to change. It ensures business continuity, thus creating added value both in the present and looking into the future, for shareholder and stakeholder alike, even in times of complex environmental change.

From this writer's point of view, resilience is a strategic objective, so called because effective emergent strategies are characterized by resilience, and ERM is a property of strategic thinking and decision-making.

Here, dear reader, you will be presented with many interconnections between the various strategy-related topics, and a relationship between developing enterprise resilience as a strategic objective and ERM as a strategic decision-making property will become evident.

K. Dindarian, *Embracing the Black Swan*, Future of Business and Finance,
https://doi.org/10.1007/978-3-031-29344-3_2

2.1 Qualifying Enterprise Resilience as a Strategic Objective

Having a sustainable strategy will enable organizations to create long-term value for their shareholders and stakeholders over the long term. Resilience as a strategic objective is designed to help an organization not only to survive but to prosper, and its connection to strategic planning is emphasized. Traditional governance and bureaucratic organization are not very well designed for overseeing risks that can suddenly arise in unexpected and frequently imperceptible ways; in its efforts to compensate, leadership tries to adjust the weaknesses of existing strategies to the realities of increased exposure to risks. The present uncertain conditions require a resilient strategy that can adjust to vulnerability and change. In this regard, strategic adaptability is about an organization's ability to handle changing circumstances successfully, even if this means moving away from its core business. Organizational resilience is not a protective procedure, but a positive, forward-looking 'strategic enabler' that enables business leaders to go out on a limb with certainty. Companies often experience failure from crises and, as a result, many businesses place resilience at the centre of their organizational strategy (Everson et al., 2012; BSI, 2014; Kerr, 2016; Davies, 2009; Lampel et al., 2014).

When top management is more likely to seek employee input in strategic decision-making and to use employee involvement to achieve tighter coupling between feedback from operations and the setting of a strategic direction for the firm, it becomes strategically advisable to build enterprise resilience into an organization. Enterprise resilience has been described as the ability and capacity to withstand systemic discontinuities and adapt to new risk environments. A resilient organization, we are advised, should align its strategies, operations, management systems, governance structure and decision-support capabilities, for identifying and adapting to changing risks and creating a competitive advantage. The corporate strategy and operating model need to be adapted accordingly, which involves cost-benefit analyses linking cross-functional risk mitigation planning with corporate strategy. Companies need to develop a more integrated approach to risk management, a one that combines business strategy with business resilience and contingency planning (Lampel et al., 2014; Starr et al., 2003).

2.2 Qualifying ERM as a Strategic Decision-Making Property

How we manage risk can be said to fall fully within the brief of strategic management, but while conventional ERM is static, the business environment is dynamic; there is, therefore, no practical connection between strategy and risk management. The integration of the changing risk profile into decision-making at both strategic and operational levels is absent. It has been pointed out by some commentators that the management of strategic risk factors has a significant impact on the realization of strategic objectives. As long as risk management remains separated from strategy, there is much less chance that ERM programmes will help in achieving strategic objectives (Everson et al., 2012; Kinman, 2012).

Strategic risk has been defined as 'the uncertainty and untapped opportunities embedded in strategic intent and how well they are executed' (Armoghan & Sykes, 2012). The response to these uncertainties and opportunities is strategic risk management, which is designed to get value from strategy such as in sales growth and service delivery. Effective risk management, it has been argued, is to understand the organizational appetite for risk—in other words, the amount of risk taken for the delivery of strategic objectives. Risk management can be addressed separately from frontline strategic assessments, decision-making, and monitoring against plans. Strategic risks can and do have an impact on executive decision-making but are, quite often, absent from many risk registers, the board thus having the responsibility for ensuring that strategic risks are included in their strategic discussions. Strategic risks include such factors as completion, customer preferences, technological innovation and regulatory or political impediments. Often, the term 'stakeholder' is used as a strategic claim group. Numerous organizations have faced real-risk events that have seriously affected them in their pursuit of strategic value for the major stakeholders. In this regard, some have argued, strategy and risk management must be closely linked so as to effectively protect shareholder value and the interests of key stakeholders (Armoghan & Sykes, 2012; COSO and C.o.S.O.o.t.T. Commission, 2004; Janisch, 1993; Frigo & Anderson, 2011).

The management of risks is based either on decentralized modules—one risk at a time—or on the management of all risks together within the strategic framework, normally known as ERM in corporations. At macro level, ERM helps the enterprise to retain its access to the capital markets and other resources necessary for implementing its strategy and business plan. At the micro level, ERM takes account of the link between managers and employees at all levels of the enterprise. In this regard, there are benefits to be gained from linking the top-down and bottom-up approaches. The group of people involved in risk identification includes not only senior executives but also the middle-management level. Those participating in risk identification should be able to cover all risk aspects of the company. They need to consider corporate focus, content such as market and market analysis, competition, product quality, aspects of research and development (R&D), procurement matters, internal processes, employee-related issues, legal and tax matters, strategy, and policy issues. It has, furthermore, been proposed that risk management be integrated into strategy development and implementation, since the risk profile of a company is fundamentally shaped by its strategic and structural decisions, and operative risks are widely triggered by these decisions (Nocco & Stulz, 2006; Denk et al., 2008).

As already mentioned, ERM can contribute to value creation and to organizational objectives such as achieving competitive advantage, attaining strategic goals, increased shareholder value and transparency in management (reduction of agency costs), decision-making, and policyholder-as-stakeholder. Moreover, the added value of ERM supports management decision-makers in their efforts to fully exploit their organization's true risk-taking capacity, complement the existing risk profile, and manage the firm's overall strategic objectives. One prerequisite that has been identified for effective risk identification and its subsequent evaluation is a uniform and comprehensive understanding of business goals and strategies. In this way, the risk management system is an integrative component of the entire controlling system and must be designed and operated by the controllers in collaboration with management (Bowen et al., 2006; Hilz-Ward & Everling, 2009).

Some observers, however, have found that companies often have difficulty implementing regulatory requirements, even though they have employed strategic ERM processes and already have flexible organizational structures. Firms with weaker ERM processes may experience even greater difficulty in implementing those requirements. In this regard, it has been argued that the risk management process generates a meaningful and future-oriented risk radar through effective use of ERM, while bearing in mind that the interactions that make up the connected world around us have increased the complexities of managing risk—in particular, the so-called emerging risks, which can change the strategic direction of companies. Furthermore, researchers argue that after the recent global financial crisis, strengthening risk management and governance are major challenges for companies. One lesson learned from the crisis has been the need for combined strategy and risk management. This better prepares companies for identifying and managing risks in a highly uncertain environment. The writers in the field offer a process for strategic risk assessment, together with recommendations for integrating risk management into strategy implementation. ERM, we are told, is directly related to what is called a 'strategy attitude'; for it to add value, it must be embedded in and directly linked to corporate strategy. Another part of this definition relates to ERM's goal of helping an organization to achieve its core objectives. If ERM is to be truly effective, it needs to be part of the strategic planning and execution processes. The management of all risks facing a company is proposed by ERM, which requires the adaptation of risk management to corporate governance and strategy. The approach to risk monitoring remains ad hoc and informal in many organizations; there is seen to be little need for increased approaches to tracking and monitoring critical exposures, notably new strategic ones. Indeed, a strong risk management culture is essential for helping a company achieve effective strategic risk management (Frigo & Anderson, 2011; McShane et al., 2011; Arnold et al., 2011; DiPiazza Jr & van Eijkern, 2009; Bromiley et al., 2015; Beasley & Hancock, 2015; Beasley et al., 2015).

Understanding the dynamics of macro-environmental change at the global business level is a growing concern for both scholars and economic practitioners. Effective decision-making strategy is an organizational capability that allows an organization to cope with changes in its macro-environment, including the social, technological, economic and legal forces that affect it. Consequently, corporate, business and operations units are adapting their strategy to cope with those changes. ERM processes and the benefits of ERM as a strategic instrument can certainly bring competitive advantages. In this regard, executives should consider the various risks when formulating their strategic plans, and the uncertainties created by the complexity of the global business environment and the speed of change must be overcome (Beasley & Hancock, 2015; Beasley et al., 2015; Neill & Rose, 2006; Bourgeois III & Eisenhardt, 1988).

For the reasons mentioned above, the following section presents a further literature review of the area of Strategy, designed to explore the characteristics and parameters of strategic management—the so-called strategic factors—in order to enhance understanding and provide a clearer grasp of strategic thinking and decision-making processes. This will, hopefully, support the overall thesis of this book that organizational resilience is an essential strategic objective for the development of an enterprise risk framework. Organizational Resilience can be measured in terms of competitive advantage, business continuity, stakeholders and shareholder values.

2.3 Strategy and Structure

Alfred Chandler defines strategy as 'the termination of the long-run goals and objectives of an enterprise and the adoption of courses of action and the allocation of resources necessary for carrying out these goals' (Chandler, 1963).

In the 1880s, organizational structures and internal control systems emerged based on new forms of transportation such as rail and on telegraph communication. The organizational form was multidivisional[1]; growth was obtained from diverse products in different markets, and the strategic decisions were made by divisional management. Chandler notes that this continued in labour-intensive industries such as tobacco, grains, metals & steel, fabrics, and glass, from the 1850s until the late nineteenth century, through to the development of transportation and communication systems (Chandler, 1963, 1977, 1991; Pass et al., 2005; Todeva, 2007).

In the late nineteenth century, Chandler points out, change came with the development of the processes of production and distribution, thus opening the way to the technological innovation that led to the Second Industrial Revolution and of the new machines used to mass produce and distribute electric power, which led to capital intensive industry.[2] The world of industry became much more capital intensive, with heavy investment taking place in new areas such as manufacturing technology and machinery, marketing, and management, especially in capital-intensive industries. This investment led to a new structure within companies: the so-called management system. Chandler concluded that capital-intensive industries expanded the market into the new geographical national and international marketing area, on the one hand, and into the related product markets that were based on 'competitive advantages of organisational capabilities developed from exploiting economies of scale', on the other hand (Chandler, 1977). As a result, it became the responsibility of lower and middle managers to coordinate the flow of products through the processes of production and distribution and of top managers to

[1]M-form (multidivisional form) organization is an organizational structure adopted by firms in which the management of that firm is decentralized, with separate groups or divisions responsible for groups of similar products or serving separate markets 28. Collins-Dictionary-of-Economics, t.e. C.P., B. Lowes, L. Davies 2005, *C. Pass, B. Lowes, L. Davies*, fourth, Editor. 2005.

[2]This means the industries with large plants were profitable because '*...the ratio of capital to labour per unit of output was much higher...*' (Chandler, 1991).

coordinate and monitor current operations and plan and allocate resources for future activities (Chandler, 1977, 1991).

By the 1950s, more and more companies were appointing the chairman of their board as their chief executive. It was recognized, through surveys of planning problems, that effective strategy planning requires the involvement of the chief executive and, generally, of top management, who must make decisions based on plans. This should be aligned with their main objectives, which normally involve the maximization of profits. Planning for profit was to be done by a critical analysis of companies' strengths and weaknesses, the threats facing them and the opportunities open to them (Steiner, 1969; Humble, 1969).

In the 1960s, the development of complex technology changed the structure of capital-intensive industries. The new organizational structure was established with two roles in mind: 'autonomous planning' as functional and 'administrative office' as overall responsible executives. These achieved, on the one hand, the creation of added value through the setting of strategies and objectives, which were facilitated by improvements in organizational skills, assets and resource allocation—explained as capital and product-specific technical and management skills—and, on the other, the prevention of losses. According to Chandler, autonomous planning and the administrative office were supposed to monitor operational performance and the correct positioning of resources, which he describes as 'strategic planning' and 'resource allocation' (Chandler, 1977). He concluded that for decision-making, the administrative office needed information about markets, technology and competition in different business areas. In this regard, Chandler argues, 'Of all the enterprise's resources, the product-specific and firm-specific managerial skills are the most essential to maintain the capabilities of its existing businesses and to take the enterprise into new geographical and product markets where such capabilities give it a competitive advantage' (Chandler, 1977, 1991).

Having a strategy is not, however, sufficient in itself; that strategy must be the correct one for making decisions. Should the environment change, intuition and analytical planning will typically be neglected. Strategic planning thus becomes necessary, and a strategic plan is needed because of changes in technological, political, economic and environmental complexity. It is, in effect, a form of continuous radar for scanning the horizon for unknown threats and opportunities (Hoopes, 1963).

The strategic plan can be successful if it is achieved by conscious, deliberate, ongoing examination of goals and alternatives, along with the potential consequences, which is necessary for coping with change. Some see strategy as a corporate goal and plan for reaching certain objectives that will be maintained essentially without regard for competitors' tactics. Management will be able to make decisions based on the integration of all information: know-how, seeing and hearing and leading the corporation to sustainable success. Operational planning could be defined as making sure that production, marketing and financial ability are matched to the expected operational needs, in both the short and long term, thereby increasing the efficiency of operating activities through analysing past performance, budgeting future costs, exercising controls over costs and efficiency, and planning and implementing future investments.

It is pointed out that the strategic plan needs to be combined with operational needs, and strategic planning refers to growth, product, customer, market, plans for product development, resources and finance. In addition, the long-term perspectives of the organization are considered in a strategy plan, but this can also have an impact in the short term, an example being cost optimization for price reduction due to a competitive position. Strategy is much more than simple formulation. It is also very much about decision-making, which is a crucial part of strategy theory. Other important factors are the efficient use of resources, a definition of corporate functions and planning on matters such as organizational development, controls and policy, as well as company leadership and the allocation of responsibilities for results (Steiner, 1969; Hoopes, 1963; Andersen, 1965; Henderson, 1964; Pitz et al., 1969).

In the 1970s, Chandler tells us, organizational structures changed because of continued expansion in the new global market, with executives becoming overwhelmed by decision-making responsibilities. Most multi-business companies, he says, build organization in three levels: at the first level, the operational level, the business is structured from the bottom up; at the second level, the divisional level, the actual business decisions are made, decisions that affect profit, market share and other measures of performance; and the third—corporate—level, where the macro decisions are made, is structured from the top down. It is at the last-mentioned (i.e. top) level that corporate executives set goals and determine the growth direction of the whole organization while at the same time interacting with government and other public organizations. Competitive position and growth are fundamental parameters for strategic planning; for example, it is through business portfolios directly set by business strategy that corporate business success is achieved. Other important information for inclusion in business plans includes competitive data and analysis, along with information on marketing, on the product and production processes, on organizational structure and on financial projections. Good strategic business planning necessarily requires investment (Chandler, 1977, 1991; Hedley, 1977; Cleland & King, 1975; Shanklin, 1979).

By the 1980s, Chandler goes on to point out, conglomerates[3] were being formed, both through mergers with and by acquisitions of diverse unrelated business entities. These unrelated companies had no business synergy per se and therefore did not require resources for manufacturing, marketing, purchasing, transport or research. Strategic decisions demanded different levels of know-how and capability, which effectively meant a new management style suited to the challenges of running much more complex organizations and business structures. Entry to the international marketplace necessitated the consideration of new approaches. Three have been particularly recommended. The first, adaptation, is about the ability of companies to adapt to new local environments. The second, standardization, concerns the export

[3] A company that owns several smaller businesses whose products or services are usually very different from each other 40. Cambridge-dictionary, in *Cambridge dictionary*. 2017.

of standard technologies. Lastly, classification and comparison apply to both standardization and adaptation. Conglomerates have been described as companies that grew almost entirely by making acquisitions in unrelated industries for the purpose of increasing their profit, 'by improving the management and hence the profit. . .(and) the value of their shares through creative, but legal, accounting that recorded on the balance sheets an inflated picture of their assets, revenues, and earnings' (Chandler, 1991; Leontiades, 1987).

It has been further suggested that there are three management styles—strategic control, financial control and strategic planning—and that the performance of a management style, and its alignment with a portfolio, is the key to its success. Some companies do not have the right mix of portfolios and management style, while other companies have a portfolio mismatch. Companies with a strategic control style have the goal of increasing added value through the alignment of strategic and financial controls. Moreover, it is important that a corporate management team has a strong instinct for what is best for the businesses in the group and in choosing where to diversify. In addition, it is recommend that companies focus on business with stable markets, relatively short-term decisions to be made and mature technologies, and that they adopt strategic management planning styles; this way, the success of that business can be ensured by focusing on one or two business areas (Goold et al., 1993).

In any broad business analysis carried out, a comprehensive market analysis assumes an increasing role thanks to the expansion of national business and the growth in foreign trade, particularly the entry into international markets after World War II. New experiences and business issues from foreign countries must be taken into consideration. International business also means operations and investment in different countries, which can ultimately limit importing and exporting and create exposure to competition and to new management challenges. Particular attention is drawn to four aspects of international business.

First, 'international risk management' relates to profit uncertainty and the financial consequences for multinational corporations. The second aspect, 'multinational conflict elements', refers to different national identities among the various stakeholders; because of differences between national interests and the business goals of multinational corporations, some conflicts occur within the international firm, while others involve the firm's relationship with the external environment. The third aspect, 'multiplicity of environment', is about tools, analytical methods and types of information. Further environmental categories related to international business are restricted to the business arena. Not all kinds of business are best suited to private enterprise (a good example would be natural resource exploitation), and among the environmental variables are cultural differences (such as with customers and suppliers), employee behaviour and communication problems, including different languages, customs and values. It is, therefore, advisable that a cultural analysis be included in the market strategy and business plan. The fourth and final aspect is 'international business and development', which concerns the need to identify, analyse and justify the contribution that a proposed international business can make (Robock & Simmonds, 1966).

Mintzberg concludes that Chandler's theory, based on the history of strategy and structure, involves a cycle of development in four stages:

1. *Acquisition of resources* (people, machines, plant and so on) through takeover and through consolidation of smaller enterprises, thus building up marketing and distribution departments (vertical integration);
2. *Improved efficiency of executives* by using the newly acquired resources and by the creation of new organizational functions (such as sales and production) for the coordination of the combined resources within the systems and processes;
3. A *period of growth through entry into new markets* and the extension or diversification of business within existing markets;
4. A *new organizational structure* (divisional form) within each division, which is managed by its own business unit, with a consolidated reporting system from each unit to the financial controller in the organizational headquarters (Chandler, 1977; Ahlstrand et al., 2001).

2.4 Strategy Formulation

This section presents an overview of strategy formulation, primarily based on the thoughts of leading strategy theorist, Henry Mintzberg, and related literature over the last few decades.

Henry Mintzberg originally defined strategy as '...a pattern in a stream of decisions' (Mintzberg, 1972) and then went on to explain that the definition for operationalizing the concept of strategy extended into strategy as a pattern in streams of actions and pointed out that '.....strategic management cannot afford to rely on a single definition of strategy...' (Mintzberg, 1972; Ahlstrand et al., 2001; Mintzberg, 1987).

The definition of strategy is highlighted in a timeline from the perspectives of both looking ahead ('strategy as plan') and looking at the past ('strategy as pattern') with two independent strategies, as shown in Table 2.1: one intended as a plan and the other realized as a pattern. Strategy is, in effect, consistent in behaviour, whether intended or not. Intentions that are fully realized can be called deliberate strategy, while those that are not realized at all can be called unrealized strategy (Ahlstrand et al., 2001; Mintzberg, 1987).

Mintzberg defines non-deliberate strategy, which has already been realized, as emergent strategy, pointing out that both deliberate and emergent strategies may be

Table 2.1 Deliberate, unrealised and emergent strategy

Concept	Case	Strategy
Strategy as plan (intended)	Intentions are fully realized	Deliberate strategy
	Intentions are not realized	Unrealized strategy
Strategy as pattern (realized)	Pattern is realized	Emergent strategy
	Not expressly intended	

conceived as two ends of a continuum where real-world strategies actually lie, and adds that both strategy concepts can be effective: deliberate strategy works with prediction, while emergent strategy '...needs to react to unexpected events' (Ahlstrand et al., 2001). Realized strategy is described as 'pattern in actions' (Ahlstrand et al., 2001), which means the strategy is perfectly deliberated. Three conditions are suggested for successful delivery of the deliberate strategy concept:

- There must have existed a precise intention in the organization;
- That organization is characterized by collective action;
- Collective intentions must have been realized exactly as intended.

In the absence of intention, a strategy with consistency of action over time is perfectly emergent, and '...some patterns come rather close, as when an environment directly imposes a pattern of action on an organisation...' (Ahlstrand et al., 2001; Mintzberg, 1987; Mintzberg & Waters, 1985).

Real-world strategy runs in both directions, namely, deliberate and emergent, rather than being a perfect form of either. This is conditioned by:

- Leadership intentions: precise, explicit and shared
- Central control over organizational actions: firm and pervasive
- Environment: benign, controllable and predictable

The combination of deliberate strategy and emergent strategy is defined as a 'concept of configuration'. Deliberate strategy by itself eliminates learning after the strategy is formulated, in contrast to the emergent strategy, which promotes learning (Mintzberg, 1972; Mintzberg & Waters, 1985).

Mintzberg presents three further kinds of strategy:

- *Strategy as a position*: this refers to the external environment, such as the number of competitors in a given market, the size and nature of the market, and so forth;
- *Strategy as a perspective* is an organization's own basic way of doing things (Ahlstrand et al., 2001) and applies to its internal environment;
- *Strategy as a ploy*: this term may be used to describe 'a specific manoeuvre intended to outwit an opponent or competitor' (Ahlstrand et al., 2001).

The most effective strategy is a mixture of both strategy as plan and strategy as pattern, since the practical reality is that it is not prudent for strategic management to rely on a single definition of strategy, according to Mintzberg, who then goes on to provide us with the 'five Ps' concept, as shown in Table 2.2 (Mintzberg, 1987).

Using his 1972 strategy definition, Mintzberg has introduced the ten schools for 'strategy formation', with the question: 'How generic should a strategy be and how controlled the process to create it?' This is given in Table 2.3 (Ahlstrand et al., 2001).

In summary, Mintzberg provides ten schools of thought for strategy formulation, from among which the strategist can choose his/her own ideas as appropriate. The overall conclusion is that deliberate strategies are rational, especially in mass

Table 2.2 Strategy definition, based on the concept of the 'five Ps for strategy'

Concept	Definition
Strategy as plan	Planning for the future
Strategy as pattern	Consistent behaviour over time
Strategy as position	Locating a particular product in a particular market
Strategy as perspective	An organization's fundamental way of doing things
Strategy as a ploy	A specific manoeuvre intended to outwit an opponent or a competitor

Table 2.3 The ten schools of strategy formulation

School	Strategy formation as a...
Design	Process conception: Decision based on result of analytical calculation
Planning	Formal process: Decision by CEO based on design process
Positioning	Analytical process: Decision by CEO based on whole process
Entrepreneurial	Visionary process: Decision by a single leader
Cognitive	Mental process: Decision based on input from environment
Learning	Emergent process: Decision based on events behaviour
Power	Process of negotiation: Decision based on organizational behaviour
Cultural	Process of social interaction: Decision based on beliefs
Environmental	Reactive process: Decision-based environmental behaviour
Configuration	Process of transformation: Decision based on plans or patterns, on positions or perspective, or on ploys

production industry, while emergent strategy is adaptive, as in dynamic high-technology industries. Indeed, this author strongly recommends reading the above-mentioned book by Mintzberg in order to gain a deeper insight into the ten schools of strategy formation (Ahlstrand et al., 2001).

Another leading strategy theorist is Michael Porter, in whose view the essential purpose of strategy formulation is coping with competition, and he relates this to the market structure and environment in which industries operate. In 1985, Porter produced his work, Competitive Advantage, in which he expresses his desire to 'build a bridge between strategy and implementation' (Porter & Advantage, 1985) Competitive advantage, he tells us, provides the architecture for describing and assessing strategy, and this is closely linked to company behaviour (Chandler, 1977; Porter & Advantage, 1985; Porter, 1979, 1980, 1990, 1996; Porter & Van der Linde, 1995; Belton, 2017).

Porter sees competition as being at the core of the success or failure of businesses, and he describes competitive strategy as 'industry attractiveness [long-term profitability] and competitive position within an industry' (Porter, 1980). Competitive strategy, therefore, is about differentiation and embarking on a different set of activities designed to deliver a unique mix of values. Porter goes on to present an analytical framework for understanding industries and competitors and formulating a competitive strategy, which describes the five competitive forces that determine the attractiveness of an industry and their underlying causes, as well as how these forces change over time and can be influenced through strategy.

Below are the five competitive forces that determine industry profitability (Porter):

- *Threat of new entrants*: these refer to the present barriers and the reaction from existing competitors that entrants can expect. Six important barriers are defined, namely, (i) economy of scale, (ii) product differentiation, (iii) capital requirements, (iv) cost advantages independent of size, (v) access to distribution channels and (vi) government policy.
- *Threat of substitute products or services*: product replacements in the market can limit entry to the market.
- *Bargaining power of buyers*: customer expectations regarding lower prices and better quality are a very important factor.
- *Bargaining power of suppliers and buyers*: price increases by suppliers, who can also reduce the quality of products and services, can have a significant impact.
- *Rivalry among existing firms*: rivalry between competitors, the slow growth of industry and a lack of products and services are all factors that can affect costs, resulting in higher fixed costs, overcapacities and price cutting, and high exit barriers (Porter & Millar, 1985; Porter & Advantage, 1985; Porter, 1980; Belton, 2017; Gumbus & Lussier, 2006).

Summary of Strategy Definition and Strategy Formulation
Strategy is defined by dictionaries in general terms. Organizational strategy, on the other hand, has been the subject of lively scholarly discussion over the past five decades by several leading strategy theorists (Chandler, 1963; Porter, 1991; Mintzberg, 1994; Whittington, 2001; Gerry Johnson & Scholes, 2011; Oxford-Dictionary, 2017).

Different scholars have defined strategy in different ways. Alfred Chandler claims that strategy is about organizational goals and objectives as well as the allocation of resources. Mintzberg claims that strategy does not always go according to conscious decisions and logical plans. Porter focuses on deliberate choices, differences and competition. Gerry Johnson, in Exploring Strategy, has discussed the definition in three parts: long term because strategy can be measured over years; direction according to long-term objectives, e.g. maximizing profits; and organization, which involves complex internal and external relationships (Chandler, 1977; Mintzberg, 1972; Porter, 1979; Gerry Johnson & Scholes, 2011).

Strategy is understood as the goals and objectives of a business, including the plans, policies and standards of conduct and the courses of action, allocation of resources, authorizations, and tasks that are pursued for at least one cycle in planning for the attainment of such goals. The value of a strategy is that it can be articulated and communicated in understandable terms; it can be analysed, tested and evaluated for rejection, modification or acceptance, all before the competition takes place, before resources are committed and risks incurred and before adverse results are realized. These many and varied definitions all highlight one or more aspects of strategy, and the relationship between vision, mission and value statements is an uncertain one. All three are general by nature and unrelated to one another. The traditional formulation of the 'think-first deliberate strategy' has long since been ineffective in terms of today's more complex and less certain context. The definition of strategy remains somewhat loose and needs more focused interpretation. Organizational strategy has been controversially discussed within academia over the past five decades (Mintzberg & Waters, 1985; Whittington, 2001; Salveson, 1974; Liyanage, 2010).

It is safe to conclude that top management is involved in strategic management for the maximization of profit, based on the SWOT (strengths, weaknesses, opportunities and threats) analysis of a variety of factors, both within and outside the company. Those threats and opportunities, however, are uncertain and unpredictable because of environmental changes, which are often complex and can reduce the usefulness of analytical planning and intuition, thus rendering ineffective the traditional strategy formulation—'think-first deliberate strategy'—when used in a complex and unstable context (Humble, 1969; Mintzberg & Waters, 1985; Porter & Van der Linde, 1995; Whittington, 2001; Liyanage, 2010; Hoopes, 1962).

The strategic plan can certainly be successful if it involves conscious, deliberate, continued, verbal examination of goals, alternatives and possible consequences, which is necessary for coping with change. Strategic thinking and decision-making processes lead us to explore and gain a better understanding of the interconnections between strategy, resilience and ERM (Henderson, 1964; Hoopes, 1962; Dindarian, 2019).

2.5 Strategic Decision-Making Levels

From the literature review, it can be concluded that it is not only the characteristics of strategic management and the parameters created by various aspects of strategic planning that determine strategic thinking and decision-making. It has become evident that the actual level of decision-making is also a critical factor. These levels, it is important to note, are applied to the clusters of proposed important factors in strategic thinking and decision-making summarized in Table 2.4. Based on the literature and for the purposes of this research study, they are modified to correspond with the broad categories of strategic management, as follows:

Level 1: all employees at this level are grouped as operational, and the business is structured from the bottom up.

Level 2: at the business level, the actual business decisions—namely, decisions that affect profit, market share and other measures of performance—are made.

Level 3: this level, structured from the top down, is considered as corporate level, where the macro decisions are made. Corporate executives set goals and are responsible for overall corporate performance while at the same time interacting with government and other public organizations.

Table 2.4 Important factors in strategic thinking and decision-making

Category	Corporate level	Business level	Operational level
Resources	Corporate resources	Business resources	Operational resources
Organization	Vertical organization	Horizontal organization	Operational organization
Processes	Policy, control and reporting systems	Implementation and execution of top-down approach	Execution of business level and top-down level
Leadership	Corporate executives set goals and are responsible for overall performance of the corporate body while at the same time interacting with government and other public organizations.		
Finance	Overall performance of the corporation	Business performance	Operational performance
Environment	Overall corporate environment	Business environment	Operational environment
Technology	Overall corporate portfolio	Business portfolio	Operational portfolio

It is important to note that the characteristics of strategic thinking and the levels of decision-making are recognized from the study of the available literature (Dindarian, 2019).

Although, according to the contingency theory, an organization performs in a stable environment, environmental change requires an organizational structure with greater connectedness among employees. The environmental changes resulting from the recent crisis have required organizations to be able to change from centralized decision-making structures to more decentralized ones, with corresponding new procedures and processes, and new ways of cooperation needing to be developed.

The study of strategy formulation helps us to understand the application of strategy theory in practice. It seems there is no single definition of strategy, which is discussed in detail in the literature review. Indeed, there are many definitions of strategy: some refer to the external environment, such as the number of competitors, the product/service, the market and the size of that market, whereas others are more about the organization's internal environment. Strategy formulation helps us to understand the relationship between the strategic thinking and decision-making processes. Competitive advantage is another concept of strategy formulation in which we learn how to deal effectively with competitors. Furthermore, by studying competitive advantage, we can better describe and evaluate corporate behaviour and link it to strategy. Thus, we get a more solid understanding of the sources of competitive advantage.

Effective emergent strategic management is a framework for analysing the environment, integrating enterprise activities, learning and adapting to change. It ensures business continuity, thus creating added value both in the present and into the future, for shareholder and stakeholder alike, even in times of complex environmental change.

The conclusion is that resilience is a strategic objective, whereas ERM is a property of strategic thinking and decision-making.

References

Ahlstrand, B., Lampel, J., & Mintzberg, H. (2001). *Strategy safari: A guided tour through the wilds of strategic mangament*. Simon and Schuster.

Andersen, T. A. (1965). Coordinating strategic & operational planning. *Business Horizons, 8*(2), 49–55.

Armoghan, M., & Sykes, R. (2012). *Sharpening strategic risk management* (Vol. 1, p. 1). PWC.

Arnold, V., et al. (2011). The role of strategic enterprise risk management and organizational flexibility in easing new regulatory compliance. *International Journal of Accounting Information Systems, 12*(3), 171–188.

Beasley, M., Branson, B., & Pagach, D. (2015). An analysis of the maturity and strategic impact of investments in ERM. *Journal of Accounting and Public Policy, 34*(3), 219–243.

Beasley, M. B., & Hancock, B. (2015). *Report on the current state of enterprise risk oversight: Update on trends and opportunities* (p. 12). Research conducted by the ERM Initiative at North Carolina State University on behalf of the American Institute of CPAs Business, Industry & Government Team.

Belton, P. (2017). *Competitive strategy: Creating and sustaining superior performance*. CRC Press.

Bourgeois, L. J., III, & Eisenhardt, K. M. (1988). Strategic decision processes in high velocity environments: Four cases in the microcomputer industry. *Management Science, 34*(7), 816–835.

Bowen, J., et al., (2006). Enterprise risk management specialty guide.

Bromiley, P., et al. (2015). Enterprise risk management: Review, critique, and research directions. *Long Range Planning, 48*(4), 265–276.

BSI. (2014). *Guidance on organizational resilience, in BS 65000* (Vol. 2014, p. 16). © The British Standards Institution.

Cambridge-dictionary, in Cambridge dictionary. (2017). https://dictionary.cambridge.org/dictionary/

Chandler, A. D. (1963). *Stretegy and structure* (p. 13).

Chandler, A. D. (1977). *Strategy and structure: The history of American industrial enterprise*. MIT Press. the visible hand, Harvard University Press. (1980) The growth of the transnational industrial firm in the United States and the United Kingdom: A comparative analysis. Economic History Review, 1962. 33: pp. 396–410.

Chandler, A. D. (1991). The functions of the HQ unit in the multibusiness firm. *Strategic Management Journal, 12*(S2), 31–50.

Cleland, D. I., & King, W. R. (1975). Competitive business intelligence systems. *Business Horizons, 18*(6), 19–28.

COSO and C.o.S.O.o.t.T. Commission. (2004). *Enterprise risk management framework*. American Institute of Certified Public Accountants.

Davies, W. (2009). *Reinventing the firm*. Demos.

Denk, R., Merkelt-Exner, K., & Ruthner, R. (2008). *Corporate risk management, 124*. Wien.

Dindarian, K. (2019). *Exploring enterprise resilience through the theoretical lens of complexity: A case study situated in the high value-manufacturing sector*. The University of Manchester.

DiPiazza, S. A., Jr., & van Eijkern, S. (2009). *Dear reader*. PWC.

Everson, M., et al. (2012). *Resilience: Winning with risk* (Vol. 1, p. 1). PWC.

Frigo, M. L., & Anderson, R. J. (2011). Strategic risk management: A foundation for improving enterprise risk management and governance. *Journal of Corporate Accounting & Finance, 22*(3), 81–88.

Gerry Johnson, R. W., & Scholes, K. (2011). *Exploring strategy. Book* (9th ed.).
Goold, M., Campbell, A., & Luchs, K. (1993). Strategies and styles revisited: 'Strategic control'—Is it tenable? *Long Range Planning, 26*(6), 54–61.
Gumbus, A., & Lussier, R. N. (2006). Entrepreneurs use a balanced scorecard to translate strategy into performance measures. *Journal of Small Business Management, 44*(3), 407–425.
Hedley, B. (1977). Strategy and the "business portfolio". *Long Range Planning, 10*(1), 9–15.
Henderson, B. D. (1964). Strategy planning. *Business Horizons, 7*(4), 21–24.
Hilz-Ward, R., & Everling, O. (2009). *Risk performance management.* GWV.
Hoopes, T. (1962). The corporate planner (New edition). *Business Horizons, 5*(4), 59–68.
Hoopes, T. (1963). The corporate planner (New edition). *Business Horizons, 5*(4), 59–68.
Humble, J. W. (1969). Corporate planning and management by objectives. *Long Range Planning, 1*(4), 36–43.
Janisch, M. (1993). *Das strategische Anspruchsgruppenmanagement.* Bern ua.
Kerr, H. (2016). Organizational resilience. *Quality, 55*(7), 40.
Kinman, B. (2012). *Resilience: Winning with risk* (Vol. 1, p. 1). PWC.
Lampel, J., Bhalla, A., & Jha, P. P. (2014). Does governance confer organisational resilience? Evidence from UK employee owned businesses. *European Management Journal, 32*(1), 66–72.
Leontiades, J. C. (1987). *Multinational corporate strategy: Planning for world markets.* Lexington Books.
Liyanage, U. (2010). Strategy and complexity. Sri Lankan. *Journal of Management,* 15.
McShane, M. K., Nair, A., & Rustambekov, E. (2011). Does enterprise risk management increase firm value? *Journal of Accounting, Auditing & Finance, 26*(4), 641–658.
Mintzberg, H. (1972). Research on strategy-making. In *Academy of management proceedings* (Vol. 1972, p. 90). Academy of Management.
Mintzberg, H. (1987). The strategy concept I: Five Ps for strategy. *California Management Review, 30*(1), 11–24.
Mintzberg, H. (1994). Rethinking strategic planning part II: New roles for planners. *Long Range Planning, 27*(3), 22–30.
Mintzberg, H., & Waters, J. A. (1985). Of strategies, deliberate and emergent. *Strategic Management Journal, 6*(3), 257–272.
Neill, S., & Rose, G. M. (2006). The effect of strategic complexity on marketing strategy and organizational performance. *Journal of Business Research, 59*(1), 1–10.
Nocco, B. W., & Stulz, R. M. (2006). Enterprise risk management: Theory and practice. *Journal of Applied Corporate Finance, 18*(4), 8–20.
Oxford-Dictionary. (2017). https://public.oed.com/new-oed-website/#
Pass, C., Lowes, B., & Davies, L. (2005). *Collins-dictionary-of-economics* (Vol. 2005).
Pitz, G. F., Reinhold, H., & Scott Geller, E. (1969). Strategies of information seeking in deferred decision making. *Organizational Behavior and Human Performance, 4*(1), 1–19.
Porter, M. E. (1979). *How competitive forces shape strategy.*
Porter, M. E. (1980). Industry structure and competitive strategy: Keys to profitability. *Financial Analysts Journal, 36*(4), 30–41.
Porter, M. E. (1990). The competitive advantage of nations. *Harvard Business Review, 68*(2), 73–93.
Porter, M. E. (1991). A conversation with Michael Porter: International competitive strategy from a European perspective. *European Management Journal, 9*(4), 355–360.
Porter, M. E. (1996, November). *What is strategy?*
Porter, M. E., & Advantage, C. (1985). *Creating and sustaining superior performance.* Free Press.
Porter, M. E., & Millar, V. E. (1985). *How information gives you competitive advantage.* Harvard Business Review, Reprint Service Watertown.
Porter, M. E., & Van der Linde, C. (1995). Toward a new conception of the environment-competitiveness relationship. *The Journal of Economic Perspectives, 9*(4), 97–118.
Robock, S. H., & Simmonds, K. (1966). What's new in international business? *Business Horizons, 9*(4), 41–48.

Salveson, M. E. (1974). The management of strategy. *Long Range Planning, 7*(1), 19–26.
Shanklin, W. L. (1979). Strategic business planning: Yesterday, today, and tomorrow. *Business Horizons, 22*(5), 7–14.
Starr, R., Newfrock, J., & Delurey, M. (2003). Enterprise resilience: Managing risk in the networked economy. *Strategy and Business, 30*, 70–79.
Steiner, G. A. (1969). Book Review: Top Management Planning. *Academy of Management Journal, 12*(1), 131–132.
Todeva, E. (2007). *Multi-divisional form.*
Whittington, R. (2001). *What is strategy-and does it matter?* Cengage Learning EMEA.

Resilience

3

In this chapter, we will explore various aspects of Resilience more closely, so that we can better understand it both in theory and in practical application.

For more than five decades, the area of Resilience has been used in different sciences, with forty definitions in different areas being given, such as physical systems, ecological systems, social systems, and a host of others in different combinations and contexts. Resilience has been variously classified as adaptation -v- resistance, as trajectory ('resilience' implies the regaining of functionality after a crisis), as predictability, as an emergent property, and as a process of responding to adversity. A further view of 'resilience' is as a necessary and dynamic trait of the community (CRRI, 2013).

There still, unfortunately, persists a school of thought that building resilience into a company can be a very costly process and therefore not worth the effort or expense. Today, a more pertinent question might be, can a business or organization afford to not become resilient? In response to such concerns, perhaps it should be borne in mind that organizations that are structurally flexible are better able to adjust when faced with unforeseen circumstances, such as a rapid fall in demand, by reallocating resources. Improved resilience is the accumulation of slack resources; these slack resources can be used instead to meet urgent needs when adverse contingencies arise unexpectedly (Lampel et al., 2014).

Resilience has been defined in post-classical framing as an emergent and adaptive procedure of subject-object interrelations. In this formulation, there is no collocation of subject and object, such as human-and-nature or culture-and-conditions; rather, the subject and object are the results of complex adaptive procedures, where subject is a governing actor while object is understood as complex. Complexity theory produces order, and order[1] and governance of complex life are emergent, which

[1] According to the dictionary, order means 'the arrangement or disposition of people or things in relation to each other according to a particular sequence, pattern, or method', Oxford-Dictionary, 2017.

K. Dindarian, *Embracing the Black Swan*, Future of Business and Finance,
https://doi.org/10.1007/978-3-031-29344-3_3

enables us to think and to govern differently. Complexity, therefore, cannot be conceived in terms of anarchy or hierarchy.

Resilience in engineering is characterized by securing and protecting physical and performance functionality against adverse and unexpected events. Generally, production and manufacturing are very closely related to engineering, and to all intents and purposes these fall under the umbrella of engineering. It should be noted, however, that they possess different elements and characteristics in terms of resilience. Technological knowledge and know-how are important both for the development of new products and the expansion and improvement of existing products. The question is, how are these utilized in the event of unexpected events, and how well prepared is the organization?

Engineering processes apply right across the spectrum, from design to commissioning and delivery. How flexible are such processes, and what possibilities do they have to organize themselves effectively for coping with unexpected change? A technical risk management system can answer the question of how these processes ensure the physical and functional properties of the product and solutions. They are concerned, after all, with the most important parts and elements. The focus on resilience is to consider emergent risks as a whole and to prevent the spreading of local risks through the system to other elements and components. The protection of the whole system, and the behaviour and functionality of that system, is extremely important.

In the 1980s, the engineering community described resilience as the ability to absorb and to recover from a hazardous event. Resilience engineering is seen by some as being concerned with building systems that can anticipate and circumvent accidents, survive disruptions through recovery, and grow through adaptation. Resilience is about the ability of a system to react to and recover from disturbances with minimal effects. Various commentators take the view that resilience is about 'bouncing back' from a disaster or crisis and about the ability of a system to adjust its functioning in order to be able to sustain operations even after a major mishap or where there is continuous stress (Chandler, 2014; Madni & Jackson, 2009; Tusaie & Dyer, 2004; Woods et al., 2006).

BSI defines resilience as the 'ability of an organisation to anticipate, prepare for, and respond and adapt to incremental change and sudden disruptions, in order to survive and prosper' (BSI, 2014). It sees the value of organizational resilience, in creating the necessary conditions for competitive 'posture', profitability and sustainability, as forming the frontispiece to a standard that emphasizes the connection of resilience to strategic planning. Essentially, BSI believes, resilience is a strategic objective that will help an organization to survive and prosper. It is about dealing with disruption, uncertainty and change with clear intent, coherence and appropriate resourcing. A highly resilient organization is also 'more adaptive, competitive, agile and robust' (BSI, 2014).

3.1 Resilience, Complexity, Uncertainty and Risk

Interest in the unified concept of resilience, complexity, uncertainty and risk is growing among both academics and practitioners. Complexity is linked to the perception of uncertainty, which in turn is related to the perception of risks and mitigation strategies (Thomé et al., 2016).

The density of global networks of people, organizations and countries has the effect of giving rise to adverse events. High-risk occurrences can damage vital infrastructure, which then triggers a domino effect on events at regional and even global levels. With conventional risk management, disruptive events cannot be mastered. For this reason, academics, managers, policymakers and politicians have shifted their attention to resilience and a system's ability to absorb—and recover from—shocks, while transforming its structures and means of functioning in the face of long-term stresses, changes and uncertainties. This requires a dynamic comprehension of risk management, so as to be able to identify where these dangers are ideal and managed, for fortifying the system parts that can deal with such risks and for seeing how the interrelation of these parts influences system behaviour (Van Der Vegt et al., 2015).

Traditional risk management approaches tend to focus on identifying risks and reducing vulnerabilities to external disruptions. Resilience, on the other hand, implies a focus on capabilities and capacities for creating or retaining resources in a way that enables systems to successfully cope with and learn from the unexpected. The notion of resilience, therefore, has the positive implication of adaptability and fortification, while the term 'defencelessness' can indicate a lack of involvement—or even total uncertainty—that is not useful for deployment activities. Re-situating from 'vulnerability' to 'resilience' also better catches the coveted result of readiness for managing unexpected troublesome occasions (Van Der Vegt et al., 2015; Sutcliffe & Vogus, 2003).

Different indicators of resilience have been offered. Risk assessments in a complex setting with vulnerabilities ought to investigate flexibility as a procedure and examine research activity, to enhance comprehension and learning among stakeholders. The traditional risk analysis has been extended because of growing complexity and uncertainty, so that any exploration of resilience is in addition to traditional risk analysis. Prevention-based and resilience-focused management strategies should be considered when we have uncertainty-induced risk issues, perhaps with some reflective discussion in an environment of uncertainty-induced risk (Johnsen & Veen, 2013; Renn, 2006).

Changes in the world are forcing executives to undertake ever-increasing risk in an attempt to create value for shareholders and for the societies among whom their organizations work, and risk management is seen as falling squarely within the brief of strategic management. The present uncertain conditions require a resilience-focused strategy that can adjust to vulnerability and change. Fast changes support a substantial number of worldwide advancements that are obliging organizations to develop solid capacities for hazard flexibility, keeping in mind that they may be falling behind their competitors and could, in the long run, come up short. Having a sustainable strategy will enable organizations to create value for shareholders and stakeholders alike over the long term. Risk assessment and risk analysis by themselves are a step in the right direction towards ensuring survival, but only in the short term. For this reason, risk resilience goes farther than conventional risk management, which means that an organization must be able to recognize changes and to adapt to these rapidly and effectively, together with the resulting risk. This in turn requires the rapid acquisition and analysis of vast quantities of information and the resulting generation of knowledge, based on the recognition patterns. It means having a versatile organization where local units have the autonomy to respond to changing circumstances, with strong risk governance procedures in place at the board and executive level. One thing is becoming increasingly clear: organizations that are risk-resilient will prosper and thrive. The cautious ones will die over time. The careless ones will die quickly (Everson et al., 2012).

3.2 Resilience and Business Continuity

Resilience describes the processes of business continuity. The notion of a stable organization is associated with the term 'resilience' in the sense that organizations quickly return to the point of equilibrium in the face of disturbances. The literature distinguishes between two views of resilience: in engineering, this means efficiency, control, fail-safe design and optimal performance. In this case, contingency planning is an important process within the system as it recovers and returns to its pre-trauma state. Resilience in biological and ecological systems, on the other hand, refers to a system's ability to deal with high levels of uncertainty. Whether in the engineering or ecological sciences, resilience is a characteristic of a whole system, not an individual part of that system (Adger, 2000).

However, to understand the resilience of a system, it is important to identify the capabilities and capacities of the individual parts of the system in terms of their integration with each other and within their environment, so that we are better able to predict performance outcomes at various levels of analysis both before and after a disruption event. Organizations need to identify and develop their dynamic capabilities in the interests of managing risk and resilience. The first significant literature on organizational resilience appeared through the study of such affected companies. Framed in this context, resilience has been described as the ability of an organization to rebound in the face of disturbance. In other words, it is not just about the survival of an organization but ensuring that that organization should keep the structure and function that it did before the event (Van Der Vegt et al., 2015; Smith & Fischbacher, 2009; Bigley & Roberts, 2001; Comfort et al., 2010).

It is generally agreed that governance forms an institutional basis for the development of organizational factors that straightforwardly add to the development of resilience. In this light, it has been observed that organizational resilience and alternative forms of governance, such as employee-owned businesses (EOBs), are important because of economic crises (Lampel et al., 2014). These can be summarized as follows:

- When employee ownership and involvement are combined, this generally brings about greater stability in business performance over a given cycle.
- The investment payback horizon of EOBs tends to be longer, as opposed to non-EOBs, across a variety of activities.

- There is a greater chance that the senior management of EOBs will look for employee involvement in strategic decision-making.
- Employee involvement is more likely to be used for strengthening the link between operational feedback and the taking of decisions on strategic direction.

These results suggest that initiatives such as employee stock ownership programmes are not sufficient in themselves to develop higher levels of organizational resilience. Managers should combine employee share ownership with employee involvement in decision-making if they are serious about building up resilience in advance of adverse economic conditions. There are many companies that have experienced failure through crises, and for this reason many businesses have placed resilience at the centre of their organizational strategy. In many cases, those crises involved unexpected natural disasters or nuclear accidents, often with significant damage and even loss of life (Lampel et al., 2014).

Companies with employee ownership form tend to have more stable business performance. Two key performance indicators are used for measurement, namely, sales and profitability. In both cases, the descending patterns in both sales and profitability for non-employee-owned business are more noteworthy than for employee-owned businesses. This leads one to conclude that non-EOBs are more affected by a downturn, but that they can survive as more resilient companies. EOBs are fundamentally more grounded regarding the creation of new business during both boom and recessionary circumstances. Human resource management practices can and do affect turnover, productivity and corporate financial performance, and investment in human resources is an important predictor of long-term performance. Having higher levels of staff engagement enables companies to thrive in times of crisis and to create a competitive advantage, especially since interpersonal connections are crucial for dealing with crises. Increased overall resilience in a firm ranks as one of the main organizational advantages resulting from an overlap between ownership and management. Openness, trust, authenticity and a proactive approach are half the battle in achieving organizational resilience, with proactiveness especially bringing the most astounding benefits, although this can be profoundly affected by trust (Lampel et al., 2014; Huselid, 1995).

The level of decision-making has a significant impact on organizational resilience. Organizations with centralized top-down decision-making are less resilient than those in which decision-making moves closer to the bottom-up and outward decision-making. The latter are better able to make sound decisions and are also better at addressing the challenge of changes in business conditions. Organizational resilience researchers have, thus far, focused mainly on exploring those internal organizational factors that directly contribute to an organization's resilience. However, the focus on the relationships between resilience and external stakeholders has been growing in recent times. In this regard, researchers have been exploring ownership patterns as internal resilience factors (Marchington & Kynighou, 2012; Gittell & Douglass, 2012; Roberts et al., 1994; Claessens, 2006; Connelly et al., 2010; Fukofuka & Loke, 2017).

Resilience is the capacity of an organization to maintain operational coherence, as well as the conservation of social and scholarly capital that is essential to the long-term achievements of that organization. Building resilience in this manner involves versatile procedures that advance competence in redesigning, all the while re-establishing productivity. These procedures are implanted in organizational structures and practices that develop coordination, raising the capacity to rapidly process feedback and adaptably rework or exchange information for managing emerging circumstances (Sutcliffe & Vogus, 2003; Christianson et al., 2009).

Traditional governance and bureaucratically inclined organizations are not very well designed for overseeing risks that arise quickly in unexpected and frequently imperceptible ways. For this reason, leadership tries to adjust the weaknesses of existing strategies to the realities of increasing exposure to hazards. In this light, the pertinent questions become:

- What are the characteristics of a resilient system?
- How do we recognize a resilient system?
- What does a 'resilient system' truly mean in practice?

Human activity, or in other words what we do and how we do it regarding the technical systems with which we work, has been extensively researched. From this point of view, the progress from observation to activity at singular, gathering, hierarchical and foundation sizes of task is basic to understanding the elements of resilience. Creating ways of measuring resilience in real situations exposed to hazard speaks to a basic assignment that is just the beginning (Comfort et al., 2010; Kerr, 2016; Herrmann et al., 2007; Hutchins, 1995; Coakes et al., 2002).

Resilient infrastructures can help a business anticipate, survive and recover from both external and internal disruptions. An infrastructure can be considered as a system, which is, in turn, made up of components, or nodes, that have a common purpose. Such infrastructures are individually owned and managed, are dependent on each other and are called systems of systems. The resilience of an infrastructure rests on four principles:

1. *Capacity*: the ability of the system to survive a threat
2. *Flexibility*: the ability of the system to adapt to a threat
3. *Tolerance*: the ability of the system to degrade gracefully in the face of a threat
4. *Cohesion*: the ability of the system to act as a unified whole in the face of a threat

How well the nodes of the infrastructure relate to one another is, at the first level of cohesion, communication ('talk to one another') and, at the second, cooperation (Jackson, 2010; Jackson & Ferris, 2013).

3.3 Organizational Resilience

Now, let us take a closer look at what exactly constitutes organizational resilience. The qualities of a resilient system are anticipation, attention, response and learning. Anticipation is about what to expect, while attention is about knowing what to look for. Response involves knowing what to do and learning concerns dynamic development and updating. Effectively, that means being able to identify and adapt to undesirable change and uncertainty before adverse events have occurred. The building of a coherent resilience framework helps an organization to understand and act on the interdependency of brand, trust and reputation. Societal and community resilience create value in that an organization supplies valuable products and services to the public. Resilience can provide assurance to stakeholders such as regulators, third parties, government, customers, partners and shareholders (Woods et al., 2006; BSI, 2014).

Organizational resilience is said to be affected by the availability and accessibility of resources and the formal organizational structure, along with the organization's relationship with other entities and its environment generally (Bell, 2007).

An important part of any organization is its workforce, and its individual employees are a source of capacity in its resilience. Such individual characteristics of employees can be said to include individual skills and abilities, behaviours, self-regulatory processes, emotional stability, openness to experience, social support, emotional recognition, self-discipline, resourcefulness and mental flexibilities, among others. These characteristics can affect the structure of the organization and are responsible for building organizational (sub)systems, such as teams and taskforces. Organizational resilience is unequivocally influenced by the relationship with other organizations and the environment, with a significant number of organizations being interconnected and reliant on each other in supply-chain network systems. Although the effectiveness and efficiency of supply chains have increased worldwide during the last few decades, disruption to them can have significant consequences for economic performance, and even a small local disruption can affect business continuity and sustainable performance, something that has motivated industry to analyse future risks and the capacity for faster recovery (Bell, 2007; Lengnick-Hall et al., 2011; Lawrence & Lorsch, 1967).

The source of an organization's potential level of resilience is the structure that is built from the character of individual employees. People are embedded in their social systems, and the relationship between individual employees and their social network allows these capabilities and resources to become available and accessible for appropriate responses as the need arises. The resilience of an organization, however, depends not only on access to resources, but also on its formal organizational structure. Moreover, the contingency theory states that the structure and process of an organization must fit its context (such as culture, environment, technology, size or role) if it is to survive or be effective. In the contingency theory, organizational performance depends on the fit between organizational context, on the one hand, and structure and process, on the other (Drazin & Van de Ven, 1985).

The contingency theory holds that an organization performs better in a stable environment, and it is noted that environmental change requires an organizational structure with greater cohesion between its employees. The environmental change resulting from the crisis has required organizations to be able to change from centralized to decentralized decision-making structures, which necessitates new procedures and processes, with new ways of cooperation having to be developed.

Versatile responses require the capacity to rapidly change the formal structure and to use a decentralized, team-based approach or build networking in order to be able to deal with emergency (Van Der Vegt et al., 2015; Lawrence & Lorsch, 1967).

The literature has recommended further research on organizational resilience, for addressing three important questions:

- How can individual employees deal with adverse events?
- What can be done to increase their (employees') resilience?
- How might the characteristics of organizational resilience, and of designs that might be used to examine the drivers of organizational resilience, be operationalized?

Given the above recent definition of resilience by BSI, the terms 'organization' and 'prosper' are important. Organizational resilience goes past mere survival, towards a more comprehensive perspective of business well-being and achievement. A resilient organization is Darwinian in that it adjusts to a changing situation with a specific end goal of staying fit for its purpose. BSI views organizational resilience as a basic essential for all companies, both vast and small. Rather than being a protective mechanism, organizational resilience is more a forward-looking strategic enabler that enables business leaders to confidently take more risks. Hearty, resilient organizations are adaptable and proactive—seeing, envisioning, making and exploiting new open doors all together, to ultimately breeze through the trial of time. Organizational resilience demands responsibility from the entire organization, including top-down bearing and bottom-up engagement, through clear correspondence with—and an eager grasp by—all employees. Resilient organizations are anxious to gain from their own encounters and those of others, to limit issues and handle openings. Distributed systems of administration and information sharing are indispensable, for instance, when they seek to put resources into new territories, present innovative items and procedures, or penetrate new markets (BSI, 2014; Van Der Vegt et al., 2015; Kerr, 2016).

The BSI model for organizational resilience involves three basic components: product excellence, process reliability and people behaviour.

Product Excellence

According to BSI, 'product excellence' can apply to all products, solutions and services that a business offers to the market. Such a business should check its capability and activities in the marketplace in which it operates, ensure its products fit both market and regulatory requirements, and distinguish its offering to enable it to remain ahead of its competitors. A truly resilient business continues to innovate, creating new products and markets, always staying ahead of the competition.

Process Reliability

Implanting best practice in creating and marketing products and services is a key lever for success. Basic business procedures in such areas as quality, conditions, health and safety, data security and business continuity must be powerful and agreeable, both inside an organization and throughout the vital parts of its supply chain. Reliable processes, delivered consistently over time, are critical in achieving and maintaining a high level of customer satisfaction.

People Behaviour

Resilient organizations look for alignment between customer requirements and employee engagement. The challenge for any organization is to comprehend, express and clearly show its qualities, with the goal that everybody 'lives' them, not so much on the grounds on which they have been advised to, but rather on the grounds that 'it's the way we get things done around here'. Long-term resilience means taking a holistic look at one's organizational capabilities, and it can be empowering to gain new ground and to make progress towards persistent change. Organizations that survive and thrive tend to have a good equilibrium between customer expectations and employee belief.

The BSI model embraces the qualities of a resilient organization. There are three clear resilience benefits: strategic adaptability, agile leadership and robust governance.

- *Strategic adaptability* concerns an organization's ability to handle changing circumstances successfully, even if this means moving away from its core business.
- *Agile leadership* involves the ability of an organization to take measured risks with confidence and its ability to respond quickly and appropriately to both opportunity and threat.
- *Robust governance* is about demonstrating accountability across organizational structures, based upon a culture of trust, transparency and innovation, thereby ensuring that that organization remains true to its vision and values.

BSI recognizes three areas that today are fundamental to accomplishing organizational resilience in all business entities, be they large or small: operational resilience, supply-chain resilience and information resilience.

3.4 Operational Resilience

A resilient organization understands the environment in which it operates and how it must adapt to that environment. The organization must not be complacent and should be constantly challenging itself to improve and grow.

3.5 Supply-Chain Resilience

As supply-chain networks expand around the globe and become more complex, the ability to quantify and mitigate risks assumes more importance. Organizations need to be able to identify serious risks.

3.6 Information Resilience

In today's world, organizations must be able to safeguard sensitive information. To be resilient, an organization must manage its information throughout its life cycle. This requires the employment of security-oriented practices that allow the gathering, storage, access to and use of information in a safe and proper way.

A question arises as to how resilience can be specified in more detail, and various theories have been explored regarding the positive characteristics of organizations and complex systems, such as resilience, a safety culture and a high degree of reliability. It has been suggested that a resilient organizational process centred on managing margins might serve to clarify organizational responsibility in terms of the overlaps and interfaces between organizations (Johnsen, 2010).

Seven principles of resilience are offered.

1. *Graceful and controlled degradation:* Proactive impact analyses must be performed, and risky behaviour should be identified and mitigated when system functions or barriers are failing.
2. *Management of margins:* The ability to manage margins is a key aspect of resilience. The effective management of margins ensures that performance boundaries are not crossed; this is accomplished using proactive indicators.
3. *Common mental models:* The use of common mental models ensures communication and collaboration across systems and organizations. Mental models play an important role in handling deviations and recovery; they also facilitate an understanding of the causes of accidents and learning from such accidents.
4. *Redundancy:* Redundancy involves having alternate ways of performing a function. The function can be carried out by different organizations, using diverse technical systems or procedures. The main role of redundancy is in supporting the ability of a system to degrade gracefully.
5. *Flexibility:* Flexibility is about diversity and having different ways of performing a function. It should incorporate a tolerance of errors, which should be immediately observable and reversible. Flexibility also involves improvisation (and thinking outside the box) during stressful situations.
6. *Reduction in complexity:* Complexity can be reduced by going from proximity to segregation, from common-mode connections to dedicated ones, from interconnected to segregated systems, from limited to easy substitution, from several feedback loops to few or even none, from multiple and interacting controls to single purpose and segregated controls, from indirect to direct information, and from limited to extensive understanding.
7. *Reduction of coupling:* Coupling can be reduced through enabling processing delays and by flexibility in sequencing, in methods used and in resources, redundancies and availability of substitutes (Johnsen, 2010).

3.7 ERM -v- Resilience

Rapid change increases the range of risks and degree of uncertainty and drives new threats. The process and procedures of conventional ERM, a reductionist approach, cannot cope with this uncertain environment; consequently, organizations need new ways of being resilient.

Activities for the most part include joint efforts at numerous levels of organizational and hierarchical silos. The procedure ought to be performed throughout the applied advancement stage and should utilize an entire risk picture that includes points of view from numerous levels of the organization, in order to ensure that safety and resilience are outlined in the framework. Diverse underlying drivers are recognized in view of various perceptions. Unique methodologies may, therefore, connect with various translations of resilience and highlight distinctive resilience standards. Plainly, there is no agreement on exactly what those standards are. What is clear, however, is the importance of standards being considered as a set rather than as individual independent ideas. Resilience is an exceptionally attractive property for basic framework resources, and resilience frameworks can respond to and recuperate from disturbances with negligible consequences for dynamic soundness (Johnsen, 2010).

Given the current rapid rate of change, coupled with the speed of information flow, the range of risks and degree of uncertainty are increasing, and new threats are continually arising. This increases the expectations of shareholders, regulators and other stakeholders, who are, consequently, challenging companies to be transparent about the risks they face and their ability to manage them. Conventional enterprise risk management (ERM) is an old idea that has gained renewed focus and relevance in the wake of the financial crisis, thus leading to a greater need for resilience on the part of companies to ensure their survival and success in such an uncertain environment. As well as anticipating and adapting to changes, resilience means being able to absorb and recover from negative events that include unexpected 'black swan' events and having, moreover, the ability to seize the opportunities hidden within those events. It is the application and embedding process that needs overhaul, and unless risk management is directly linked to strategy, ERM programmes do not help to achieve strategic objectives. Conventional ERM is static, while the business environment is dynamic; there is, therefore, practically no connection between strategy and risk management. It becomes unnecessary to bother with another type of ERM to deal with the dynamic business environment, although it is still needed to be able to ensure operational dynamics, address unexpected risk and deal with the more extensive business environment. The management of strategic risk factors, on the other hand, has a much greater impact on the realization of strategic objectives (Kinman, 2012).

Strategic risks have also been described as the uncertainty and unexploited opportunities embedded in strategic intent and how well they are executed. The response to these uncertainties and opportunities is strategic risk management, whose purpose is to obtain strategic value such as sales growth and service delivery. It has been noted that effective risk management involves an understanding of the organizational risk appetite, meaning the amount of risk taken for the delivery of given strategic objectives, and that risk management can often be run separately from frontline strategic assessments, decision-making and monitoring against plans (Armoghan & Sykes, 2012). Four business risks have been discussed:

1. *Financial risks:* These include debt, changing interest rates, poor financial management, asset losses, (loss of) goodwill, amortization and various accounting problems. Information about financial risks is seen as a key pillar of stakeholder communication, performance measurement and strategic delivery.
2. *Operational risks:* Cost overruns, operating controls, poor capacity management, supply-chain issues, employee issues (including fraud or corruption), regulation issues and commodity prices would be among these. The focus of operational risks is on health and safety issues arising from industry regulations and standards, which can be managed from within the business.
3. *Hazard risks:* Examples would be macroeconomic factors, political issues, terrorism and natural disasters. Many hazard risks are not controllable and can have a serious impact on the operating environment of the business, with the result that all too often, management does not even consider them in its strategic thinking.
4. *Strategic risks:* These might include a fall-off in demand, a failure to retain customers, integration problems, pricing pressures, regulation, R&D, industry or sector downturns, and joint venture or partner losses. Although strategic risks have an impact on executive decision-making, they are often missing from many risk registers, with the board thus having the responsibility for ensuring that strategic risks are included in their strategic discussions.

A company needs to develop its own capabilities for dealing with inherent uncertainty, which must include the ability to recognize, take and rapidly and effectively adapt to changes and resulting risk. This is vital if that business is to become truly resilient. The researchers offer a different way of dealing with uncertainties, such as scenarios and contingency planning, which are used to identify risks as well as opportunities for building organizational resilience. Engineering companies, for example, focus on their economic strategy, which can include treasury, finance, sales, procurement, legal and IT functions or indeed any other factors related to financial return or reward. Resilience is, moreover, linked to the ability of leaders to get their people's attention and get things done. Resilience supports transparency and efficiency in getting such things done, but it depends on a strong relationship between public and private sector stakeholders (Everson et al., 2012; Kinman, 2012; Armoghan & Sykes, 2012; Chesley, 2012).

It is not just organizations that need to become resilient; even countries face risks. A resilient country is one that can adapt to changing international circumstances, withstand sudden shocks and recover to a desired equilibrium, all while maintaining the continuity of its operations. The abilities to recover from crises and to adapt to changing environments are both crucial. What is referred to as 'system thinking' is used for the conceptualization of a country as a system, which is, in turn, both a part of a larger system and comprised of smaller ones. Those larger systems include the global economy, climate and communication networks. A diagnostic tool has been developed by the World Economic Forum's Risk Response Network for assessing the resilience of countries (national resilience) against global risks, using three sets of measurement criteria. The first of these is the country as macro system, using five subsystems: economy, environment, governance, infrastructure and society. The second set comprises three components of resilience: robustness (having fail-safes and firewalls, including the ability for decision-making to become either more hierarchical or more modular, as and when necessary), redundancy (having excess capacity and diverse ways of accomplishing the same objectives) and resourcefulness (having networks of trust that enable flexible self-organization, to adapt to crises in novel ways). Then, there is resilience performance, with two subsystems: response (having good feedback mechanisms that enable the early recognition of emerging issues and the ability to mobilize quickly) and recovery (the capacity to rebound from a crisis by absorbing new information and adapting quickly to new circumstances). This set of diagnostic tools is used to make assessments based on both quantitative statistical data and perception-based data (Howell, 2012).

Organizations need people with the adaptive capability to respond quickly and effectively to changes if they are to give themselves a significant competitive advantage. Employees are often faced with both internal and external changes in daily business, and they need to learn how to be resilient and how to quickly develop positive adaptive behaviours matched to the immediate situation. Such behaviours can help employees to spontaneously meet customer needs, avoid missed opportunities and generally avert adverse events by thinking quickly and acting decisively in crisis situations. Resilient employees find it easier to adapt to organizational change and are therefore better able to improve both productivity and quality (Mallak, 1998)

The five principles of organizational resilience sets out a framework for creating a highly agile, synchronized and knowledge-based organization (Mallak, 1998; Bell, 2002):

1. Leadership is about setting priorities, the allocation of resources, a commitment to resilience, and support with investment (facilities, security systems, controls and technology enhancement).
2. Culture involves empowerment, trust and accountability.
3. People who are properly selected, motivated, equipped and led will overcome almost any obstacle or disruption.
4. Systems characterize a resilient organization built on an infrastructure of extensive enterprise connectivity and information robustness and organizations that achieve agility and flexibility by combining a highly distributed workplace model with a robust and collaborative IT infrastructure.
5. Setting concerns workplace safety and security, such as the identification of high-risk locations, the distribution of the workplace into multiple, dispersed settings ('goodbye to the corner office' and 'the network is the workplace') and workplace agility.

A resilient organization is (i) characterized by dispersed people, knowledge, systems and workspaces; (ii) electronically integrated across employees, partners, buyers, external sources and communities; (iii) deliberately designed to adjust quickly to misfortune, shock or major change; and (iv) able to operate at full speed, even in the face of adversity and under conditions of cautiousness. It is also claimed that resilient people possess three characteristics: the ability to accept reality and to face it down, an ongoing search for meaning (they hold a deep belief—often buttressed by strongly held values—that life is meaningful), and ritualized ingenuity, i.e. a strong ability to improvise (Morello, 2002; Coutu, 2002).

Resilience indicators given in the literature are leadership, situational awareness, innovation and creativity, a proactive posture, a stress-testing plan, planning strategies, a unity of purpose, braking silos, leveraging of knowledge, internal resources, effective partnership, decision-making and staff engagement. The International Consortium for Organizational Resilience (ICOR) provides an organizational resilience framework for risk management, which is identified in a range of management disciplines, including business continuity, continuity of operations, crises management and communication, critical environments, financial health and viability, HR management, incident response, information security, legal and compliance, organizational behaviour and risk management.

A trio of resilience standards, such as those below, has been put forward:

1. *Management principles:* An organization must be resilient not only in systems, data and work design, but also in its people, management structures and analysis of risk and financial personality.
2. *Infrastructure principles:* Designing resilience into networks, operations, data architecture, wireless communication and data centres means going beyond event-induced disaster recovery. It means designing systems for quick recovery and bounce-back. An infrastructure designed for resilience is an excellent foundation for business continuity and agility.
3. *E-Work principles:* For people to be able to work seamlessly across time, distance and boundaries after shock or disaster, they must have at their fingertips a range of collaboration tools and services that will jumpstart productivity and enable them to recover quickly (Nelson & Abcp, 2007).

Summary of Resilience

There is overall agreement that resilience can be understood in different ways and, certainly, it is applied in a variety of fields in human (social) systems, in engineering and in management science. Resilience can, it is widely agreed, be regarded as a process that responds to adversity and there is, in general, a strong consensus that it relates to disaster, crises, disruptions and unexpected changes. Increasingly, resilience is seen as a strategic objective that should help an organization not only to survive but, indeed, to thrive.

Broadly speaking, resilience is concerned with adaptive processes and is an emergent property, which is a characteristic of complexity. It is widely agreed that the term 'resilience' can be used to describe an organization's ability to deal with uncertainty and to respond and adapt to sudden changes and disruptions to be able to survive and to succeed. Companies must, therefore, constantly strive to overcome the uncertainties created by the complexity of the global business environment and the speed of change, and a strong risk-management culture is essential for helping a company achieve effective strategic risk management (McShane et al., 2011; Beasley et al., 2015).

Traditional governance and bureaucratic organizations are not very well designed for overseeing risks that rise quickly in unexpected and, frequently, imperceptible ways (Kerr, 2016). Two vital questions arise in this regard:

- What are the characteristics of a resilient system?
- What does this really mean in practice?

Conventional ERM is wholly inadequate for dealing with today's highly uncertain environment. There is a lack of integration of the ever-changing risk profile with decision-making at both the strategic and operational levels. Modern companies need to develop a strong risk resilience culture if they are to ensure their success or, indeed, their very survival. Such a culture will allow organizations to anticipate and adapt to change. In this regard, five questions for improving conventional ERM are offered (Everson et al., 2012; Kinman, 2012; Starr et al., 2003).

1. Who owns risk?
2. How effective is the board in overseeing risk management?
3. How proactively is risk managed?
4. Can 'black swan' risks be managed?
5. What is the return on risk management?

Most organizations are exposed to—and exhibit varying degrees of—complexity. This complexity, it is argued, should be embraced in the context of fostering greater degrees of resilience within the organization. The assessment of organizational resilience and risk management can and should be aligned, to close the dangerous gap in the resilience profile of an enterprise.

3.8 Analysis of Resilience

The study of resilience helps us to understand the theoretical application of the knowledge domain of resilience, in practice. An analysis of the domain, in turn, helps us to identify the factors of organizational resilience. The resilience domain is clustered into ten sub-categories in the order shown in Table 3.1. This allows us a better understanding of the characteristics of resilience from these proposed factors, and it improves our grasp of their relationship with further aspects of organizational resilience (Dindarian, 2019).

Table 3.1 Summary of the factors of Organizational Resilience

Leadership	Organization	Environment (stakeholders)
Agile leadership	Ability	Capacity
Control	Absorption and recovery	Flexibility
Decision-making	Adaptability	Information (finance)
Efficiency	Adaptive response	Internal and external stakeholders
Employee involvement in decision-making	Behaviours	Networking and communication
Employee involvement in firm governance	Bounce back	**Processes**
Employee involvement in strategy setting	Capacity	Process availability
Employee stock ownership	Cognitions	Process reliability
Mobilization of resources	Cognitive flexibilities	Process that responds to adversity
Motivation	Communication	Processes of crisis management
Strategic adaptability	Context	Robust governance
Trust and delegation	Coping with change	**Information**
People	Dealing with complexity	Exchange of information
Adaptability	Dealing with uncertainty	Information resilience
Authenticity	Emergence	**Uncertainty**
Efficiency	Emotional recognition	Natural uncertainty
Employees resources and capacity	Emotional stability	Local financial uncertainty
Engagement	Finance	Global financial uncertainty
Innovation	Functionality	Environmental uncertainty
Involvement	Innovation	
Know-how	Lessons learned	
Openness	Networking	
Ownership	Openness to experience	
People behaviour	Overcoming uncertainty	
Performance	Performance	
Pro-action	Process	
Trust	Recovery	
Technology	Resourcefulness	
Product excellence	Responsibility	
Operational	Self-discipline	
Operational resilience	Self-efficacy	
Supply chain	Self-regulatory processes	

(continued)

Table 3.1 (continued)

Leadership	Organization	Environment (stakeholders)
Supply-chain risks	Skills	
Efficiency	Social support	
Supply-chain disruption	Structure	
Supply-chain resilience	Tolerance	

References

Adger, W. N. (2000). Social and ecological resilience: Are they related? *Progress in Human Geography, 24*(3), 347–364.
Armoghan, M., & Sykes, R. (2012). *Sharpening strategic risk management* (Vol. 1, p. 1). PWC.
Beasley, M., Branson, B., & Pagach, D. (2015). An analysis of the maturity and strategic impact of investments in ERM. *Journal of Accounting and Public Policy, 34*(3), 219–243.
Bell, M. A. (2002). *The five principles of organizational resilience.* Gartner Research.
Bell, S. T. (2007). Deep-level composition variables as predictors of team performance: A meta-analysis. *Journal of Applied Psychology, 92*(3), 595.
Bigley, G. A., & Roberts, K. H. (2001). The incident command system: High-reliability organizing for complex and volatile task environments. *Academy of Management Journal, 44*(6), 1281–1299.
BSI. (2014). *Guidance on organizational resilience, in BS 65000* (Vol. 2014, p. 16). © The British Standards Institution.
Chandler, D. (2014). *Resilience: The governance of complexity*. Routledge.
Chesley, D. (2012). *Resilience: Winning with risk* (Vol. 1, p. 1). PWC.
Christianson, M. K., et al. (2009). Learning through rare events: Significant interruptions at the Baltimore & Ohio Railroad Museum. *Organization Science, 20*(5), 846–860.
Claessens, S. (2006). Corporate governance and development. *The World Bank Research Observer, 21*(1), 91–122.
Coakes, E., Willis, D., & Clarke, S. (2002). *Knowledge management in the sociotechnical world. Computer supported co-operative work*. Springer.
Comfort, L. K., Boin, A., & Demchak, C. C. (2010). *Designing resilience: Preparing for extreme events*. University of Pittsburgh Pre.
Connelly, B. L., et al. (2010). Marching to the beat of different drummers: The influence of institutional owners on competitive actions. *Academy of Management Journal, 53*(4), 723–742.
Coutu, D. L. (2002). How resilience works. *Harvard Business Review, 80*(5), 46–56.
CRRI. (2013). *Definition of community resilience: An analysis*. Available from: http://www.resilientus.org/publications/carri-special-reports/.
Dindarian, K. (2019). *Exploring enterprise resilience through the theoretical lens of complexity: A case study situated in the high value-manufacturing sector*. The University of Manchester.
Drazin, R., & Van de Ven, A. H. (1985). Alternative forms of fit in contingency theory. *Administrative Science Quarterly, 30*, 514–539.
Everson, M., et al. (2012). *Resilience: Winning with risk* (Vol. 1, p. 1). PWC.
Fukofuka, P. T., & Loke, D. T. (2017). Predictors of organizational resilience: A path analysis. *Global Journal of Human Resource Management, 5*(9), 31–42.
Gittell, J. H., & Douglass, A. (2012). Relational bureaucracy: Structuring reciprocal relationships into roles. *Academy of Management Review, 37*(4), 709–733.
Herrmann, E., et al. (2007). Humans have evolved specialized skills of social cognition: The cultural intelligence hypothesis. *Science, 317*(5843), 1360–1366.
Howell, L. (2012). *Resilience: Winning with risk* (Vol. 1, p. 1). PWC.

Huselid, M. A. (1995). The impact of human resource management practices on turnover, productivity, and corporate financial performance. *Academy of Management Journal, 38*(3), 635–672.
Hutchins, E. (1995). *Cognition in the Wild*. MIT Press.
Jackson, S. (2010). The principles of infrastructure resilience. *DomPrep J, 2010*.
Jackson, S., & Ferris, T. L. (2013). Resilience principles for engineered systems. *Systems Engineering, 16*(2), 152–164.
Johnsen, S. (2010). Resilience in risk analysis and risk assessment. In *International Conference on Critical Infrastructure Protection*. Springer.
Johnsen, S. O., & Veen, M. (2013). Risk assessment and resilience of critical communication infrastructure in railways. *Cognition, Technology & Work, 15*(1), 95–107.
Kerr, H. (2016). Organizational resilience. *Quality, 55*(7), 40.
Kinman, B. (2012). *Resilience: Winning with risk* (Vol. 1, p. 1). PWC.
Lampel, J., Bhalla, A., & Jha, P. P. (2014). Does governance confer organisational resilience? Evidence from UK employee owned businesses. *European Management Journal, 32*(1), 66–72.
Lawrence, P. R., & Lorsch, J. W. (1967). Differentiation and integration in complex organizations. *Administrative Science Quarterly, 12*, 1–47.
Lengnick-Hall, C. A., Beck, T. E., & Lengnick-Hall, M. L. (2011). Developing a capacity for organizational resilience through strategic human resource management. *Human Resource Management Review, 21*(3), 243–255.
Madni, A. M., & Jackson, S. (2009). Towards a conceptual framework for resilience engineering. *IEEE Systems Journal, 3*(2), 181–191.
Mallak, L. (1998). *Putting organizational resilience to work* (pp. 8–13). Industrial Management-Chicago Then Atlanta.
Marchington, M., & Kynighou, A. (2012). The dynamics of employee involvement and participation during turbulent times. *The International Journal of Human Resource Management, 23*(16), 3336–3354.
McShane, M. K., Nair, A., & Rustambekov, E. (2011). Does enterprise risk management increase firm value? *Journal of Accounting, Auditing & Finance, 26*(4), 641–658.
Morello, D. T. (2002). *The blueprint for the resilient virtual organization spurred by the needs for security, protection and recovery, enterprises are taking on the new challenge of deliberately designing resilience into their management of people, places, infrastructure and work processes*.
Nelson, J. I., & Abcp, C. (2007). *Building resilient communities: One organization at a time*. The International Consortium for Organizational Resilience.
Oxford-Dictionary. (2017).
Renn, O. (2006). Risk governance: Towards an integrative framework. In *International Disaster Reduction Conference, Davos*.
Roberts, K. H., Stout, S. K., & Halpern, J. J. (1994). Decision dynamics in two high reliability military organizations. *Management Science, 40*(5), 614–624.
Smith, D., & Fischbacher, M. (2009). The changing nature of risk and risk management: The challenge of borders, uncertainty and resilience. *Risk Management, 11*(1), 1–12.
Starr, R., Newfrock, J., & Delurey, M. (2003). Enterprise resilience: Managing risk in the networked economy. *Strategy and Business, 30*, 70–79.
Sutcliffe, K. M., & Vogus, T. J. (2003). Organizing for resilience. *Positive Organizational Scholarship*, 94–110.
Thomé, A. M. T., et al. (2016). Similarities and contrasts of complexity, uncertainty, risks, and resilience in supply chains and temporary multi-organization projects. *International Journal of Project Management, 34*(7), 1328–1346.
Tusaie, K., & Dyer, J. (2004). Resilience: A historical review of the construct. *Holistic Nursing Practice, 18*(1), 3–10.
Van Der Vegt, G. S., et al. (2015). Managing risk and resilience. *Academy of Management Journal, 58*(4), 971–980.
Woods, D., Hollnagel, E., & Leveson, N. (2006). *Resilience engineering* (p. 350).

Complexity

4

In this book, we draw on information from my PhD research study (Dindarian, 2019), gained from both the literature that formed the basis of the thesis and the findings of my research. Methods of building enterprise resilience through the theoretical lens of complexity are presented. This will, hopefully, allow us to gain a better insight into the underlying theory that can, hopefully, be applied in practice. Our primary purpose in this section is to give the reader an overview of the complexity theory, an understanding of which allows management to start improving decision-making capabilities and processes.

The research field of complexity has been growing and discussed at length during the last four decades. Complexity science is connected to emerging science and the chaos theory. Innovation can be said to be creativity in organizational behaviour that has been researched based on the complexity theory. Social behaviour and the group process are also subject to complexity research. Research has also considered complexity theory in the categories of knowledge management and general management, as well as complex responsive processes in organizations, organizational change, networks, computer science, and physics & biology. Other sciences, such as sustainability & ecology, and society & philosophy have also been researched and explored based on complexity science (Alhadeff-Jones, 2008; Mitchell Waldrop, 1992; Lewin, 1999; Stacey et al., 2000; Olson, 2002; Buchanan, 2002; Buchanan & Aldana-Gonzales, 2003; Barabási & Bonabeau, 2003; Allen, 2012; Lansing & Kremer, 1994; Johnson, 2002; Bentley, 2002; Kauffman, 1995; Capra, 1996; Byrne, 1998; Cilliers & Spurrett, 1999).

The complexity theory can be applied to solving complex decision-making problems based on uncertain information, strategy, project performance and supply-chain management. The complexity of strategy is associated with the extent of information processing and of managerial interaction and integration of information such as ideas, roles, skills and knowledge (Floricel et al., 2016; Liyanage, 2010; Padalkar & Gopinath, 2016; Thomé et al., 2016; Neill & Rose, 2006; Miller & Cardinal, 1994; Bielza et al., 2011; Ambulkar et al., 2015; Brusset & Teller, 2017; Elleuch et al., 2016).

K. Dindarian, *Embracing the Black Swan*, Future of Business and Finance,
https://doi.org/10.1007/978-3-031-29344-3_4

The complexity theory has been described as a science of complexly interacting systems that explores the nature of interaction and adaptation in such systems and how such areas as emergence, innovation and performance have been influenced by them (Schneider & Somers, 2006).

Systems

The capability of a given device can be measured by its connection with one or more other devices, resulting in a system or subsystem. A physical system is built from tangible elements that may be static or dynamic in nature, with their own properties, functions and capabilities, which in turn relate to their original elementary properties and functions. An example of 'system' is a typical computer setup, consisting of devices (hardware) such as the CPU, keyboard and monitor, a vast range of software—operating system, firmware and various apps—and accessories such as a mouse, printer, camera and speakers. In fact, the performance of a computer system depends on the capabilities of those interconnected devices. Two or more systems build up to a solution as a 'system of systems', a collection of systems that interoperate with each other to achieve additional desired capabilities, but each of which is capable of independent operation as well. We can see the functionality of a system-within-systems in our daily lives, such as in commuting from home to workplace or elsewhere, for which we use bicycle, motorbike, car or public transport. Each vehicle is a mechanical system, while the road-traffic control centres that regulate such movement include hardware, software and many people and they incorporate traffic lights, GPS and so on. This system of systems governs our movement from A to B. Similarly, we can see systems in both the natural sciences (e.g. biology, astronomy) and human sciences, such as the departments within organizations or communities within larger societies.

Complexity is born of the nature of large interconnected systems and is escalated by the background, personal characteristics and perspectives of the individuals designing such systems. It is important for designers to understand complexity and how complexity affects our understanding and prediction of system behaviour. Complexity must be managed in such a way that it does not overwhelm the design effort or hinder the development of effective solutions (Maxwell et al., 2002).

Reductionism is a form of research logic in which parts of a system are isolated and studied independently of the system from which they are derived. Holism, on the other hand, sees things differently: the whole is different from the sum of the parts. Complexity science moves us away from the reductionist perspective, taking a more holistic approach. Instead of viewing leadership just as merely an interpersonal influence, complexity theory sees leadership as providing links to 'emergent structures' within and among organizations. Complexity is about independent systems interacting with each other, and it is characterized by uncertainty, unpredictability and non-linearity (Mitchell Waldrop, 1992; Schneider & Somers, 2006; Costanza et al., 1993; Tetradian glossary, 2016).

4.1 Complicated -v- Complex Systems

Systems formed from many components fall into two types: complicated and complex.

A complicated system has been described as a system of many parts, whose behaviour is that of an automaton, i.e. the individual components and the relationships between the components remain largely unchanged. A mechanical clock is a typical complicated system. Complex systems are rarely in equilibrium, and hence, they must change over time. Since the system is, by definition, complex, emergent behaviour appears from it unannounced. A system is complex when there are strong interactions among its elements, so that current events heavily influence the probabilities of many kinds of later events. It has also been said that the parts of a complex system cannot be separated and that it continues to have the same properties. Complex systems are comprised not only of interacting parts, but interdependent parts as well (Mansfield, 2010; Axelrod & Cohen, 2000; Bar-Yam, 2003).

It is worth noting that complexity theory explores systems. Essentially, systems are built from independent parts that are all interconnected, whose output after integration and interaction is uncertain, unpredictable and non-linear. People can be defined as a system, composed of many different parts from the smallest cell to the whole body, including its intangible parts such as thoughts and its behaviour and personal characteristics in its environment. In engineering science, a designer works in a team as a system within a system. It is very important for an engineer to understand complexity and how complexity affects the understanding and prediction of system behaviour. It is even more important to be able to cope with complexity so that it does not prevent the development of effective engineering solutions or overwhelm the engineering effort. Social, technological, economic and legal setups can all be characterized as systems.

Change within complex systems is inevitable, and even small local changes can cause major changes in behaviour within an entire larger system. The impact of these changes is referred to as 'emergent behaviour' and is an important characteristic of change. At this point, we will look at a few different kinds of system to give the reader better clarity regarding systems and complexity.

4.2 Natural and Artificial Systems

Systems are either 'natural' or 'artificial'. Natural systems are created without human intervention. Weather, for example, is a complex natural system consisting of many variables and interconnected components. Its emergent behaviour is unpredictable. Artificial systems, on the other hand, are created by humans, who can generate them either intentionally or by chance, and this may happen either through action or evolution. John Mansfield describes three kinds of artificial systems: social systems, technical systems and socio-technical systems (Mansfield, 2010).

4.3 Social, Technical, and Socio-Technical Systems

A social system can be described as the interaction of people with each other, such as a commercial organization, non-government communities, sports clubs, education systems such as schools or colleges, a belief community such as a religious system or a political community such as local or regional government. The behaviour of social systems is governed by rules, whether these have been formally established by law or have simply come into existence through common knowledge, practice and general agreement. Social systems can be either intentionally and formally established, or they may evolve.

Technical systems, on the other hand, are all purposely made by man. Social and technology-based systems (socio-technical systems) may be built by a whole variety of people and groups, including legislators, engineers, cyber-tech forces, the Internet of Things, artificial intelligence, economists and even shamans, parish priests and pastors. A common characteristic among such systems is that they have a specific purpose, with requirements to be met and objectives and goals to achieve. Society is shaped by using tools, which in turn are made to fulfil the needs of society. As those needs continue to grow, so does the demand for more and larger tools. Socio-technical systems, which are found everywhere in human society, can be understood as 'complex adaptive systems' that are a special case type of complex system. Economic systems are similarly classified. They are complex in their nature because the components of which they are comprised are constantly interconnected, and these generate dynamic impact (Mansfield, 2010). In our next section, we will speak a little more about complex adaptive systems.

4.4 Complex Adaptive Systems

A complex adaptive system (CAS) is one that contains component subsystems that all interact in such a way as to co-evolve. This perspective not only helps us to understand more clearly the factors that underline the complexities of socio-technical systems, but it allows for a new approach to systems design predicated on unpredictable adaptive processes. CASs exhibit complexity theory characteristics, which are specified in six components: interrelationship, adaptability, self-organization, emergence, feedback and non-linearity (Mitchell Waldrop, 1992; Lewin, 1999; Smith, 2005; Phelan, 2001; Holland, 1992; Holland & Miller, 1991; Aritua et al., 2009; Kaplan & Seebeck, 2001). Figure 4.1 presents a simple illustration of CAS components.

The multi-causal dynamic within organizations can be better understood through CASs that can help us to develop ways to manage, plan, design, implement and evaluate regarding the degree of complexity of the issue in question. The study of CASs has led to a better understanding of projects in the context of their environment. Moreover, complexity theory provides a CAS for the assessment of the holistic view and is applied to gain a better understanding and to address complex issues. A project's environment is characteristic of a CAS and is most appropriately

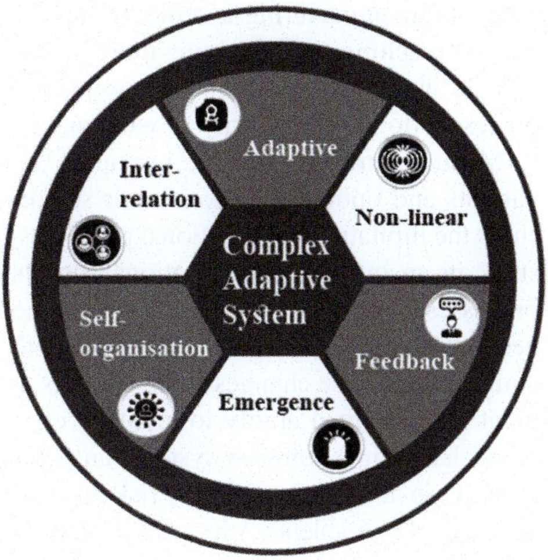

Fig. 4.1 Components of complex adaptive system

assessed through a holistic approach that can be applied to better understand and address complex issues (Holland, 1992; Aritua et al., 2009; Van Beurden et al., 2011).

The risks inherent in complicated systems can be easily assessed based on detailed system parts, expert knowledge and previous experience. The situation is different for complex systems, where the risks lie beyond the parts and expert knowledge or for which there is a lack of experience, such as emergent behaviour and properties. Such examples are already known from the world of pharmaceuticals and drug development. In a comparison of complicated versus complex systems, risk and uncertainty management are handled differently.

4.5 Manufacturing and Product Complexity

4.5.1 Complexity in Technology Development and Application

In the following section, we look at how complexity in the real world of business evolves from marketing to production and administration and what lies in between. The aim is to show the complexities in commercial reality and to illustrate complexity characteristics, including clarification of the adaptation process.

The internationalization of the economy, including the globalization umbrella, has influenced the process landscape of business development and the development of products and system solutions. Technological requirements are coming more and more into line with the needs of end users, and the requirements for complicated systems are therefore shifting towards the complex system. The more individual the requirements become, the more complex they become. As Henry Ford once said, a customer can have any colour car he wants, provided it is black! Assembly-line production has been improved over the years to increase productivity, while industrial manufacturing is still striving for leaner processes. In recent years, production machines are becoming more intelligent through digitalization, thus increasing the interconnectivity in the production chain, with the result that traditional processes do not necessarily fit with current process requirements.

Manufacturers and service providers today face the challenge of creating more variants and options alongside their standard products and services. This tends to show the limitations of traditional processes, which tend to be inflexible and perhaps stuck in an outdated organizational structure. Changes in one area through such processes are not necessarily reflected in the impact on other areas, so entrepreneurs need to be more flexible when designing their processes for better management of complexity. These changes bring benefits as well as risks. Traditional risk management has a limited ability to identify, capture and manage complexity risks. Any local change in a complex system can potentially affect the behaviour of the whole system, so a holistic view of risk management is now required. Complexity is governed by resilience, through an adaptation process that concerns a system's ability to cope with a high degree of uncertainty and adapt to threats.

The most widely accepted world of enterprise risk management is the Committee of Sponsoring Organizations of the Treadway Commission (COSO), whose approach is considered holistic. Yet, users of COSO find that complexity risks and emerging risks are difficult to represent, and new approaches are therefore encouraged.

Within the whole area of commercial complexity, the purpose of the resilience concept is to govern that complexity, for greater competitive advantage and business continuity, the protection of stakeholders' investments and interests, and the creation of value for shareholders. Resilience is a feature in the alignment of processes and procedures in individual organizations, in the business environment generally and in technology, leadership and other important areas such as resources and finance.

In the complex process landscape, the most important areas of resilience are market data, sales and bidding, execution, supply chain, norms and standards and, perhaps most importantly, the complexity of customer requirements.

Within the broad business environments, complexity can be divided into two areas: internal and external. Internally, the process and procedures of business should align with further organizational elements such as the structure of an organization and the decision-making levels. Externally, complexity can apply to customer behaviour, market share and position, and the level of competition.

In multinational business environments, it is necessary to consider factors such as social and cultural behaviour, geographic and climatic conditions and, most importantly, the political system and the process and procedures of political decision-making. Resilience in a complex business environment means being able to provide protection against adverse events and emergent risks, which in turn depends on the extent to which an organization is prepared to adapt to the environment during and after unexpected changes. The organization must have both the capability and capacity for this, as well as a sound knowledge of its operational business environment. Resilience in business environments is about addressing the complexity of each business area through measures such as the gathering of data and information, the creation of hypothetical scenarios around unexpected changes in the environment, and the preparation of an effective emergent strategy and decision-making structure, plus a comparison of such new measures with current business strategy. Questions will inevitably arise as to whether the traditional organizational structure and processes of companies can cope with internal and external complexity through a suitable process landscape. New processes and procedures incur costs, which can be summarized as the price of complexity. Individual and specific requirements will likely increase the degree of complexity of new measures that have to be processed, using market data and information. This means the modification and renewal of standard products as variants, which can give rise to additional costs across the various business areas.

4.6 Cost of Complexity

It should be noted that the product itself—any product—is a complicated system. The costs of such systems are predictable, and the experts can calculate all costs including risks of change. This differs from a complex system, in which people from different departments are interconnected, who work and make decisions at different levels. This transforms the complicated production system into a complex system. The fact of people being involved from different departments, together with their interactions, increases complexity. In effect, we can say, whereas a product is a complicated system, the design and production of that product is a complex system. The processes of complicated systems differ significantly from those complex systems but often, in practice, these differences are not taken into consideration. This means that the cost increases and emergent problems must be addressed and resolved in the long run. People always try to solve the problems of complex systems using the processes of complicated systems and then wonder why it costs more time and money.

Market and customer requirements place considerable demand on the development of diversity and the number of variants, and this increases complexity. The costs of this complexity include design development, increased production and manufacturing costs, and quality control, as well as other interrelated costs such as the procurement and possible development of new parts or internal/external subsystems. External supply parts cause additional costs if they deviate from standard products, and this applies to every change and deviation. Further costs arise from testing and commissioning, including approval and customer acceptance.

In international business, the complexity and risks increase due to the approval and acceptance processes, which are dependent on the respective standards, regulations and specifications of given regions and countries. External complexity continues to increase with the number of participating and partner companies and the degree of their activities. There are many examples of this, such as in the rail transport sector, where several external contractors work with each other; these include construction companies, planning companies, architects, civil and structural engineering suppliers/providers and mechanical and electrical companies, together with their sub-suppliers, not to mention other involved organizations and parties, be they private or public sector. It is worth mentioning that even the indirect partners within the system themselves have requirements that strongly influence the final product's requirements. In the rail transport system, the most important parties are the end customers, the passengers and their representatives, who set requirements for safety and comfort. A complex system cannot be controlled by reduction, the main reason being that any local changes or external influences in the system causes changes in overall system behaviour, the outcome of which is unclear and can have positive or negative results.

Looking at these system behaviours using the above example of customer-related complexity drivers, we can see that a reduction in demand can have a range of consequences. These can include a neglect of customer needs (as illustrated by Henry Ford's comments), a slowing down in market dynamics, a renunciation of country specifics, a reduction in the number of customers that may affect turnover, a failure to take demand fluctuations into account (thereby increasing performance risk) and a decrease in supplier diversity through renouncing innovation and greater dependence on monopolists. These are just a few examples of the positive or negative effects of reducing external complexity, because external complexity affects internal processes and organizational structure. Resilient organizations are ideally able to adapt to external complexity and organize themselves and respond to external changes.

Internal complexity drivers include organizational structure, people, processes, resources and finances, all of which are interlinked both structurally and procedurally. Internal complexity is increased by, among other things, communication among individuals. As we have seen, external complexity influences internal structures, such as in the establishment of new departments because of new requirements, unforeseen market demands or new market trends. As the number of departments increases, so does internal complexity, which in turn affects the organizational structure, which is directly related to the humans within it. This means that individuals can react positively or negatively to the changes, in terms of commitment, responsibility, competence, skillsets, career prospects and their general social and personal behaviour. Furthermore, such structural changes require an adjustment in functional, commercial and technical resources, which in turn has a direct influence on decision-making and control processes. All changes affect finances as internal complexity costs. Resilient organizations function as complex systems, so they are sufficiently able and flexible to adapt to external complexity within manageable risk boundaries.

4.7 Complexity -v- Product Variant Cost

As already mentioned, while a product itself may be a complicated system, its production is a complex system. In other words, external complexity influences product variations and departures from standard product designs to satisfy individual customer needs, market demands, and market trends. However, with a growing number of variants and increasingly different product functions, features and values, the complexity of the manufacturing process can and does increase, with both positive and negative effects:

- Positive effects can include an increased market share and improved market position, while simultaneously creating market entry barriers for competitors.
- Among the negative effects, on the other hand, are greater raw material requirements in terms of both type and quantity, a growing number of sub-suppliers, logistical pressures, more resources all round, the need for additional investments, and new commercial and financial structures having to be put in place.

Reducing complexity is favoured by some business analysts and scholars, and this approach is promoted as the key to success by many industry consultants. This reasoning, I would contend, is in fact flawed, because a proper understanding of the concept of complexity is lacking. One suggested way of dealing with complexity is to 'reduce variations, avoid and manage'. Managing complexity is, however, different from risk management, so such recommendations are misplaced, both in academia and in practice. Complexity cannot be reduced but must be dealt with, or at least coped with.

4.8 Complexity Cost -v- Complexity Reduction

Let us assume that a sales department carries out a customer analysis based on market data and information; there are various methods, tools and processes for this, which we need not go into in detail. The result of this analysis shows that an excessive number of customers can increase the number of variants and, thus, internal complexity. By reducing the number of variants to reduce complexity, however, there is a risk that the actual market share will diminish and that the market position will be compromised. This will likely result in some lag in the market dynamics and a loss of reputation. There is a school of thought that suggests simply reducing sales complexity by eliminating the less profitable customers and products. There are various methods, procedures and tools for achieving this (which we need not discuss in detail here). Market segmentation with a suitable portfolio and thus optimization of the variants can certainly make the number of demands more manageable and allow greater focus on specific customers. This strategy can create sales advantages, but it does not necessarily achieve its objective of reducing complexity.

The automotive industry, for example, pursues a strategy of variant optimization and market segmentation, and it adjusts the portfolio accordingly in the global market. This takes customer needs into account by offering a product range that matches the culture and behaviour of customers and end consumers. Market needs influence technological usability and values. Rather than serving to reduce complexity, however, it merely increases complexity costs. This is in line with the international business strategy, in which globalization plays an important role.

In the last four decades, traditional target markets have been transformed into the global marketplace, challenged by customer and market demands, especially with more localized requirements. Sponsors and investors, especially in developing and third-world countries, are demanding more local added value, which is being used to gain a competitive advantage in the global market. The products in themselves do not become more complex, but the supply chain makes the business processes more so. Localization is associated with investment, assets, technology transfer, training and other factors. This complexity increases with the involvement of sub-suppliers, with outcomes that can be positive or negative. Larger suppliers can localize their business partially or completely, whereas smaller companies lose their competitive capabilities, because a lack of resources and finances normally results in fewer variants of their products. The complexity of global business processes is increasing due to local content in regions with less expertise and manufacturing know-how, and fewer local suppliers. Cost drivers include the functional costs of human resources such as sending experts to the regions and the matter of logistics and the supply chain. This author does not recommend optimizing and/or reducing process complexity but, rather, advocates for developing the ability to cope with complexity, thus creating added value for the stakeholders.

4.9 Complexity Cost -v- Outsourcing

Industry is setting internal goals for dealing with the complexity of global business, the strategy being to increase the degree of modularization, use a greater number of standards and reusable parts and pursue a platform strategy, which will be discussed in more detail later. These goals are extended by localization and the outsourcing of production to so-called low-wage countries, with the aim of reducing costs and thus creating competitive advantage. This strategy of outsourcing production is a consequence of globalization, where industry often underestimates the complexity that arises. However, it is worth noting that industry has made many advances in recent decades through process improvements, manufacturing and product management systems, and other processes designed to increase competitiveness. The positive and successful implantation of such processes helps the industry to improve its competitive position and quality, but the complexity does not become any less than before; if anything, it increases in many cases because of the interactions of several processes that are linked to each other and which influence each other.

The processes with technical, commercial and operational characteristics, as well as customer and social characteristics, create new interactions. These and other processes cannot be viewed in siloed terms. They are part of the whole system, whose behaviour can be influenced by each change in local processes.

Traditional manufacturing processes are linear (meaning complicated) systems, but in practice, systems change through human imagination and decision-making, which makes them complex. We can illustrate this with examples from the praxis: variant make-or-buy and simultaneous engineering.

Manufacturing processes are clearly defined and have been improved over the years, one example being lean management. Inevitably, there comes a time when the make-or-buy decision will be called into question.

The automotive industry has largely defined the battery as a purchased part depending on the required performance. For each vehicle type, platform and variant, a standardized kit has been integrated into the product design. In one variant, the required power is changed according to the customer's wishes (for example, the air-conditioning system is to remain in operation for longer when the engine is switched off). On the one hand, a battery with the same mass and higher power is needed, which means that the requirements must be met by a third party; on the other hand, this can mean increased development time and costs. In addition, there are also risks that must be considered with a newly developed product, such as the product's dependence on a particular supplier. Outsourcing or purchasing means that no internal changes are required if it is a standard product. Another option might be to choose a standard product to save time and costs while achieving quality. In this case, the battery does not fit into the standardized installation space, which may affect other interfaces. Thus, interface changes or adaptations become necessary, so that internal changes are required. These changes can affect the entire process chain in the design, development and production start-up phases. There is a constant need for coordination between all departments involved, which increases the coordination effort and additional labour costs, which may also require new investment. By introducing simultaneous engineering, however, measures can be taken to reduce costs and keep the effort to a minimum. It means simultaneous development of the product and the associated processes, which makes the system complex. This is because any decision to change one process can affect other processes and vice versa. Those changes can create new conditions that did not exist before. Simultaneous engineering means early consideration of requirements in all areas, which increases the interactions between those areas. The people involved in product development can change the system's behaviour, namely, human imagination and decision-making, in connection with the process changes, which makes complexity management important. In the next section, we will look at complexity management as related to lifecycle engineering.

4.10 Complexity Cost -v- Modularization

Complexity increases in line with a greater number of variants and higher customer and market demands. Industry has been addressing the rising cost of complexity through modular product development and platform strategies designed to increase competitiveness, especially in the wider transport industry: automobiles, rail vehicles, aircraft and marine vessels.

Modular components are not limited to mechanical parts, because there are the hardware and software components of mechanical, electrical, pneumatic and hydraulic devices, systems and subsystems. Systems function both independently and within the overall system, such as the air-conditioning and braking systems in a car. Subsystems are the functional parts of the system, such as the control unit (both software and hardware) of a braking system, which enables the braking system as a unit to communicate with other systems and subsystems. The final product is the overall system, namely, a motor car consisting of parts, components, devices, systems and subsystems. The car, for example, is not itself complex although it can be a highly complicated system. What is undeniably complex, however, is the processes of manufacturing that car in combination with people in many different roles and capacities.

4.11 Complexity Cost -v- Platform Strategy

In recent decades, more and more companies have opted for a platform strategy because of environmental requirements such as reusable parts, product waste engineering and sustainability. The platform strategy distinguishes between, on the one hand, the long-term orientation of research and development towards the creation of new technologies and, on the other, support for short-term product development. The platform strategy focuses on the development of new technologies, whereby it is important to bundle the organization's know-how for shortening development times and enabling a greater variety and variants of standard products, thereby reducing development and manufacturing costs. It is crucial to adapt purchasing processes to the platform strategy to optimize subcontractor costs, especially once-off costs for new developments or changes and modifications to standard products, and to reduce costs incurred by manufacturing processes, machine set-up and changeover and workflows.

Unquestionably, technology development based on platform and module development brings advantages in terms of cost reduction. However, this does not reduce complexity; on the contrary, it creates a complex system through process characteristics, in which the know-how of differently thinking people and different machines are bundled. Such organizations function and react to risks in a network more productively than other forms of organization. Technology development with platform and module development strategy have higher technical risks in the beginning, which are reduced with more knowledge over time. In the long run, platforms and modules make the risks in product development low and controllable.

There is a perception that without a product management system or configuration of parts, modules and a platform strategy, the product supply chain becomes more complex, thus increasing the complexity and manufacturing costs. For this reason, various ways of working, together with different methods, processes and tools, are being developed as part of a drive to reduce complexity costs, among other outgoings. Those reductionist approaches are now reaching their limits, because of the rigid linear processes that have evolved over time. The traditional ways of working and the methodologies associated with them are summarized under the term 'quality function deployment' (QFD). The composition of the processes of QFD is linear, including the processes of failure mode and effect analysis, make-or-buy, simultaneous engineering and other preferred process chains such as pre-development from design to manufacturing and maintenance-and-service and, at the end, dismantling and disposal. The mapping of such processes to product properties is also linear.

In some literature, product descriptions are confined to technical, operational and commercial properties. In these processes, the possibilities are limited to certain characteristics and to the customer's personal preferences. Such characteristics include safety, health preferences, quality, comfort, aesthetics and luxury, to name just a few. At that point, it is already important to distinguish between complicated and complex systems. Cost reduction in linear processes with the reductionist approach refers to complicated systems, such as the final product. Non-linear systems, on the other hand, are complex systems, such as the creation of a new technology by humans in combination with machines. Human imagination and decision-making function as a complex system, and these therefore influence the development and design of a product. A system in a complex state should be manageable without needing to be reduced. Managing complexity, indeed, makes sense as an act of prevention that takes into consideration the changes in a system's behaviour.

4.12 Complexity Cost -v- Lifecycle Engineering

The development and design of a product is referred to by some sources as lifecycle engineering. The effort and cost involved in lifecycle engineering are referred to as complexity costs, so models and processes are developed for complexity reduction. However, the process of lifecycle engineering starts with customer requirements and market acquisition and continues through design, development, product lifecycle and ultimate disposal. The costs of those processes are not merely routine complexity costs.

4.13 Complexity Cost -v- Economic and Accounting Cost

The distinction between 'economic' and 'accounting' cost is also worth making at this point. In some literature, economic and accounting costs are lumped together as total costs, which leads to silo thinking. The costs in a complicated system are not the same as those in a complex one. The described strategies, such as modularization, platform and lifecycle engineering, are used primarily as a means of reducing costs. Failure to distinguish between 'economic' and 'accounting' costs can lead to uncertainty and to confusion between different measures. In order, therefore, to look at complexity costs across the entire value chain, it makes sense to consider these classifications of costs separately. An important reason for this is that complexity costs persist because of their characteristics, including functional costs such as wages, materials, operating costs and rent, all of which depend on various internal and external factors, so that any change in factors can affect the overall cost position, especially during times of uncertainty, such as during energy crises.

4.14 Complexity Cost -v- Productivity

A fundamental characteristic of production is 'productivity', which describes the relationship between the output and input of a system and is accordingly used as a measure in various scientific fields. In turn, a vital element in productivity has, historically, been the use of energy to create and deliver a product or even a service. In the early days, the main energy sources were muscle power, water and wind. Productivity has a local effect with fluctuating results caused by complex processes. The output was lower compared to the input, the energy consumption. Muscle power depended on the food people ate, which in turn depended on nature and other human elements such as health and diligence. Waterpower depended on its source and accessibility and was influenced by natural events. Wind power depended on climatic conditions and the season. Such processes have the characteristics of a complex system.

The importance of productivity has, however, grown enormously between the first and fourth industrial revolutions. New energy sources and electricity-generating machines have increased the level of productivity over the last century and a half. In effect, new technologies have steadily increased productivity from the time of steam engines up to the use of electricity. Productivity in transport and logistics has increased due to infrastructure—productivity being a measure of energy consumption. Energy consumption in road transport is relatively higher than in water and rail transport, but lower than in air transport. Roads, motorways and traffic regulations influence the productivity of the transport sector, as do waterways, from transport by sailing ships to the propulsion of shipping vehicles by machinery and fossil fuels. Transporting oil, gas and other liquids through pipelines is very energy efficient. Machines have increased productivity in all sectors: agriculture, industry, toolmaking, mining and others.

In the world of work and processes, productivity occupies a special place, which has been evident through the industrial age. The notion of productivity can be applied to work, to production, to the supply chain and to business continuity. This also applies to the processes of administration and management. It is worth noting that productivity has also steadily increased within communication systems, from the telegraph right through to today's satellite systems. Since the development and use of automated systems and the associated process landscape, productivity in industrial sectors has increased to an enormous extent. This has expanded through computers, data processing and information technology. It is still in the implementation phase in the global industrial world but is being overtaken by digital technology and Industry 4.0. It does not make sense to fully implement automation technology, but in combination with advanced technologies, automation processes will further increase productivity.

Productivity is a vitally important factor in lifecycle engineering, where it applies to the entire value chain of a product. Output-input relations are process-dependent operations of human and machine resources whose characteristic behaviour corresponds to that of a complex system. There are other factors too that are related to lifecycle engineering, including the social factor, which determines and influences the processes of product lifecycle engineering. Those function like a complex system. Society, in demographic terms, is an important factor for product lifecycle engineering. This is explained in more detail in the section 'Demographics'. In terms of the environmental, product lifecycle engineering refers to eco-design, waste engineering, nature and ecosystem processes. Lastly, in the realm of technology, product lifecycle engineering is subject to manufacturing, efficiency and innovation. In the above discussed areas, lifecycle engineering is all about understanding and governing complexity.

4.15 Complexity Cost -v- Supply Chain

In the technological arena, complexity of procurement is a particular challenge for the industrial and manufacturing sectors. In manufacturing, procurement of standard parts runs along linear processes. However, variants and customer-specific requirements can result in a complex system, which cannot be managed with conventional processes. The procurement department purchases the raw materials, components, and system and subsystem parts. Any change in the purchasing specification can have an impact on technological systems and their interfaces. In some literature, the complexity of procurement is limited to 'avoid and reduce'. This approach is a projection of risk management in the procurement process. Reducing a complex system changes the behaviour of the whole system, with an unclear outcome. Such procedures can have disastrous consequences, such as delays in delivery, problematic interfaces, rising costs and even interruptions in production.

Procurement is directly related to the supply chain in the global market. Transport and logistics are an important part of a procurement process. The complexity of the supply chain is partly explained in some literature by linear processes. Complex processes require an understanding of the actors and their role within the supply chain. The disruption and interruption of supply chains leads to uncertainties, and subsequent risks can have significant consequences for companies.

As already noted, in the manufacturing and production industry, variants and changes increase complexity thanks to the increased number of areas involved and their interactions with each other. A system becomes more complex when the number of involved elements increases. These include sales resources, R&D and engineering, internal and external orders, integration of new and changed purchase items, production orders, machine upgrades and retrofits, and logistics and transportation, just to mention a few. The complexity effort and its associated costs are distributed to all areas and functions of the company along the entire value chain. In sales, this can mean additional effort and resources for variant and change management and additional one-off costs for new or changed parts. In R&D, it can result in additional engineering effort, documentation, and timing and coordination, together with possible technological work in production such as the processing of interfaces and changes to standard products. In the area of production, additional machines and equipment, as well as possible changes in work processes, all increase complexity costs. The same holds true in purchasing, with its additional contracts and work plans, production coordination, technology and the number of parties involved, along with possible further quality assurance through variants and changes, not to mention increased disposal processes, warehousing, logistics and transport. In the service area, additional specifications, documents, repairs, equipment, spare parts, special tools and education & training all incur extra costs.

It is recommended that case studies be conducted on complexity in the manufacturing and production industry to contribute to the management of complexity and possibly increase the resilience—and thus the competitiveness—of companies. These have special relevance in the areas of product variants, module and platform strategy, R&D and related processes, purchasing and procurement, manufacturing and the execution of complex projects.

We will now consider recent research in the fields of project complexity and the management of complex projects, which are of special relevance to this book, to help us to better understand and explore the delivery of complex portfolios into the global market. This bottom-up approach was part of the case study in the author's PhD and builds a basis for the conceptual framework (enterprise resilience framework), as well as providing a reference base for discussion.

4.16 Projects and Project Management Complexity

The theoretical study of Complexity helps us in gaining a better understanding of the area in practice. The research fields of project complexity and the management of complex projects are growing and have merited much discussion over the course of the last four decades.

Most current project management has been enriched by reductionist techniques and hard paradigms such as PRINCE2®, PMBoK®, APM and PMI. The hard paradigm provides well-approved frameworks for, and approaches to, the execution of single projects (Aritua et al., 2009; Pryke & Smyth, 2012; Wideman, 2002; Bentley, 2010).

In practice, most projects are executed in a multi-project environment, with a large part of such projects being executed within the portfolio and program. Bearing this in mind, it can be argued that the complexity theory provides a holistic view of multi-project management and indeed gives us a basis for a deeper understanding of the multi-project environment.

Project execution using the reductionist approach in multi-project environments can lead to failure or, at best, limited success. The reasons for such failure or limited success of projects are related to either soft paradigms, which cannot be measured using the qualitative and quantitative approach, or to hard paradigms (Blismas et al., 2004; Pollack, 2007).

The relationship between complexity theory and multi-project management is less widely discussed than might be expected. For this reason, there is a need to explore the perceptions of practitioners of complexity within the multi-project environment. Within that environment, practical knowledge of the implications of the complexity theory mindset is limited. Given that the application of hard paradigms is cited as a common reason for the failure of projects in multi-project environments, it is important to understand and identify the project execution methods used in such environments, both in theory and in practice. In order to do this, the application of complexity theory is recommended, because it provides a holistic view of multi-project management (Aritua et al., 2009; Blismas et al., 2004; Maylor et al., 2006).

It is generally acknowledged by project management professionals that while complexity can create planning obstacles, it can help considerably in the identification of goals and objectives and the selection of project organization. Also, it is often used in the selection of project acquisitions, and two types of project complexity are suggested. Organizational complexity is related to the interaction between the organizational elements of a project. Technological complexity, on the other hand, refers to the transformation process, which involves operations (the provision and arrangement of activities), techniques (characteristic of materials) and knowledge and skills. The perception and elements of complexity in large infrastructure projects have been investigated, and a new framework for project complexity has emerged, with extended project constraints in terms of resources and objectives. Six different types of project complexity are defined: technical, social, financial, legal, organizational and temporal. The complexity of a project has a bearing on the process of project management, which extends to project organization, resource planning, procurement and project performance, regarding time, cost and quality. The organization of large and complex projects is multidimensional and ever-changing. Organizational complexity has already been discussed in terms of differentiation and interdependency. The vertical (hierarchical) structure and horizontal (organizational units) structure are two dimensions of organizational complexity by differentiation. It is, therefore, safe to conclude that the main problem with taking the reductionist approach to project execution in multi-project environments is that all too often it leads to failure or, at best, limited success (Dunović et al., 2014; Bosch-Rekveldt et al., 2010; Baccarini, 1996; Williams, 1995; Hertogh & Westerveld, 2010; Bennett, 1991).

As mentioned earlier, projects can be characterized as complex socio-technological systems; the project management process, project organization, resource planning, procurement and project performance regarding time, cost, and quality and uncertainty of goal and methods all characterize project complexity. The application of complexity theory has expanded to organizational change, network and design effort, with the result of preventing the development of effective solutions (Olson, 2002; Buchanan & Aldana-Gonzales, 2003; Barabási & Bonabeau, 2003; Allen, 2012; Maxwell et al., 2002; Baccarini, 1996; Williams, 1995; Bennett, 1991).

It is worth discussing project environment complexity in relation to the various stakeholders in the following section. This will hopefully help readers to visualize the different complexity factors and their effect on projects and project management processes.

4.17 Project Stakeholder Complexity

Companies must be able to respond quickly and flexibly to any changes in their environment in a fast-changing dynamic market. Stakeholders and their behaviour are project-related environmental factors that can have an important influence on the success or failure of a project. Project managers must be able to know and involve their environment in project planning, project control and project monitoring. For this reason, a detailed understanding of possible stakeholders and their possibilities of influence can have a major impact on successful project management. According to ISO 26000, transparency, reliability, credibility, accessibility, legal compliance, competence, commitment, flexibility, profitability, stability, increase in value and business security are all stakes. ISO 21500 states that the purpose of managing stakeholders is to provide appropriate understanding and attention to those stakeholders' needs and expectations, and according to ISO 10006, stakeholders are defined thus: 'Interested party: Individual or group with an interest in the performance or success of an organisation' (ISO, 2003). Instead of the term 'interested party', however, the more common term 'stakeholder' is used in this book, since this is what is more frequently used both in the literature and in practice (Abresch, 2003; ISO, 2010, 2012).

In recent decades, researchers have characterized 'stakeholders' in various categories. Primary stakeholders are suppliers, customers and functional supervisors, while secondary stakeholders would include competitors and environmental protection groups. Internal stakeholders include the project management team and its members and the human resources department, whereas external stakeholders, who are not part of the company, might include customers, suppliers and professional associations. Current stakeholders have been identified and are known, while potential stakeholders have not yet made themselves known as stakeholders but are potential stakeholders. Active stakeholders exert a direct influence on the project, whereas passive stakeholders remain in the background and, initially at least, do not exert any influence. Stakeholders with contractual obligations are directly linked to the project, while public stakeholders do not have any contractual obligations (Pinto, 1998; Litke, 1995; Clarkson et al., 1994; Rowley, 1997; Clarke, 1998).

Both direct and indirect technical environment factors can have a significant bearing on the outcome of a project. It is important to be able to identify factors that might have a direct influence, such as sales development, on the entire company, or that have an indirect impact, such as exchange-rate fluctuations, on the project.

There may also be both internal and external socio-environmental factors at play: direct socio-environmental factors are directly linked to the investors, whereas indirect socio-environmental factors are normally not directly related to the project but can still have a high impact on it. This group includes market competitors, local politicians and organized individuals with an interest in the project (Abresch, 2003).

Internal and external organizational-social factors can also affect a project's outcome. Within the organizational-social groups, a further distinction is made between groups that belong to the company (internal) and groups outside the company (external). Organizational-social factors include all influencing factors that are introduced to the project by individuals and institutions (Patzak & Rattay, 2004).

Another category of factors is objective content-related factors. These factors are not directly generated by the actions of individuals, but they can still influence a project. This group includes concurrent projects and routine applications in the company. The value creation and value enhancement of companies and projects largely depend on the degree of support and satisfaction among associated stakeholders. This highlights the embedding of the company in the broader environment as well as its necessary orientation to the outside and to the network relationship of project and environment (Patzak & Rattay, 2004; Freiling, 2013).

It is vitally important for companies that they be able to respond to any changes in their environment in a fast-changing, dynamic market quickly and flexibly. Stakeholders and their behaviour are project-related environmental factors that can have an important bearing on the success or failure of a project. Project managers must know how to include their environment in project planning, project control and project monitoring. For this reason, a detailed understanding of potential stakeholders and their possible spheres of influence can have a massive impact on successful project management.

In the literature, there is a common understanding of project complexity and its elements and of the interconnectedness and mutual dependencies between those elements and how they interact. There is not so much evidence, however, regarding the application of complexity theory in practice, such as in large engineering organizations. This is something we will look at more closely in this book, in particular the model and process for supporting an effective emergent strategy against undesirable changes. At this point in time, it is difficult to find a practical answer to the question, 'How do you measure complexity in a robust manner that takes account of structural, dynamic and interaction elements?' (Baccarini, 1996; Whitty & Maylor, 2009).

4.18 Characteristics of Project Complexity

The characteristics of complexity—the so-called complexity factors—are listed and linked to the concept and characteristics of the complex adaptive system, to the various categories of complexity and to the factors contributing to project complexity shown in Table 4.1.

Table 4.1 Characteristics of complexity as identified from the literature

Concept of CAS	Category of complexity	Factors contributing to project complexity
Interrelationships	• Organizational • Technological	• Number of stakeholders • Number of requirements • Number of specialists • Number and variety of tasks • Number of components • Interrelationships between technical processes • Number of locations • Number of specifications, different norms and standards • Organizational risks • Technical risks
Adaptability	• Organizational/stakeholders • Environment	• Variety of stakeholder perspectives • Political influence • Requirements • Uncertainty in scope • Environmental risks
Self-organization	• Organizational	• Response to changing business environments • Experience with parties involved
Emergence	• Organizational• Technological	• Trust in contractor • Internal company support • Trust in the project team • Experience with technology • Availability of resources and skills
Feedback	• Organizational	• Variety of stakeholders' perspectives • Response to changing business environments • Internal strategic pressures
Non-linearity	• Organizational• Technological• Environmental	• Uncertainty in technical methods • Newness of technology • Changing business environments • Availability of resources and skills

References

Abresch, J.-P. (2003). *Projektumfeld und Stakeholder*. GPM [Hrsg.]: Projektmanagement Fachmann.

Alhadeff-Jones, M. (2008). Three generations of complexity theories: Nuances and ambiguities. *Educational Philosophy and Theory, 40*(1), 66–82.

Allen, P. M. (2012). *Cities and regions as self-organizing systems: Models of complexity*. Routledge.

Ambulkar, S., Blackhurst, J., & Grawe, S. (2015). Firm's resilience to supply chain disruptions: Scale development and empirical examination. *Journal of Operations Management, 33-34*, 111–122.

Aritua, B., Smith, N. J., & Bower, D. (2009). Construction client multi-projects–a complex adaptive systems perspective. *International Journal of Project Management, 27*(1), 72–79.

Axelrod, R., & Cohen, M. D. (2000). *Harnessing complexity: Organizational implications of a scientific frontier*. Basic Books.

Baccarini, D. (1996). The concept of project complexity--a review. *International Journal of Project Management, 14*(4), 201–204.

Barabási, A.-L., & Bonabeau, E. (2003). Scale-free networks. *Scientific American, 288*(5), 60–69.

Bar-Yam, Y. (2003). When systems engineering fails-toward complex systems engineering. In *Systems, man and cybernetics*. IEEE International Conference on. 2003. IEEE.

Bennett, J. (1991). *International construction project management: General theory and practice*. Butterworth-Heinemann.

Bentley, P. J. (2002). *Digital biology. The creation of life inside computers and how it will affect us*.

Bentley, C. (2010). *Prince2: A practical handbook*. Routledge.

Bielza, C., Gómez, M., & Shenoy, P. P. (2011). A review of representation issues and modeling challenges with influence diagrams. *Omega, 39*(3), 227–241.

Blismas, N., et al. (2004). A typology for clients' multi-project environments. *Construction Management and Economics, 22*(4), 357–371.

Bosch-Rekveldt, M., et al. (2010. In Press, Corrected Proof). Grasping project complexity in large engineering projects: The TOE (technical, organizational and environmental) framework. *International Journal of Project Management, 29*, 728.

Brusset, X., & Teller, C. (2017). Supply chain capabilities, risks, and resilience. *International Journal of Production Economics, 184*, 59–68.

Buchanan, M. (2002). *Small world: Uncovering nature's hidden networks*.

Buchanan, M., & Aldana-Gonzales, M. (2003). Nexus: Small worlds and the ground-breaking science of networks. *Physics Today, 56*, 71–72.

Byrne, D. S. (1998). *Complexity theory and the social sciences: An introduction*. Psychology Press.

Capra, F. (1996). *The web of life: A new synthesis of mind and matter*. HarperCollins.

Cilliers, P., & Spurrett, D. (1999). Complexity and post-modernism: Understanding complex systems. *South African Journal of Philosophy, 18*(2), 258–274.

Clarke, T. (1998). The stakeholder corporation: A business philosophy for the information age. *Long Range Planning, 31*(2), 182–194.

Clarkson, M., et al. (1994). The Toronto conference: Reflections on stakeholder theory. *Business and Society, 33*(1), 82.

Costanza, R., et al. (1993). Modeling complex ecological economic systems. *Bioscience, 43*(8), 545–555.

Dindarian, K. (2019). *Exploring enterprise resilience through the theoretical lens of complexity: a case study situated in the high value-manufacturing sector*. The University of Manchester.

Dunović, I. B., Radujković, M., & Škreb, K. A. (2014). Towards a new model of complexity–the case of large infrastructure projects. *Procedia-Social and Behavioral Sciences, 119*, 730–738.

Elleuch, H., et al. (2016). Resilience and vulnerability in supply chain: Literature review. *IFAC-PapersOnLine, 49*(12), 1448–1453.

Floricel, S., Michela, J. L., & Piperca, S. (2016). Complexity, uncertainty-reduction strategies, and project performance. *International Journal of Project Management, 34*(7), 1360–1383.

Freiling, J. (2013). *Gemeinsame Werteschaffung durch engste vertikale Kooperation* (p. 229). Perspektiven einer stakeholderorientierten Unternehmensführung.

Hertogh, M., & Westerveld, E. (2010). *Playing with complexity. Management and organisation of large infrastructural projects*. AT Osborne/Transumo.

Holland, J. H. (1992). Complex adaptive systems. *Daedalus*, 17–30.

Holland, J. H., & Miller, J. H. (1991). Artificial adaptive agents in economic theory. *The American Economic Review, 81*(2), 365–370.

ISO, E. (2012). 21500: 2013–06. (2013). Leitlinien Projektmanagement (Entwurf) ISO. 21500.

ISO, I., 10006. (2003). *Quality management systems-guidelines for quality management in projects* (p. 2003). International Organization for Standardization (ISO).
ISO, I., FDIS 26000. (2010). *Guidance on social responsibility*. ISO.
Johnson, S. (2002). *Emergence: The connected lives of ants, brains, cities, and software*. Simon and Schuster.
Kaplan, S., & Seebeck, L. (2001). Harnessing complexity in CSCW. In *ECSCW 2001*. Springer.
Kauffman, S. (1995). *At home in the universe: the search for laws of selforganization and complexity* (Vol. 1996, p. viii). Oxford University Press.
Lansing, J. S., & Kremer, J. N. (1994). Emergent properties of Balinese water temple networks: Coadaptation on a rugged fitness landscape. In *Santa Fe institute studies in the sciences of complexity-proceedings volume* (Vol. 95, p. 97). Addison-Wesley Publishing CO.
Lewin, R. (1999). *Complexity: Life at the edge of chaos*. University of Chicago Press.
Litke, H.-D. (1995). *Projektmanagement: Methoden, Techniken, Verhaltensweisen* (3rd ed.).
Liyanage, U. (2010). Strategy and complexity. Sri Lankan. *Journal of Management*, 15.
Mansfield, J. (2010). *The nature of change or the law of unintended consequences: An introductory text to designing complex systems and managing change*. World Scientific.
Maxwell, T. T., Ertas, A., & Tanik, M. M. (2002). Harnessing complexity in design. *Journal of Integrated Design and Process Science, 6*(3), 63–74.
Maylor, H., et al. (2006). From projectification to programmification. *International Journal of Project Management, 24*(8), 663–674.
Miller, C. C., & Cardinal, L. B. (1994). Strategic planning and firm performance: A synthesis of more than two decades of research. *Academy of Management Journal, 37*(6), 1649–1665.
Mitchell Waldrop, M. (1992). *Complexity*. Touchstone Books Simon & Schuster.
Neill, S., & Rose, G. M. (2006). The effect of strategic complexity on marketing strategy and organizational performance. *Journal of Business Research, 59*(1), 1–10.
Olson, R. E. (2002). Facilitating organization change: Lessons from complexity science. *Quality Progress, 35*(6), 112–112.
Padalkar, M., & Gopinath, S. (2016). Are complexity and uncertainty distinct concepts in project management? A taxonomical examination from literature. *International Journal of Project Management, 34*(4), 688–700.
Patzak, G., & Rattay, G. (2004). *Projektmanagement. 4., wes. überarb. Aufl.* Linde.
Phelan, S. E. (2001). What is complexity science, really? *Emergence, A Journal of Complexity Issues in Organizations and Management, 3*(1), 120–136.
Pinto, J. K. (1998). *The project management institute project management handbook (Jossey-Bass Business & Management Series)*. Jossey-Bass.
Pollack, J. (2007). The changing paradigms of project management. *International Journal of Project Management, 25*(3), 266–274.
Pryke, S., & Smyth, H. (2012). *The management of complex projects: A relationship approach*. John Wiley & Sons.
Rowley, T. J. (1997). Moving beyond dyadic ties: A network theory of stakeholder influences. *Academy of Management Review, 22*(4), 887–910.
Schneider, M., & Somers, M. (2006). Organizations as complex adaptive systems: Implications of complexity theory for leadership research. *The Leadership Quarterly, 17*(4), 351–365.
Smith, A. C. (2005). Complexity theory for organisational futures studies. *Foresight, 7*(3), 22–30.
Stacey, R. D., Griffin, D., & Shaw, P. (2000). *Complexity and management: Fad or radical challenge to systems thinking?* Psychology Press.
Tetradian glossary. (2016).
Thomé, A. M. T., et al. (2016). Similarities and contrasts of complexity, uncertainty, risks, and resilience in supply chains and temporary multi-organization projects. *International Journal of Project Management, 34*(7), 1328–1346.

Van Beurden, E. K., et al. (2011). Making sense in a complex landscape: How the Cynefin framework from complex adaptive systems theory can inform health promotion practice. *Health Promotion International, 28*(1), 73–83.

Whitty, S. J., & Maylor, H. (2009). And then came complex project management (revised). *International Journal of Project Management, 27*(3), 304–310.

Wideman, R. M. (2002). *Comparing PRINCE2® with PMBoK®*. AEW Services.

Williams, T. (1995). A classified bibliography of recent research relating to project risk management. *European Journal of Operational Research, 85*(1), 18–38.

Enterprise Risk Management 5

In this section, we will look at how companies maintain their share values and protect their stakeholders' interests and how enterprise risk management (ERM) is taken into account when meeting legal, regulatory and standard obligations and requirements. We will consider the various definitions of ERM and its processes and clarify the distinction between ERM and enterprise resilience. The nature of ERM will also be explained, in order to better understand the interdependencies of the risks that companies face and how those companies align their strategy and objectives with those risks, along with the processes of decision-making and progress measurement.

5.1 Need for Enterprise Risk Management

The objective of enterprise risk management is to develop a holistic view of the most serious risks facing the achievement of the entity's most important goals.

In today's dynamic global environment, the management of risk is vital. The ERM-integrated approach has become important because of increased volatility in the business world, and the risk situation of many companies has significantly worsened. Globalization, high pressure from international competition, the trend of company networking and modern information technologies are all parameters that characterize the company environment. These changes are taking place quickly and frequently, with less time for preparation and response. It is, therefore, becoming increasingly difficult to keep a company under control. Increasing cost and performance pressures, progressive automation and complexity of production facilities, as well as strong turbulence in the financial markets; all combine to make it difficult to deal with potential opportunities and risks (Denk et al., 2008; Gordon et al., 2009; Quon et al., 2012; Beasley et al., 2010).

The drivers of change and development in ERM frameworks are regulatory development, rating agency views, economic capital, conglomerates, the convergence of financial products, markets, globalization and board attention to public

K. Dindarian, *Embracing the Black Swan*, Future of Business and Finance,
https://doi.org/10.1007/978-3-031-29344-3_5

demands for certain assurances. The impact of ERM on management practices is about crisis planning and liquidity crisis management (Bowen et al., 2006).

There are further triggers for the need for structured risk management:

1. Discontinuities and turbulence in the corporate environment as the primary driver of risk management;
2. Institutional frameworks as secondary drivers of risk management, such as COSO-II (COSO-ERM), the first set of standards on risk management, which was prepared by the Committee of Sponsoring Organizations of the Treadway Commission (COSO), with a draft on enterprise risk management to create a standard for risk management systems and standardize terminology in this area;
3. Gaps in existing risk management systems (Denk et al., 2008).

Traditional risk management, known as the risk-management-with-silo approach, is subject to several limitations. These include the fact that interlinking risks between silos are not considered as well as the possibility that some risks may affect a multiplicity of silos, not to mention that the response of individual silos may have an impact on the whole organization. Because of these potential shortcomings in risk management, there was a need for improvement in the concept of risk management (Beasley et al., 2010; McShane et al., 2011; Arnold et al., 2011; Frigo & Anderson, 2011).

Recent events such as Lehman Brothers, the Enron collapse, WorldCom, the 9–11 terrorist attacks, MF Global, Hurricane Katrina and the Covid pandemic, among others, have all served to remind us of the importance of having successful procedures in place, for identifying, evaluating and reacting to vital risk incidents that can negatively influence the success of an undertaking. As a result of having to face various hazard occasions, many organizations have started to identify risks and make appropriate improvements. In this regard, it has been argued that conventional ERM methods should be used to address emergent risks, but it must be borne in mind that conventional ERM frameworks are limited, and expansion of the whole concept of ERM is necessary in order to be able to address emergent risks and establish organizational resilience (DiPiazza Jr & van Eijkern, 2009; DiPiazza, 2008; Beasley et al., 2015).

As to the question of whether there is a greater need for ERM, enterprises with effective ERM enjoy long-term competitive advantages, thus creating added value for shareholders at both macro and micro levels. It has been suggested that companies can improve their performance by using an ERM framework and that the relationship between ERM and a company's performance is affected by five identified factors: environmental uncertainty, industry competition, the size of the firm, the level of complexity and the degree of monitoring by the board of directors. Recent studies have indicated that companies with a higher level of maturity in their ERM processes are characterized by higher operating performance than those having less developed ERM processes (Gordon et al., 2009; McShane et al., 2011; Nocco & Stulz, 2006; Callahan & Soileau, 2017).

5.2 ERM Frameworks

Enterprise risk management can be defined as an integrated framework for managing risks—credit, market and operational—as well as economic capital and risk transfer, all designed to maximize enterprise value. It is also said to be a decision-making discipline that addresses differences in company goals (Lam, 2000; Makomaski, 2008).

There are a number important ERM frameworks, each describing an approach for identifying, analysing, responding to and monitoring risks and opportunities in the organization's environment. Management selects a risk-response strategy for specific risks that have been identified and analysed, which strategy may include different ERM frameworks. ERM in business includes the methods and processes used by organizations for managing risks, so that opportunities related to the achievement of objectives can be better exploited. ERM provides a risk management framework that involves identifying and assessing events or circumstances that can have a bearing on the organization's objectives, determining a response strategy and monitoring progress. This enables business enterprises to create value for their stakeholders, including the community at large, and to protect everyone's interests.

Normally, the components of those frameworks are as follows:

- *Avoidance:* exiting the activities giving rise to risk;
- *Reduction:* taking action to reduce the likelihood or impact related to the risk;
- *Alternative actions:* considering other feasible steps for minimizing risks;
- *Share or insure:* transferring or sharing a portion of the risk for financing purposes;
- *Acceptance:* no action being taken, due to a cost/benefit decision.

Monitoring is typically performed by management as part of its internal control activities, which can include a review of analytical reports or management committee meetings with relevant experts, in order to understand how the risk response strategy is working and whether the objectives are being achieved (D'Arcy & Brogan, 2001).

Attributes might include the following:

- Balancing qualitative and quantitative tools
- Providing early warnings and escalations
- Influencing business activities
- Reflecting environmental changes
- Incorporating risk interdependencies (Lam, 2003)

In 2004, the Committee of Sponsoring Organizations of the Treadway Commission (COSO) issued an integrated framework that defines ERM as '. . .a process, effected by an entity's board of directors, management and other personnel, applied in strategy setting and across the enterprise, designed to identify potential events that may affect the entity, and manage risk to be within its risk appetite, to provide reasonable assurance regarding the achievement of entity objectives' (COSO and C. o.S.O.o.t.T. Commission, 2004). There is a focus on four categories that influence the business objective(s):

1. *Strategic risks* include such factors as completion, customer preferences, technological innovation and regulatory or political impediments.
2. *Financial risks* cover potential losses due to changes in financial markets, including interest rates, foreign exchange rates, commodity prices, liquidity risks and credit risks.
3. *Operational risks* cover a wide variety of situations, which may include customer satisfaction, product development, product failure, trademark protection, corporate leadership, information technology, fraud and information risk.
4. *Compliance risks* resulting directly or indirectly from regulatory measures are varied and can include health and safety, human rights protection, labour law, anti-bribery laws and environmental risks.

The COSO framework builds on eight interrelated components in order to establish effective ERM: internal environment, objectives, event (risk) identification, risk assessment, risk response, control activities, information and communication and monitoring (COSO, The (COSO), 2004).

5.3 The ERM Process

As part of the risk management process, it should be ensured that any risks facing a company are identified and managed and that risk-relevant information is routed systematically and in an orderly way to decision-makers, so that risk management measures can be taken in time. Four phases are identified in the risk management process:

1. *Systematic risk identification:* Risk classification, deliberate search for risks;
2. *Risk assessment and aggregation:* Quantitative or qualitative risk assessment, risk aggregation;
3. *Risk control and monitoring:* Risk avoidance, reduction, diversification, transfer, and prevention and the setting up of early warning systems;
4. *Risk reporting:* Both internal and external reporting (Denk et al., 2008).

The aim of risk identification is the timely, regular, quick, willing and economical recording of all opportunities and risks in the company that may have an impact on its corporate goals and/or target system. This involves a range of tasks that include a systematic and structured survey of all relevant risks (including risk sources, effects and time of occurrence) together with the categorization and grouping of risks, and these in turn form the basis for further steps in the risk management process. To achieve the goals of risk management, a systematic, process-oriented approach is necessary. The quality of the risk identification depends on the scope of the information that has been obtained. Depending on the company, this identification can be carried out from the perspectives of different personnel, as well as from different content perspectives, such as the opportunities and types of risk (for example, economic, financial and external risks), the level of the processes (projects, core and supporting processes) and the business areas (such as services, IT and production). Two approaches to the risk identification process are offered, namely, the top-down and bottom-up approaches, both of which are described in the following section (Denk et al., 2008).

Executives are expected to maintain a detailed record of the company in all its aspects, including any opportunities or risks that have occurred or have the potential to do so. With the top-down approach, the risks are not identified in the necessary depth and granularity, because executives do not, as a matter of course, probe into such details and, in any event, they have limited time. Although a top-down identification of risk may be more cost-effective, it is argued, this approach will by no means succeed in creating broad risk awareness within the company (Denk et al., 2008).

The view has also been expressed that the bottom-up approach integrates deeper hierarchical levels in the risk identification process, thereby creating a company-wide risk management culture. It is important to ensure that employees at all levels of the company take the matter of risk seriously and actively participate in the risk management process. In any event, valuable information, analysis and experience can be gained from employees in both the operational and central units, who work daily at the customer interface and as part of the internal service process. Too little information or room for manoeuvre, it is argued, can lead to exaggerated attention to detail and corresponding exaggerated granularity, which leaves the overall picture of risk identification lacking. In terms of cost, this approach is certainly the more expensive (Denk et al., 2008).

There are benefits to linking the top-down and bottom-up approaches. The group of people involved in risk identification includes not only the senior executives but also the middle management level. The group of people participating in risk identification should be able to cover all risk aspects of the company. They need to consider corporate focus, market analysis, competition, product quality, aspects of R&D, procurement matters, internal processes, employee-related issues, legal and tax matters, strategy and policy issues. To encapsulate as many relevant risks as possible, the risks are systematized into so-called risk areas. These serve as a basis for the cause-related identification of risks. Both internal and external factors have been identified for the implementation of ERM, which refer, respectively, to the maximization of shareholders' wealth and to globalization, corporate governance and technological progress (Denk et al., 2008; Hilz-Ward & Everling, 2009; Razali & Tahir, 2011).

5.4 ERM -v- Enterprise Resilience

Over the last four decades, management accounting reports have evolved and developed in line with both the internal and external changes faced by companies in their operating environments. The internal environment includes factors such as financial pressures from, for instance, senior management initiatives, while external factors could be globalization, competition and differentiated products. Companies today can hardly afford to ignore the risks presented by environmental changes. Management accounting can be an important tool for dealing with change and it can help senior management in situations of considerable uncertainty and complexity. It does not, in itself, eliminate risk—but it can force key agents to explain their assumptions (Cooper, 1996; Burns & Vaivio, 2001).

Current rapid changes and the fast speed of information flow serve to increase risks and uncertainty and to drive new threats. This, in turn, increases the expectations of shareholders, regulators and other stakeholders, and companies are thus being challenged to be more transparent about the risks they face and their ability to manage them. They view conventional ERM as a rather old notion that has gained renewed focus and relevance in the wake of the financial crisis and stress the need for companies to develop strong risk resilience to ensure survival and success in today's increasingly uncertain environment. Risk resilience, they argue, allows an organization to anticipate and adapt to change. Furthermore, it enables the absorption of—and recovery from—risk events, including unexpected black swan events. Moreover, risk resilience enables companies to seize the opportunities hidden within those risk events. It is the application and embedding process that needs overhaul. There is no need to bother with another type of ERM to overcome the dynamic business environment as such; however, what is important is to ensure the dynamic of an operation, along with the ability to deal with unexpected risks and handle confrontation with the more extensive business environment (Everson et al., 2012).

Companies view risk as a threat to their financial portfolios and therefore focus their enterprise risk management on securing their portfolios against losses. Enterprise resilience, on the other hand, has a broader and increasingly important role. Although many enterprises have expanded, thus creating potential competitive advantages, their vulnerabilities have correspondingly increased. The assessment of organizational resilience and risk management can—and indeed should—be aligned, in order to close the dangerous gap in the resilience profile of an enterprise (Starr et al., 2003).

Enterprise resilience is the ability to withstand systemic disruptions and adapt to new risk environments. A resilient organization aligns its strategies, operations, management system, governance structure and decision-support capabilities in order to identify and adapt to changing risks and to create a competitive advantage. Resilience must be built up by increasing the company's reliance on a global financial, operational and commercial infrastructure and by making legal and regulatory changes to ensure the security and continuity of the business. We now have vastly more networks, such as policy networks, ownership networks, collaboration networks, organizational networks and network marketing. Despite this, the conventional risk management model has not kept up with the shift from central to networked organizations. It is now clear that an organization cannot protect the various nodes in its network individually; threats will simply migrate from a protected node to more vulnerable points. In this light, three steps to forming a resilient enterprise are outlined:

1. *Diagnose enterprise-wide risks and interdependencies*; this is related to the identification of companies' earning drivers.
2. *Adapt the corporate strategy and operating model*; this is done through carrying out cost-benefit analyses that link cross-functional risk mitigation planning with corporate strategy.
3. *Endure increased risk and complexity*, mainly through building an organizational structure that integrates business intelligence and risk monitoring.

In a nutshell, the resilient organization, through an enhanced sensing capability, integrates business intelligence so that it can improve situational awareness (Starr et al., 2003).

Companies need to develop a more integrated approach to risk management that combines business strategy with business resilience and contingency planning. Businesses have always faced risks that are real, and not all of which can be expected, but these can be managed by having leaders, boards and stakeholders work together to create resilient companies. With dramatically increased shareholder expectations, it is claimed, resilient companies will reap rewards, ranging from increased partner and customer loyalty to improved earnings consistency (Starr et al., 2003).

For managing a range of risks holistically, a well-regulated system is needed. ERM consists of two parts: traditional risk management and risk governance. A traditional risk management process is less formal, lacks structure and is not centralized; it is concerned with individual risks or those in a single silo (rather than holistically) and includes the identification of risks, the measurement of risks and the monitoring and, possibly, reporting of risks. With the increase in the amount and complexity of the risks and surprises encountered by management in the operations of the business, there is a need for many companies to assess their existing risk management processes (Beasley & Hancock, 2015; Lundqvist, 2015).

5.5 ERM Analysis

The study of enterprise risk management helps us to understand the theoretical application of the knowledge domain, ERM, in practice. This analysis of the ERM domain, in turn, helps us to identify the existing ERM frameworks, processes and procedures.

The ERM domain supports the main aims and objectives of this research study. It can be concluded from the literature review that ERM is a property of strategic thinking and decision-making. Further objectives of this research study are the

Table 5.1 Summary of proposed risk framework processes

Risk framework process
• Avoidance: Exiting the activities giving rise to risk. • Reduction: Taking action to reduce the likelihood of impact related to the risk. • Alternative actions: Deciding and considering other feasible steps to minimize risks. • Share or insure: Transferring or sharing a portion of the risk to finance it. • Acceptance: No action is taken, due to a cost/benefit decision.
• Balancing qualitative and quantitative tools. • Providing early warnings and escalations. • Influencing business activities. • Reflecting environmental changes. • Incorporating risk interdependencies.
• Internal environment. • Objectives. • Event (risk) identification. • Risk assessment. • Risk response. • Control activities. • Information and communication. • Monitoring.
• Systematic risk identification. • Risk assessment and aggregation. • Risk control and monitoring. • Risk reporting.
• Diagnose enterprise-wide risks and interdependencies. • Adapt the corporate strategy and operating model. • Endure increased risk and complexity.

provision of a methodology for the integration of emergent risks with strategic risks and for recognizing the interconnectedness of risks, thus enabling practitioners to interrelate emerging risks through robust analytical methods, and the application of complexity thinking (the holistic view) to enterprise risk management processes.

It has been argued by researchers on risk management that the concept of ERM is a holistic one, which can help in solving important practical problems. Table 5.1 presents selected processes of risk framework that cover, in the view of this author, the most relevant literature on the area of risk framework.

Risk Identification

An analysis of further literature has led the author to determine risk identification. The quality of risk identification depends on the scope of the information that has been obtained.

The presented risk factors resulting from the literature research, which can be considered as important risk indicators, are clustered into nine categories in Table 5.2 below.

Table 5.2 Summary of proposed risk factors ordered by sub-category

Risk factor category	Risk factors
Compliance risks	Anti-bribery laws
	Management fraud
Environmental and social	Competitors
	Environmental risks
	Health and safety
	Human rights
	Customer
	Political impediments
	Competition
	Market and market analysis
	Employee-related issues
	Maximization of shareholder wealth
	Globalization
Financial	Commodity prices
	Credit risk
	Foreign exchange rates
	Interest rates
	Liquidity risks
	Legal and tax matters
	Economic capital
Information technology	Information technology
Information, communication	Information risk
Operational risks	Corporate leadership
	Projects
	Procurement matters
	Operational risk
Process	Labour laws
	Trademark protection
	Regulatory compliance
	Core and supporting processes
	Internal processes
	Policy issues
	Corporate governance
Strategic	Completion
	Customer preferences
	Strategy
Technological	Product development
	Product failure
	Technological innovation
	Aspects of R&D
	Product quality
	Technological progress

References

Arnold, V., et al. (2011). The role of strategic enterprise risk management and organizational flexibility in easing new regulatory compliance. *International Journal of Accounting Information Systems, 12*(3), 171–188.

Beasley, M., Branson, B., & Pagach, D. (2015). An analysis of the maturity and strategic impact of investments in ERM. *Journal of Accounting and Public Policy, 34*(3), 219–243.

Beasley, M. S., Frigo, M. L., & Frameworks, E. (2010). *Enterprise risk management* (Vol. 7, pp. 97–124).

Beasley, M. B., & Hancock, B. (2015). *Report on the current state of enterprise risk oversight: Update on trends and opportunities* (p. 12). Research conducted by the ERM Initiative at North Carolina State University on behalf of the American Institute of CPAs Business, Industry & Government Team.

Bowen, J., et al., (2006). *Enterprise risk management specialty guide.*

Burns, J., & Vaivio, J. (2001). Management accounting change. *Management Accounting Research, 12*(4), 389–402.

Callahan, C., & Soileau, J. (2017). Does Enterprise risk management enhance operating performance? *Advances in Accounting, 37*, 122–139.

Cooper, R. (1996). Costing techniques to support corporate strategy: Evidence from Japan. *Management Accounting Research, 7*(2), 219–246.

COSO and C.o.S.O.o.t.T. Commission. (2004). *Enterprise risk management framework.* American Institute of Certified Public Accountants.

COSO, The (COSO). (2004). *Enterprise risk management-integrated framework: Executive summary.*

D'Arcy, S. P., & Brogan, J. C. (2001). Enterprise risk management. *Journal of Risk Management of Korea, 12*(1), 207–228.

Denk, R., Merkelt-Exner, K., & Ruthner, R. (2008). *Corporate risk management, 124.* Wien.

DiPiazza, S. (2008). *Exploring emerging risks.* PWC. Annual Global CEO Survey 2008, 2009.

DiPiazza, S. A., Jr., & van Eijkern, S. (2009). *Dear reader.* PWC.

Everson, M., et al. (2012). *Resilience: Winning with risk* (Vol. 1, p. 1). PWC.

Frigo, M. L., & Anderson, R. J. (2011). Strategic risk management: A foundation for improving enterprise risk management and governance. *Journal of Corporate Accounting & Finance, 22*(3), 81–88.

Gordon, L. A., Loeb, M. P., & Tseng, C.-Y. (2009). Enterprise risk management and firm performance: A contingency perspective. *Journal of Accounting and Public Policy, 28*(4), 301–327.

Hilz-Ward, R., & Everling, O. (2009). *Risk performance management.* GWV.

Lam, J. (2000). *Enterprise-wide risk management and the role of the chief risk officer.* White paper, erisk.com, 25.

Lam, J. (2003). A unified management and capital framework for operational risk. *RMA Journal, 85*(5), 26–29.

Lundqvist, S. A. (2015). Why firms implement risk governance–Stepping beyond traditional risk management to enterprise risk management. *Journal of Accounting and Public Policy, 34*(5), 441–466.

Makomaski, J. (2008). So what exactly is ERM? *Risk Management, 55*(4), 80.

McShane, M. K., Nair, A., & Rustambekov, E. (2011). Does enterprise risk management increase firm value? *Journal of Accounting, Auditing & Finance, 26*(4), 641–658.

Nocco, B. W., & Stulz, R. M. (2006). Enterprise risk management: Theory and practice. *Journal of Applied Corporate Finance, 18*(4), 8–20.

Quon, T. K., Zeghal, D., & Maingot, M. (2012). Enterprise risk management and firm performance. *Procedia–Social and Behavioral Sciences, 62*, 263–267.

Razali, A. R., & Tahir, I. M. (2011). Review of the literature on enterprise risk management. *Business Management Dynamics, 1*(5), 8–16.

Starr, R., Newfrock, J., & Delurey, M. (2003). Enterprise resilience: Managing risk in the networked economy. *Strategy and Business, 30*, 70–79.

Building the Conceptual Enterprise Resilience Framework

6

Analysis of the four knowledge areas of strategy, resilience, complexity and ERM has allowed us to raise our understanding of their relationship with each other.

The theoretical background starts out from the premise that changes in the business and operating environment influence strategic thinking and decision-making, thereby making strategic planning essential. The big question, however, centres on the effectiveness of the employed strategy at a time of uncertainty caused by complex environmental change; such change affects businesses continuity, and this requires organizational resilience.

6.1 Points Worth Noting

The identified characteristics of strategic management and critical factors of strategic decision-making in seven categories are processes, organization, environment, technology, finance, resources and leadership. It is important to establish the relationships between each of the strategic factors and resilience, the factors of which are also identified in nine categories: process, organization, stakeholders, technology, people, operations, leadership, information and supply chain. Uncertainty has a bearing on resilience in different contexts, such as financial and environmental uncertainty, and it is therefore listed in the table among the factors that contribute to the area of resilience.

The factors contributing to complexity are the result of recent research clusters in nine categories, namely, organizational, social, economic, legal, financial, technological, environmental, uncertainty of goal and uncertainty of method.

Finally, based on the available literature, the processes of different ERM frameworks and risk factors have been ordered into nine categories: compliance, environmental and social, financial, information technology, information and communication, operational risks, process, strategic and technological.

From the above analysis, Table 6.1 presents a summary of the factors that are clustered based on information obtained from the literature.

K. Dindarian, *Embracing the Black Swan*, Future of Business and Finance,
https://doi.org/10.1007/978-3-031-29344-3_6

Table 6.1 Summary of strategy, resilience and complexity factors

Strategy	Resilience	Complexity
Processes	Information	Economic
Environment	Leadership	Environment
Finance	Operations	Financial
Leadership	Organization	Legal
Organization	People	Organizational
Resources	Process	Social
Technology	Stakeholders	Technology
	Supply chain	Uncertainty of goal
	Technology	Uncertainty of method
	Uncertainty	

Table 6.2 Proposed factors for enhancement of BSI resilience framework

Framework	Basic components	Resilience benefits	Critical Resilience Area
BSI framework	Product excellence	Strategic adaptability	Operational resilience
	Process reliability	Agile leadership	Supply chain resilience
	People behaviour	Robust governance	Information resilience
Result of this author's research (Dindarian, 2019)	Organizational flexibility	Financial credibility	Environmental resilience
	Resource availability	Economic sustainability	
	Innovative technology		
	Social integrity		

Further analysis of the above results in 18 factors that can be used for the purpose of building the framework. It should be noted that since 'uncertainty' appears in different contexts, it should be considered in relation to matters such as the uncertainty inherent in methods embedded in processes and leadership goals. Furthermore, the *legal* factor is assumed to be known matter and not contributing to the notion of resilience.

In addition, it was decided to compare and, if possible, to integrate these factors into the BSI resilience framework; the result of this is presented in Table 6.2. The BSI areas of basic components, the qualities of a resilient organization (resilience benefit) and critical resilience area are all covered by information from the literature. Current research contributes with additional components such as organizational flexibility, availability of resources, innovative technology and social integrity. In addition, the benefits of resilience extend into financial credibility and economic sustainability. Finally, the critical resilience area is supplemented with environmental resilience.

From the above discussion, our understanding can be concluded as in the following paragraphs.

6.2 Resilience and Strategic Management

Within the literature, important reasons for the various changes in the world are offered, and the consequent need for resilience is emphasized. It is suggested that to countenance this level of change, having a sustainable strategy will enable organizations to create value for both their shareholders and stakeholders over the longer term. It becomes clear that the nature and degree of change and the present uncertain conditions facing us globally all require a resilient strategy that can adjust to such vulnerability and change. The value of organizational resilience in creating the necessary conditions for competitive positioning, profitability and sustainability forms the frontispiece to a standard that emphasizes the connection between resilience and strategic planning. It has been argued that an emergent strategy reacts to unexpected events; such a strategy, to be effective, must be characterized by resilience.

6.3 Resilience and Decision-Making

According to the contingency theory, an organization performs in a stable environment. However, environmental changes require an organizational structure with greater connectedness among employees. The environmental changes resulting from the recent crisis have required organizations to be able to change from centralized decision-making structures to more decentralized ones, with corresponding new procedures and processes, and new ways of cooperation needing to be developed.

6.3.1 Resilience and Complexity

One school of thought evident throughout the theoretical literature argues that resilience is an emergent and adaptive procedure of subject and object, such as human and nature or culture and conditioning, and that these are the results of complex adaptive procedures and processes. The complexity theory creates order. It is important to note what the literature teaches us about complex life that can be seen as emergent, a concept that makes people think and govern differently. Complexity cannot be formulated merely in terms of hierarchy. An organization may be seen as a community, as a system or as 'life' in its own right. In this regard, we understand an organization as something complex. In this light, emergence is applied for the purpose of this book. Thus, resilience is concerned with emergence, and emergence is a characteristic of complexity.

6.4 Resilience, Risk and Uncertainty

Traditional risk management, both bottom-up and top-down, focuses on external disruptions. Emergent risk management is a top-down process. Both uncertainty and risk are examined in the context of complexity, and indeed, uncertainty is seen as one of several dimensions of complexity; that being said, uncertainty and risk are often considered synonymous.

Resilience implies a focus on many factors, as discussed earlier. Researchers on organizational resilience recommend that organizations be able to manage both risk and uncertainty. It can be inferred, therefore, that risk and uncertainty are not quite the same thing. Risk events are known and need to be identified, mitigated and monitored. Uncertainty, on the other hand, refers to events that are unknown and can be emergent. Resilience is, in essence, a system's ability to deal with high levels of uncertainty and is concerned with emergence, a characteristic of complexity.

6.5 Enterprise Resilience

One major objective of this book is the development of an enterprise risk framework suitable for the purposes of establishing organizational resilience.

Organizational resilience is an important term in the light of what has been discussed above. The consensus is that resilience as an emergent property ensures the ability of an organization to survive and to succeed by facing up to disaster, crisis, disruption and unexpected change. The existing body of research regarding organizational resilience, however, not to mention standards, policies, processes and procedures in the area, is rather limited.

There is strong broad consensus that a highly resilient organization is adaptive, competitive, agile and robust and that such organizations quickly return to the point of equilibrium—they 'bounce back' as it were—in the face of disaster, crises, disruptions and unexpected changes.

Resilience, as can be seen from the literature, is a characteristic of a system rather an individual part of that system, whether one is speaking about the engineering or ecological sciences. For us to better understand the resilience of a system and, more importantly, to be able to predict performance outcomes at various levels of analysis before and after a disruption event, it is important to identify the capabilities and capacities of the different components of that system in terms of both their integration with each other and with their environment, in that order. Since an organization can be seen as a system, it is, in effect, vital that we understand the whole structure of that organization.

A relationship between the areas of resilience and of strategic thinking, decision-making, complexity and risk and uncertainty has been established. The characteristics of a resilient system are explored and identified not only from an analysis of the literature and from desk study, but also from the author's own research findings.

The opinions overall are consistent that resilience can be understood in different ways and that it is widely applied in various scientific fields.

The relationship between resilience and strategic thinking is examined, leading to the conclusion that the changed environment resulting from the recent crisis has required organizations to be able to move from centralized decision-making to decentralized decision-making structures, which require new procedures and processes.

The relationship between resilience and complexity is understood and explored; an organization can be seen as a community, as a system or as a form of 'life'. In this regard, it can be inferred that an organization is complex by its very nature.

The relationships between the areas of resilience, risk and uncertainty are investigated, and an effort is made to understand them. We can conclude that while risk events are known, and can be identified, mitigated and monitored, uncertainty events are unknown and can be emergent. Resilience is, in essence, a system's ability to deal with high levels of uncertainty, and it is concerned with emergence, which is, as mentioned earlier, a characteristic of complexity.

From our understanding of enterprise resilience, it can be said that an organization might be seen as a system, which must be understood in its entirety.

6.6 The Enterprise Resilience Framework Concept

The conceptual enterprise resilience framework (ERF) is designed based on analysis, discussion and findings, supported by the important argument that effective emergent strategies are characterized by resilience. Resilience, in turn, is concerned with emergence, a characteristic of complexity. Making sense of complexity lies at the heart of 'holism', a key concept in ERM. This concept approach can be presented diagrammatically, as shown in Fig. 6.1.

The arrows represent the system as a self-contained unit, with ERM shown as a strategic property and resilience as a strategic objective and, also, a governing process of complexity. Coping with complexity is a matter of strategy, and the approach is both top-down and bottom-up. The arrow around the concept is intended to illustrate the process of continuity and improvement. It is recommended that complexity thinking be embedded into ERM.

6.7 Embedding Complexity Thinking into ERM

The area of enterprise risk management is explored using the current literature and desk study, which have helped the author to highlight the decision-support capabilities of enterprises. ERM is the link that exists between strategy and risk management, among others, to effectively protect shareholder value, and it is a part of a company's risk management and internal control systems. The COSO framework for ERM is applied for the purpose of this book, because this framework provides a sound, practical basis on which to approach our objectives.

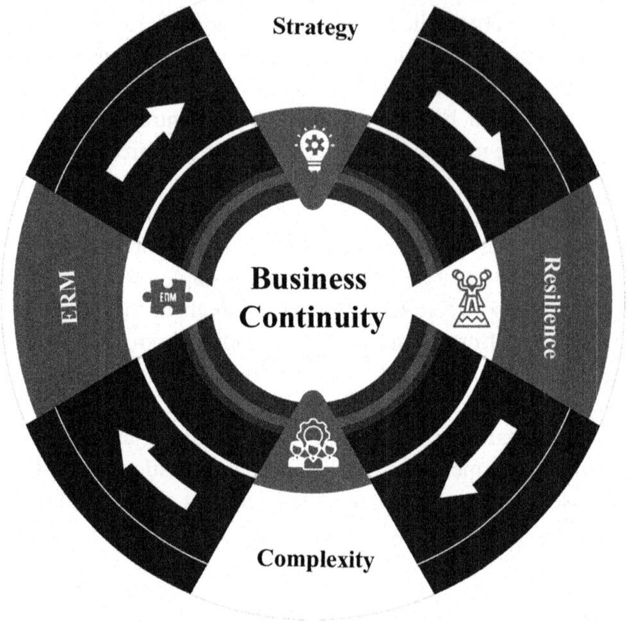

Fig. 6.1 Conceptual approach of enterprise resilience

Governance ensures the correct structures and issues guidelines and procedures for ERM within an organization. There are ERM stakeholders at each level in all corporate entities: there is governance, and there are risk owners, both of which groups work closely together. ERM requires defined contact persons in all countries where the company operates. Bodies concerned with ERM within an organization maintain regular communication with other governing bodies, particularly in relation to identifying new risks. Risks are identified, from both the top-down and bottom-up perspectives, at all levels of an organization, from the most senior level, through the various business units and divisions, right down to the lowest level. The risk owners are members of senior management, who make decisions and determine risk strategies as appropriate. Decisions on project portfolios involve a top-down process, which involves the assessment and evaluation of some business risk aspects such as legal and compliance, commercial and various technical areas.

In summary, the information and the results of analyses support the proposal for the development of an enterprise risk framework suitable for the purposes of establishing organizational resilience. This is outlined in Fig. 6.2.

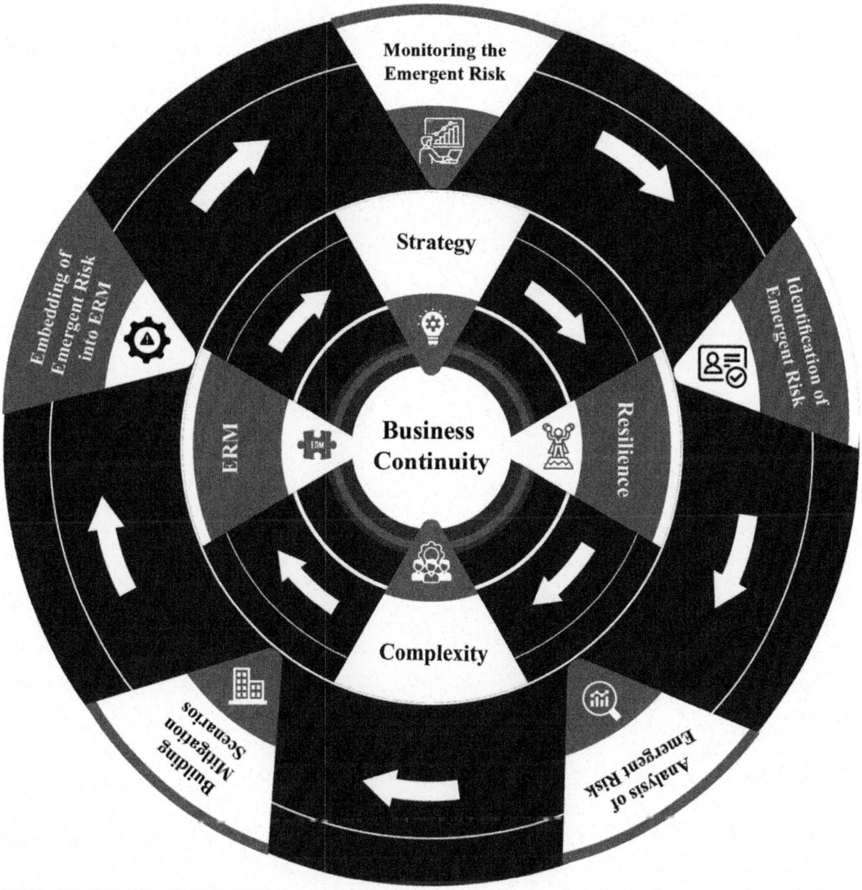

Fig. 6.2 Embedding complexity thinking into ERM

Reference

Dindarian, K. (2019). *Exploring enterprise resilience through the theoretical lens of complexity: A case study situated in the high value-manufacturing sector*. The University of Manchester.

Part II

Case Studies and the Enterprise Resilience Framework

Case Study I: Delivery of a Complex Railway Programme

7

This chapter presents a case study of the delivery of a complex programme, the Class 185 Diesel Multiple Unit for TransPennine Express trains in the UK. The requirements of the programme are outlined and an overview of the scope of the project is presented. The complexity of delivery of the portfolio is discussed, especially how the train design could meet the requirements of external stakeholders, and the ability of the organization to deal with the complexities that manifested themselves is also considered.

Here, we will be focusing on the application of the complexity theory in practice, on the science of complexly interacting systems and, on an operational level, on how the complexity theory provides a basis for understanding the delivery of projects—such as the delivery of complex portfolios into the global market. Such projects are characterized by the variety of different elements involved, by their interconnection and mutual dependencies and by how they interact. In more recent times, research on complexity in projects has considered many aspects, and several viewpoints have emerged, some of which are concerned with complex projects per se, while others are more interested in the management of project complexity. The term 'system' is applied to enhance our understanding of complexity (Allan et al., 2013; Mansfield, 2010; Dunović et al., 2014; Whitty & Maylor, 2007; Crawford et al., 2006; Baccarini, 1996).

The subject of the case study is the delivery of a complex portfolio, a branch railway project. Typically, the requirements of such projects are influenced by many elements,[1] including a range of different stakeholders such as government, contractors, suppliers and consultants, a variety of technical, commercial and financial influencers and various social, legal and watchdog bodies concerned with standards, processes and organizational structures. This is not to mention other factors such as project environment, resources (human, financial and natural) and,

[1] In this case study, the term 'element(s)' is used synonymously with 'components', 'constituent', 'part', 'section', 'portion', 'piece', 'bit', 'aspect', 'factor' and 'feature'.

K. Dindarian, *Embracing the Black Swan*, Future of Business and Finance,
https://doi.org/10.1007/978-3-031-29344-3_7

last but certainly not least, the project objectives. The makeup and interactions of those elements and stakeholders are not always clear-cut or well-defined, and the relationships and structures that are crucial to the success of a project such as this are indeed complex. These issues have been included in this case study, dealing with the various aspects of complex portfolios: process complexity, organizational complexity, environmental complexity and technological complexity.

7.1 British Rail: The Oldest Rail Network in the World

A brief history of the privatization of British Rail is presented here to help the reader gain a better understanding of today's decision-making processes and organizational structure.

The British railway network is the oldest in the world. It covers 16,536 km of normal track (1435 mm gauge), of which one-third is electrified, and three quarters consist of double- or multitrack line. Following the opening of the first passenger transport route in 1825, hundreds of railway companies were established, which in 1922, after numerous mergers, were consolidated into four companies. In 1948, the railways were nationalized, in the wake of which the stretch network was reduced to less than half.

After various political sea changes, British Rail was once again privatized between 1994 and 1997, when the company was divided into almost 100 different companies, effectively bringing about the end of a single British railway system and triggering the initiation of industrial competition. The degree of success of this privatization is questionable, not least because of the multiplicity of aims and objectives. Furthermore, it has been argued that privatization came about because the railway had lost its market share and could not compete with increased road transport, all while debts were accumulating, and use of the ailing rail network was greatly reduced, thus increasing the loss in value of both infrastructure (fixed assets) and rolling stock. However, the UK government claimed in its white paper that the goal of British rail privatization was '. . .to see better use made of the railways, greater responsiveness to the customer, and a higher quality of service and better value for money for the public who travel by rail' (Glover, 1998; Gibb et al., 1996; Charlton et al., 1997; Gibb, 2000; Yvrande-Billon & Ménard, 2005; The UK Government, 2017; TheNationalAuditOffice, 2017; Department-of-Transport, 1992).

Nowadays, in place of the old British Rail is a chain of companies that offer interconnected services to the railway stakeholders, in which companies constitute the organization and decision-makers of the railway sector with which this case study is concerned. As a result of British railway privatization, the structure of British Rail has changed and is now divided into five different groups of companies, namely, those handling infrastructure, maintenance, rolling stock, passenger transport and freight. The infrastructure itself, including tracks, stations and depots, as well as most of the signalling systems, is owned and maintained by Network Rail, which was established in 2002 by the government as a non-profit company. A variety of passenger and freight transport services are operated by several companies, none of whom get any state financial support. Most train operators in the UK lease their rolling stock from leasing companies, which own most of the passenger coaches, locomotives and freight cars. The maintenance and servicing of this rolling stock are carried out by the train manufacturers, such as Siemens (Glover, 1998; Gibb et al., 1996; Charlton et al., 1997; Gibb, 2000; Wellings, 2015).

In the UK, the Department for Transport is responsible for the strategic and financial management and planning of the railways.

7.2 UK Government: Department for Transport (DfT)

The DfT has stated that the vision of the organization is 'to provide world class train services that drive economic growth and exceed passenger expectations' (The UK Government, 2017).

The DfT Rail Group was set up under the Railways Act 2005, with Royal Assent. This group is responsible for the overreaching strategic and financial management of the railways.

The DfT itself is a ministerial department whose brief is to work with agencies and partners to support the transport network designed to move people and goods around the country. This government department works with the railway industry to ensure the rail network is safe, efficient and sustainable. It is responsible for designing and procuring new and replacement rail franchise services on the national rail network. One of the main responsibilities of DfT is 'strategy for the rail industry in England and Wales, funding investment in infrastructure through Network Rail, awarding and managing rail franchises, and regulating rail' (The UK Government, 2017).

7.2.1 Complexity of the DfT Organization

In terms of structure, DfT has been built as a top-down organization around a so-called Central Department, which is led by a Board of Executives that includes non-executives and ministers and chaired by the Secretary of State. Below this is the Permanent Secretary, who is above the Executive Committee, in which the latter group leads the different Central Departments: Roads, Traffic and Local; High Speed Rail (with an arm's-length body, High Speed 2 Ltd); Highways England; Resources and Strategy; International, Security and Environment; and the Rail Executive, which incorporates a number of arm's-length bodies: British Transport Police Authority, Transport Focus, Directly Operated Railways, and Network Rail.

The DfT is responsible for setting rail policy and partly funds the rail services, which are delivered through four bodies, namely, passenger services, rail infrastructure, new rail projects and the regulator. Network Rail Limited has been established with subsidiaries for separate functions. Its most significant components are Network Rail Infrastructure Limited.

7.3 Rail Franchising

Franchises were initially led by the Office of Passenger Rail Franchising, which was in turn replaced by the Strategic Rail Authority (SRA) in 1997. According to the Transport Act of 2000, the new organization, as a 'non-departmental public body' in the UK, is obliged to provide a strategic direction for the railway industry. As a result of the Railway Act of 2005, the Strategic Rail Authority was dissolved, and its tasks and responsibilities were assigned to the Department of Transport. The aim of franchising is, on the one hand, to achieve a competitive market within the passenger rail sector and, on the other, to ensure quality, value for money services for passengers and cost-effectiveness.

A further stated aim is to be a world-class railway with innovation that will create the opportunity for both people and business. It is also a government objective to boost the efficiency and sustainability of the railway with passenger experiences (Department-Of-Transport, 2017).

The following section gives an overview of the programme, Class 185 DMU TransPennine Express.

7.4 The TransPennine Express Programme

In 2003, the Strategic Rail Authority (SRA) announced that the new TransPennine Express franchise would operate intercity services by a consortium of FirstGroup plc and Keolis SA across the North of England (The UK Government, 2003).

The design specifications for the Class 185 trains included a new door arrangement for each car, air-conditioning, disabled toilets, gangways between carriages, luggage-and-bicycle storage spaces, CCTV, spaces for wheelchair passengers and first-class seating. Other requirements had been specified regarding the train's performance, including 37,700 miles per breakdown, and the service was to start with the first unit into general traffic in March 2006, with the entire fleet becoming operational by November the same year. The main requirements were (i) the introduction of trains capable of 100 mph (160 kph), (ii) the improvement of both passenger capacity and quality of services, (iii) greater performance, (iv) high efficiency and (v) the reliability of rail services. Furthermore, the construction of two modern traction maintenance depots at Manchester Ardwick and York Holgate facilities was planned (The UK Government, 2003).

7.5 Rolling Stock Order

In September 2003, Siemens Transportation System Division signed a contract with the operators First/Keolis TransPennine Ltd. and lessors HSBC Rail (UK) Ltd. for delivery of 56 three-car trains. The contract value was £260 million including maintenance and services.

In 2004, the Strategic Rail Authority reduced the train requirement from 56 to 51 units. The business division of Siemens Transportation System manufactured, assembled and tested the trains in Germany. In 2005, the first train was tested successfully at the Siemens Railway Test Centre. The Class 185 trains for the TransPennine Express are diesel multiple-unit (DMU) passenger trains, which are part of the Desiro UK train family designed exclusively for the UK Market. The trains were delivered during 2006 and 2007. This project involved the use of maintenance facilities at Ardwick Rail Depot in Manchester and York Depot, being a joint initiative between Siemens, First TransPennine Express, the government and HSBC Rail (TransportFocus, 2007).

Siemens' new £30m train maintenance depot for First TransPennine Express was officially opened by the then transport secretary, Douglas Alexander MP, who said, 'This is great news for passengers in the north of England and I welcome the investment. It should allow for trains to be maintained to a high standard and raise the quality of rail journeys' (BBC-NEWS, 2004; RailwayGazette, 2005a; Railwaypeople, 2006).

Our next section outlines the requirements of the programme and gives an overview of the scope of the project.

7.6 Train Requirements

Faster regional travel and a greater level of passenger comfort have been the cornerstone of customer demand over the last decade. In turn, state-of-the-art technical innovations and reliability, greater added value for passengers, better heating, ventilation and air-conditioning, more comfortable seating (particularly in first class), CCTV and GPS-based communication and information systems have all been central to operator requirements. In addition, passenger requirements have expanded to operational considerations, including easy access to trains, overall cleanliness, passenger information systems, catering services, more and improved luggage space and toilet facilities.

To meet those needs, trains were designed to operate in formations of three carriages, with the design of doors and their positioning on the cars being a key accessibility factor. Seating was arranged to allow for more legroom, with priority seating, including handrails, for elderly and disabled passengers. Technical requirements would be met by the introduction of a fleet of diesel multiple-unit (DMU) trains capable of 100 mph, with increased capacity, high reliability, greater assurance of availability, easy maintenance and high levels of safety. Furthermore, the construction of two modern depots and state-of the-art maintenance facilities was planned. Details of the requirements appeared in the tender documents, TransPennine Express: Invitation to Tender, issued by DfT in 2003. In addition to all of this, there were expressed customer demands, country-specific regulations and various other requirements on the part of stakeholders not directly involved in the projects, e.g. the Rail Safety and Standards Board (The UK Government, 2003; RSSB, 2003; Health & Safty Commission, 2000a; Health & Safty Commission,

2000b). Some major requirements are included in, but are not limited to, those listed below:

Selected requirements for supporting cross-industry groups in national programmes:

- Manage railway group standards on behalf of the industry.
- Propose changes through the facilitation of a research and development programme, so that education and awareness would lead the development of a long-term safety strategy for the industry, including the publication of annual Railway Strategic Safety Plans.
- Measure, report and inform on health-and-safety performance, safety intelligence, trends, data and risk.
- The facilitation of effective representation of the UK rail industry in the development of European legislation and standards that could have an impact on the rail system.
- Railway group standards.
- Safety strategies and strategic safety plans.
- Learning from accidents.

There are also unclaimed requirements, for example, the cultural requirements of the end users, such as the passengers, train drivers and service employees. The requirements that were central to scope of supply were laid out in the relevant contracts.

The technical requirements are described in the following sections on specifications for more detailed clarification and understanding. Examples of these are the specifics on end-product trains both as a whole system and as subsystems, such as the traction systems, interior design, livery, auxiliary control systems, CCTV, passenger information systems, train management systems, energy meters, bogies, braking, door-control mechanisms and heating and air-conditioning.

The trains were to be designed for operation within the United Kingdom. Full operability would be determined by conditions such as average daily temperature and maximum temperatures throughout the year. The equipment had to comply with UK, European and international standards relevant to railway operation at the time of submission of the bid.

7.6.1 Railway Group Standards

'Standards are a vital element in ensuring the safety of a complex interactive system such as a railway. As the railway command structure of British Railways has changed from the former monolithic functional operating and engineering directorates to the increasingly fragmented, autonomous and, eventually to be privatised, individual businesses of the railway industry in the UK, management by a robust standards regime assumes a position of critical importance. Without good standards the industry cannot be managed safely, reliably, or cost-effectively. It is essential that the safety of the railway is maintained and improved. A key component of this activity is the mandatory observation of the common core standards. Railway Group Standards represent these core standards and are produced by an open consultative process of all parties involved. They are high level performance-based standards. How their requirements are met is the responsibility of the individual companies, who will need to adopt or create further related tiers of documents-specifications, procedures, instructions etc. The development of quantified risk assessment to aid decision-making and determination of standards is important and welcome but the need for experienced professional judgment in matters concerning safety remains a critical factor' (Burrage, 1995).

7.6.2 Requirement Summary

The diversity of customer requirements was very high. Generally, requirements included the reduction of journey times, high service capacities and quality, safety and security, low lifecycle cost, technology trends, environmental considerations and sustainability. UK railway regulations were changed shortly before the announcement of the project, resulting in few or no references for new requirements being available. The number of units and stakeholders involved was high, as was the extent of their links to and interaction with each other, with considerable variability in actions and relationships. The target of Siemens was to design a complex product without any compromise in terms of meeting all requirements. Within a very short time, managing the requirements from design process to commissioning phases became the primary challenge.

7.6.3 Specifications

The contractual, technical and other specifications for the design of trains were extensive. A train is composed of a complex network of small and large parts, comprising mechanical, hydraulic, pneumatic and electrical components, equipment, devices, systems and subsystems. All these systems are engineered and integrated as one complete, unitary system that we know as 'the train'. There are necessary stable and approved processes for issuing concepts for initial ideas, and design specifications follow production specifications. The specifications are strictly applied to highly detailed systems that must adhere to contract requirements, with the result being a high-performance train as required and fully adaptable to the particular railway operational system, known as an integrated system. The train specifications form the basis for the design and build of the train.

7.7 Railway Vehicle Specifications in the UK

In both the UK and Europe, there are multiple and highly detailed specifications relating to the manufacture and operation of trains. Technical specifications were divided into two major groups, mechanical and electrical, applying to both the exterior and interior, in three levels: the roof of the train, the interior and the underfloor.

7.8 Train Concept and Specifications

The train was ordered as required in formations of three carriages. The train-car body shell is specified in aluminium, and the trains are powered by diesel engines mounted under the floor. The specifications were engineered according to requirements; for example, a part of the comfort requirement was that the vestibules and disabled access should lead into the first-class area with a large vestibule that included one of the two toilet modules on the train. The vestibule was to include a large wheelchair space, with foldaway seating and tables for disabled passengers.

The layout of the standard class was specified as a mixture of bays and two-abreast seating. The windows for the first class were specified at a generous size. The concept of the passenger information system was to be loud and clear with the same kind of visual displays in operation. The toilet modules would be installed in the first and centre cars. Door controls would be fitted with open/close push-button and a locking control (TransportFocus, 2007; RailwayGazette, 2005a; Siemens Transportation System, 2006).

7.8.1 Rolling Stock Design: Vehicle Concept

7.8.1.1 Interior Equipment

The Desiro UK DMU Class 185 was designed around the idea of shortening travel time while at the same time satisfying demands for high levels of passenger comfort. The train was developed at the request of the UK operator to cover the regional traffic demands of the UK market. The Desiro UK was designed for the UK market with a state-of-the-art and high-quality coach interior, including air-conditioning, a seating arrangement with more legroom and a first-class section that would all make a big difference for passengers and offer superior services on the TransPennine Express service. The train was designed with electric and diesel drive systems, and the Class 185's diesel drive system would make it the first Diesel Multiple Unit within the portfolio (TransportFocus, 2007).

7.8.2 Design Energy Consumption and Product Life Cycle

The train was developed by Siemens for operation on the hilly TransPennine Express lines, with hill-driving having already been taken into consideration at the design stage. For this purpose, strong diesel engines with integrated 'Eco-Mode' were designed, which switched off part of the engines on a non-hilly track and shut them down completely at depots, for saving on fuel. Furthermore, this system requires relatively little maintenance and extends the service life of the engine (NetworkRail, 2017; Tovey, 2016; RailwayGazette, 2007; RailwayGazette, 2008).

7.8.3 Design and Concept of Monitoring and Safety

The trains contain a significant amount of monitoring and safety features. The security closed-circuit television enables an optimal monitoring of the train interior through colour CCTV cameras. The safety of the vehicle is also ensured by a train protection warning system and the 'European Rail Traffic Management System' (Siemens Transportation System, 2006).

7.8.4 Train Manufacture and Assembly

A train's dynamic is considered an operational environment. Primarily, its main variables are the condition of the train itself (such as weight and rotating mass), the crash laden weight, traction and braking effort, redundancy in operation and the effects of failures, all of which are applied to the computer simulation of the train prior to manufacture. Based on requirements and design specifications, the manufacturing orders for construction and assembly are issued. Train manufacture is considered in terms of its major components, such as the mechanical and electrical systems, as well as the bogie systems and their interfaces. The hydraulic and pneumatic systems are subsystems of the whole train.

7.8.5 Mechanical System

The mechanical system is split into many subsystems. The main part is the car body shell.

7.8.6 Car Body

The car body shells, like the Siemens Desiro UK Portfolio Classes 350, 360 and 450, were manufactured from aluminium using the mechanical design by CAD automated production technology in 'three-dimension(s) in conjunction with virtual reality technology' (IC.IDO, 2017). The structure of aluminium material, along with strength, deflection, weight, abrasion and corrosion and the level of vibration, were taken into consideration and tested (RailwayGazette, 2005a; IC.IDO, 2017; Kim et al., 2007; Wang & Zou, 2011; Cai & Jianhui, 2011).

7.9 Commissioning and Delivery

The trains were commissioned and tested at the Siemens test centre in Germany, to a top speed of 160 km/h as required, and delivery of the first train took place in late July of 2005 (RailwayGazette, 2005a). Drivers would be trained before the delivery of trains in two full-cap simulators located in Manchester and York. The initial introduction of Class 185 was presented through simulation software, Train Discovery Application, whereby staff could learn fault diagnostics, along with health-and-safety procedures and rules. The train management system and its interfaces were included in the simulator, which allowed personnel to be trained, through computer programmes and simulation software, in the procedures and rules of complete train set-up. In 2006, Siemens delivered 51 three-car Class 185 diesel trains for TransPennine Express operation and service (TransportFocus, 2007; RailwayGazette, 2005b).

7.10 Maintenance and Servicing

Siemens would provide a full-service package for the maintenance and servicing of the new Class 185 fleet, and the full-service programme would involve carrying out preventive and corrective maintenance and services, including the repair of defective parts. The maintenance and servicing of Class 185 trains were to be carried out in two state-of-the-art newly built depots in Manchester and York. Siemens has committed to the maintenance and servicing of the trains for the lifetime of the contract franchise and beyond.

In the UK, Siemens built two state-of-the-art depots for the first TransPennine Express: a main depot at Ardwick, in Manchester, which opened in 2006, and another in York in 2007. All the required infrastructure, machinery and tools were provided by Siemens for both depots. The delivery of the 51 trains was finalized in 2007.

Since then, Siemens has built three further depots for the maintenance of later Desiro UK fleets (electrical multiple units) at Northam in Southampton, at Acton in West London and in Northampton.

Subsequently, both the employees and passengers of the first TransPennine Express expressed their satisfaction with the new vehicles.

7.11 Delivery of a Complex Portfolio

The train is a complex portfolio for the UK market, designed for the global market. The challenge in this case was to design a train to meet the requirements of external stakeholders. Technical complexity arose from the diversity of requirements: the train end-user (i.e. passenger) demands modern and comfortable seating, with ample stowage space for items such as luggage, bicycles, and pushchairs and a range of up-to-date communication facilities. The UK's own national—along with European and international—standards and regulations have had a large impact on train technical complexity. Moreover, train operating companies require train configuration flexibility; in this instance, a total fleet of 51 three-coach Class 185 trains were required, which could either be used singly or joined together to form six-carriage trains. To make matters even more complicated, services between Manchester and Scotland were normally operated by Class 350 electric trains consisting of four carriages, which can be coupled together thus providing eight carriages, resulting in high reliability and low consumption, as well as less maintenance and servicing, which can all have a direct impact on train design and technical complexity. Network Rail required the light and environmentally friendly trains to protect its infrastructure assets. Last, but not least, the supply chain concept had to fit into the UK portfolio programme. All of this involved outsourced sub-supplies, which would be provided in the form of small parts, components, devices, systems and subsystems (RailwayGazette, 2005a).

From an engineering point of view, the main challenge was to design and build a train that would cut down on the maintenance of rail vehicles through a reduced-weight body shell, which would have a bearing on the fitting of further large components as well as the various systems and subsystems. Reducing the weight of the body shell has an impact on traction, resulting in the need for less force and power with, therefore, little frictional force on the rails, thus ultimately reducing the maintenance on rail wheels and bearings. This reduces the number of parts required, simplifies assembly and usually offers a more lightweight design (Kim et al., 2007; Wennhage, 2001).

The diversity of customer requirements is very high. Generally, requirements include the reduction of journey times, high service capacities and quality, passenger safety, low lifecycle cost, technology trends, environmental considerations and sustainability. A train is a complex network of small and large parts, comprising mechanical, hydraulic, pneumatic, and electrical components, equipment, devices, systems and subsystems. All of these are engineered and integrated as a complete, unitary system that we know as 'the train'. There are necessary stable and approved processes for issuing concepts for initial ideas and for design and production specifications. These specifications are strictly applied to highly detailed systems that must adhere to contract requirements, with the result being a high-performance train as required and fully adaptable to the railway operation system, known as an integrated system. The train specifications form the basis for its design and build.

The target of Siemens in this instance was to design a complex product without any compromise in terms of meeting requirements. Within a very short time, managing the requirements from design process to commissioning phases became the primary challenge. The UK railway regulations were changed shortly before the announcement of the project, resulting in few or no references for new requirements being available. The number of units and stakeholders involved was high, as was the extent of their links to and interaction with each other, with considerable variability in actions and relationships. The contractual, technical and other specifications for the design of trains were extensive.

The train itself is complicated; however, the delivery of that train is highly complex.

References

Allan, N., et al. (2013). A review of the use of complex systems applied to risk appetite and emerging risks in ERM practice: Recommendations for practical tools to help risk professionals tackle the problems of risk appetite and emerging risk. *British Actuarial Journal, 18*(1), 163–234.

Baccarini, D. (1996). The concept of project complexity–a review. *International Journal of Project Management, 14*(4), 201–204.

BBC-NEWS. (2004). *First profits to hit expectations.* Available from: http://news.bbc.co.uk/2/hi/uk_news/england/3578297.stm

Burrage, K. W. (1995). Railway safety standards. In *International Conference on Electric Railways in a United Europe.*

Cai, Y., & Jianhui, L. (2011). Study on car body vibration transmissibility analysis approach for railway passenger carriage. In *Second International Conference on Mechanic Automation and Control Engineering.*

Charlton, C., Gibb, R., & Shaw, J. (1997). Regulation and continuing monopoly on Britain's railways. *Journal of Transport Geography, 5*(2), 147–153.

Crawford, L., Pollack, J., & England, D. (2006). Uncovering the trends in project management: Journal emphases over the last 10 years. *International Journal of Project Management, 24*(2), 175–184.

Department-of-Transport. (1992). *New opportunities for the railway: The privatisation of British Rail White Paper New Opportunities for Railways, in government white paper*, HMSO, D.o. Transport.

Department-Of-Transport. (2017). *Aims of rail franchising and what we expect from our delivery partners?* [cited 2017 06/01/2017]; Available from: http://webarchive.nationalarchives.gov.uk/20160520141653/https://www.gov.uk/government/publications/rail-franchising-aims-and-expectations/aims-of-rail-franchising-and-what-we-expect-from-our-delivery-partners

Dunović, I. B., Radujković, M., & Škreb, K. A. (2014). Towards a new model of complexity–the case of large infrastructure projects. *Procedia-Social and Behavioral Sciences, 119*, 730–738.

Gibb, R., All change: British railway privatisation, Roger Freeman, and Jon Shaw (Eds); McGraw-Hill, 2000. Journal of Transport Geography, 2001. 9(3): p. 224–226.

Gibb, R., Lowndes, T., & Charlton, C. (1996). The privatization of British rail. *Applied Geography, 16*(1), 35–51.

Glover, J. (1998). *Privatised railways.* Ian Allan.

Health & Safty Commission. (2000a). *The ladbroke grove rail inquiry: Part 1 report 2000.*

Health & Safty Commission. (2000b). *The ladbroke grove rail inquiry: Part 2 report 2000.*

IC.IDO. (2017). *leading virtual reality-based collaborative decision-making solution.* Available from: http://virtualreality.esi-group.com/

Kim, J.-S., Lee, S.-J., & Shin, K.-B. (2007). Manufacturing and structural safety evaluation of a composite train carbody. *Composite Structures, 78*(4), 468–476.

Mansfield, J. (2010). *The nature of change or the law of unintended consequences: An introductory text to designing complex systems and managing change.* World Scientific.

NetworkRail. (2017). *Route plans.* Available from: http://www.networkrail.co.uk/aspx/4451.aspx

RailwayGazette. (2005a). *Trans Pennine Express DMU starts commissioning trials.* Available from: http://www.railwaygazette.com/news/single-view/view/transpennine-express-dmu-starts-commissioning-trials.html

RailwayGazette. (2005b). *Simulating the world's railways.* Available from: http://www.railwaygazette.com/news/single-view/view/simulating-the-world39s-railways.html

RailwayGazette. (2007). *DMU Eco-Mode fuels savings at TPE.* [cited 2007 21 Dec 2007]; Available from: http://www.railwaygazette.com/news/single-view/view/dmu-eco-mode-fuels-savings-at-tpe.html

RailwayGazette. (2008). *Trans-Pennine trains get greener.* [cited 2008 03 Oct 2008]; Available from: http://www.railwaygazette.com/news/single-view/view/trans-pennine-trains-get-greener.html

Railwaypeople. (2006). *First Trans Pennine's new maintenance depot opens.* Available from: https://www.railwaypeople.com/Page/news-article-first-transpennine-s-new-maintenance-depot-opens-1062

RSSB. (2003). *Rail safety and standards board: Who we are?* [cited 2003 April 2003]; Available from: http://www.rssb.co.uk/whoweare/index.asp

Siemens Transportation System. (2006). *Desiro UK DMU Class 185, Technical inforamtion.*

The UK Government. (2003, July 28). *D.f.t., SRA announce preferred bidder for TransPennine express franchise (PDF).* Press release, Department of Transport.

The UK Government. (2017, Jan 6). *D.f.t. Department for transport.* Available from: https://www.gov.uk/government/organisations/department-for-transport

TheNationalAuditOffice. (2017). *Departmental-overview-2015-16-Department-for-transport.* [cited 2017]; Available from: https://www.nao.org.uk/

Tovey, M. (2016). *Conclusions: Transport design in the future. design for transport: A user-centred approach to vehicle design and travel.* p. 353.

TransportFocus. (2007, May 16). *The Pennine Class 185 experience–What do passengers think?* Available from: http://www.transportfocus.org.uk/research-publications/publications/the-pennine-class-185-experience-what-do-passengers-think/

Wang, H. C., & Zou, Z. Y. (2011). Design of optimization of gear train weight based on reliability simulated annealing. In *Proceedings 2011 International Conference on Transportation, Mechanical, and Electrical Engineering (TMEE).*

Wellings, R. (2015). *It's time for Network Rail to be privatised.* [cited 2017 04 February 2017]; Available from: http://www.telegraph.co.uk/news/uknews/road-and-rail-transport/11702664/Its-time-for-Network-Rail-to-be-privatised.html

Wennhage, P. (2001). *Structural-acoustic optimization of sandwich panels.*

Whitty, S. J., & Maylor, H. (2007). *And then came complex project management. in 21st IPMA World Congress on Project Management.*

Yvrande-Billon, A., & Ménard, C. (2005). Institutional constraints and organizational changes: The case of the British rail reform. *Journal of Economic Behavior & Organization, 56*(4), 675–699.

8 Case-Study Analysis

The focus of my PhD study was on the internal and external factors that contribute to project complexity, on how the complexity factors in a project can be identified and, finally, on how already-identified project complexity factors can be dealt or at least coped with.

The data on which the analysis is based are the result of research carried out in relation to four categories of project complexity, namely, processes, organizational, environmental and technological. These categories are justified and examined within the study of the knowledge domains of strategy, resilience and complexity. Further categories of complexity, identified from the literature, are integrated in the case study; these include—but are not limited to—leadership, resources, information, operational, people, stakeholders, economic, financial, legal, social and risk and uncertainty.

8.1 Quantitative Analysis

For the quantitative part of the study, the participants were asked to indicate to what extent they agreed or disagreed with a series of statements, all directly related to project complexity, concerning complexity factors. The choices ranged from 'strongly disagree' to 'strongly agree'. In addition, the participants were requested to elaborate in more detail in semi-structured interviews. It should be noted that qualitative analyses of semi-structured interviews are given at the end of this section, where relevant data and detailed information can be found, as well as details about the applied methods and methodology for the data analysis of my PhD research (Dindarian, 2019).

K. Dindarian, *Embracing the Black Swan*, Future of Business and Finance,
https://doi.org/10.1007/978-3-031-29344-3_8

8.2 Process Complexity

The characteristics of process complexity were explored using five questions in statement form, whose purpose was to determine the extent to which, in the opinions of the respondent practitioners, certain process-related elements are complexity factors.

1. The communication of business management processes (such as strategy, financial, planning and controlling), and their links to the project management processes, can have a positive/negative impact on project complexity.
2. The customer-relationship management process practiced in the project and its links to the project management processes can have a positive/negative impact on project complexity.
3. The supply-chain management process practiced in the project and its links to the project management processes can have a positive/negative impact on project complexity.
4. The product-lifecycle management process practiced in the project and its links to the project management processes can have a positive/negative impact on project complexity.
5. The support processes (quality management, environmental health and safety, human resources, intellectual management, financial management, accounting, procurement, IT management, communication, export control and customs, technical regulations and standardization) practiced in a project, and their links to the project management processes, can have a positive/negative impact on complexity.

8.3 Organizational Complexity

The characteristics of organizational complexity were similarly investigated, using 15 questions (in statement form) whose purpose was to determine the extent to which, in the opinions of respondent practitioners, organizational or organization-related elements are complexity factors.

1. The planned duration of a project affects that project's complexity.
2. The compatibility of project management methodology or project management tools contribute to project complexity—in relation both to the customer/consortium client and to sub-suppliers.
3. The financial objective of minimizing engineering costs (thus resulting in fewer engineering hours) contributes to project complexity.
4. An increased number of production/engineering locations involved in a project contributes to its complexity.
5. Project delivery criteria (e.g. target cost, quality and schedule) can all have a positive or negative effect on complexity.

6. At the start of the actual project (as opposed to the bid phase) and during its lifecycle, the resources (material, human and skills) required may have a positive or negative impact on complexity.
7. The involved parties' level of awareness of health and safety, security and environmental importance can have a positive/negative impact on complexity.
8. The level of interfaces between the different disciplines involved in a project (e.g. mechanical, electrical, chemical, civil, financial, legal, communication) can lead to complexity.
9. The number of different financial resources invested in the project (such as own investment, bank, JV parties, subsidies) can lead to complexity.
10. The number of different main contract types involved can contribute to a project's complexity.
11. The number of different locations, teams and engineering departments involved can contribute to a project's complexity.
12. The number of different nationalities involved in a project affects its complexity.
13. The number of languages used during a project for work-related communication has a bearing on complexity.
14. The level of trust between different disciplines involved in a project (e.g. between team members on deliverables and between contractors and project teams) can lead to complexity in that project.
15. Uncertainty in project organization contributes to complexity.

8.4 Environmental Complexity

The characteristics of environmental complexity were investigated using 11 questions, whose purpose was to investigate the extent to which, in the opinions of respondent practitioners, given environmental or environment-related elements are complexity factors. The number of stakeholders involved in a project (e.g. internal and external suppliers, contractors, governments, etc.) can contribute to complexity.

1. Stakeholders having different objectives contribute to project complexity.
2. Different dependencies on the part of the various stakeholders can contribute to project complexity. (Such dependencies include the lack of empowerment or authority to make decisions, and uncertainties on the part of hired consultants who must report to their clients.)
3. The influence of a political situation on a project leads to complexity.
4. The level of management support in project deliverables can in turn have a positive or negative impact on project complexity.
5. Coordinating a project remotely leads to project complexity.
6. The experience and knowledge of a project team about the countries in which the project is being delivered can have a positive or negative impact on project complexity.

7. Having internal strategy-related pressures from the business contributes to project complexity.
8. The stability of the project environment (e.g. exchange rates, raw material pricing) can have a positive or negative impact on project complexity.
9. The levels of competition (related to market conditions) can lead to a positive or negative impact on project complexity.
10. Uncertainty or risks in the project environment contribute to project complexity.

8.5 Technological Complexity

The characteristics of technological complexity were investigated using 11 questions, whose purpose was to investigate the extent to which, in the opinions of respondent practitioners, given technological or technology-related elements are complexity factors.

1. The number of detailed technical requirements contributes to project complexity (longer and more-detailed customer or internal specifications, versus short, high-level, more generalized specifications).
2. The number of different areas of expertise involved, together with the number of different technical experts, increases the complexity of a project.
3. Uncertainties in project goals and project strategy lead to complexity.
4. Poor communication of project goals and strategies between or among the project team and stakeholders leads to project complexity.
5. Uncertainties in the scope of a project contribute to complexity.
6. Strict quality requirements contribute to project complexity.
7. Uncertainties in the technical methods applied in a project contribute to complexity.
8. Conflicting design standards, along with the country-specific norms applied in a project, contribute to complexity.
9. New technology (non-proven technology) can contribute to project complexity.
10. The experience of the project team in the use of technology can have a positive or negative impact on project complexity.
11. Conflicts between customer requirements, local customer safety standards, the objectives of special-interest groups and design standards all contribute to project complexity. (Special interest groups would include drivers, guards, bicycle users, handicapped people and mothers with children.)

8.6 Qualitative Analysis

The complexity theory provides a basis for understanding complex projects. In general, the complexity of a project is characterized by the number of different elements involved, by their interconnection and mutual dependencies and by how these elements interact. This study explores those points using our railway engineering project case study.

Presented below is the set of questions posed to respondent practitioners as the basis for our qualitative analysis.

1. What does 'complex project' mean to you? How would you define it?
2. Based on your experience and/or perception, was your project complex?
3. Based on your definition and experience, is it possible to assess project complexity at the start of, and during, the lifecycle of a project?
4. Based on your experience, can complexity affect the performance of your project?
5. What were the internal and external factors that contributed to project complexity?
6. How did you identify the complexity factors in your project?
7. How did you deal/cope with identified project complexity factors?
8. Were there any variations in project complexity during project life cycles?

8.6.1 Complexity of the Project Business

It is important to mention at this point that practitioners were asked to address the definition of 'project complexity' from their own point of view. According to their responses, the definition of project complexity is given based on four major aspects: process, organization, environment and technology. Two further aspects of project complexity that arise within the practitioners' definitions are risk and uncertainty.

8.6.2 Definition of Project Complexity

Project complexity is defined based on human interaction and on different objectives and expectations, in addition to the involvement of a number of different parties and stakeholders, such as numbers of customers, of train-leasing companies and of train-operating companies. Thus, a multinational project with different authorities is, by definition, a complex project.

In terms of technology, technical challenges such as the amount and ratio of proven -v- unproven technology are further terms that serve to define project complexity, according to the responses of interviewees. Furthermore, the number and interactions of involved divisions and their relevant tasks contribute to a project's complexity. The definition of 'project complexity' is seen in terms of technical systems and system interfaces.

In the opinion of one respondent practitioner, the level of complexity is determined by a range of key factors such as the number of technical work packages and their level of interconnectivity, the number of divisions, the number of technical systems and system interfaces, the stakeholders, the amount of risk, the nature of a new market, the profiles of new customers and the types of new product.

Project complexity often depends on technological novelty, such as the development of new vehicles/trains. Some practitioners define project complexity based on business extensions, a case in point being entry into a new country or into a new territory without experience; we can conclude, therefore, that country-specific standards, and the culture of the new customer, can make or break a project.

In addition, project complexity can be defined through the application and interaction of different processes within the organization and its projects.

The financing of major projects is a further important aspect of project complexity, as reported by some practitioners:

> . . . a multinational project with different authorities. For me, this is a vehicle project with a three-digit million amount. . .of course, a small-scale project can be complex, but usually it's a complex project in the hundreds of millions. . .low volume, raw volume, bucket costs. . . .

It is important to note that the number of risks and changes in the scope of a project cause uncertainties during that project's execution, and this contributes to the definition of project complexity, as reported by several practitioners.

> Challenging technical and time requirements, the number of involved parties, changes or uncertainties during the project, new market without experience. . . .

The definition of project complexity is justified through the working experience of the respondent practitioners, working on complex projects in high-technology engineering manufacturing organizations.

> One of our European projects was complex; the stakeholders were complex, the technology was complex, and it was a new product. It was a complex product, yes. . . .

> Yes, in different locations in more than two European countries; some suppliers were distributed within Europe and others outside Europe; a very fast-moving project. . . .

The definition of complexity is given as a set of key terms by all interviewees. The most relevant of these are summarized thus:

- Number of interfaces
- Different or conflicting objectives
- Ratio of proven to unproven technology
- Amount of unproven technologies
- Number of stakeholders
- Number of risks
- New territory, i.e. new customer, new product—ignorance or lack of knowledge
- A multinational project with different authorities
- Finance, e.g. a vehicle project with a 'three-digit million' amount
- Low-volume, raw-volume bucket costs
- Technological novelty
- New vehicles/trains

- New components/development
- Different processes used by people
- Entry into new countries: local standards, customer culture, etc.
- Variety of technologies used
- Technical complexity (number of works)
- Number of divisions
- Complexity in terms of technical systems
- System interfaces
- Challenging technical and time requirements
- Number of involved parties—contracts
- Changes or uncertainties during the project
- New market without experience
- Amount of input and output within the process
- Many stakeholders
- New products to be developed during project execution
- Different mentalities due to a variety of countries involved
- Numbers of customers, e.g. train-leasing companies, train operators
- Number of locations, e.g. different countries

8.6.3 Assessment of Project Complexity

The respondent practitioners were also asked about their experiences regarding the assessment of project complexity in practice. This assessment is given from practitioners' experience and on the correct balance between deep dives and the broader experience of general management, namely, an individual project manager.

The practitioners assess project complexity in different ways, without any formal process. It appears there is a marked absence of procedures, processes and tools for the assessment of project complexity. The respondents highlight the importance of setting up processes for assessing project complexity at the very beginning of the project.

8.6.4 Complexity and Project Performance

The performance of a project is a characteristic of market reputation and business continuity. Practitioners were asked, therefore, about the impact of complexity on a project's performance.

There was general agreement to the effect that complexity increases the level of risk in that project and that it has an impact on the project's result. Furthermore, underestimating the degree of complexity can negatively affect project performance.

> Yes. If I have a complex project, I must ask how I can deal with it. I must have the ability - and capability - to deal with complexity; planning is very important.

> Yes, complexity has an impact on the result; if it is not well-managed, then it has a negative impact. . .a new country with immature technology; if I take that into account at the beginning of a project, and proceed to set up the project, then I can master that.

> Yes, for example an objective conflict regarding the selection of suppliers. . . .

The practitioners' experiences and opinions are, in this case, strongly aligned that complexity has an impact on a project's performance.

8.6.5 Complexity Factors

The respondents were asked about the internal and external factors that contribute to complexity in a project in order to gain a better understanding of practitioners' opinions.

The external factors identified by practitioners include a lack of experience in the market, notably a knowledge (or lack thereof) of local standards, the involvement of external stakeholders such as owners and operators, unfamiliar people, and relationships with customers, interfaces, stakeholders and the environment.

Internal factors identified by practitioners include technical interfaces between systems, internal processes, internal interfaces, organization, physical resources, a lack of proper communication, the skills of the project team, teamwork between different departments and project management.

8.6.6 Identifying Complexity Factors

The practitioners were asked about their practical experience of identifying project complexity factors. Generally, they use their own experience—or learn from that of others, even external partners—to identify the factors that contribute to project complexity. Some of the practitioners use tools other than their own experience.

> Read the tender documents, reflect on your own solutions (such as which technologies are used) and your own experience (one has carried out various projects already and can assess).

Additionally, project complexity is identified by project managers and their team members.

8.6.7 Dealing with Complexity

Using their experiences, humans often must rely on their own ingenuity to find solutions to problems. When respondents were asked about dealing with identified project complexity factors, they reported that they dealt with complexity by drawing upon the appropriate resources and detailed analysis and planning in the earlier part of the project.

> Try to react early . . .
>
> Deployed appropriate resources . . .
>
> With detailed analysis and planning . . . .
>
> Manpower, assessing the details. . .

Furthermore, they deal with complexity through mitigation plans, networking with stakeholders and reducing uncertainty.

> Close cooperation in the organisation, trying to define countermeasures, being prepared for risks, approval, talking to authorities in a new country and getting a picture, meetings with stakeholders, applying processes that are given in a transparent way so that all members know and work together, defining processes that help to master complexity. . . .
>
> We have designed countermeasures. A countermeasure is, for example, if you have a problem in a country, you get local people to solve it. The most difficult part is when support processes do not fit; that is something the project manager cannot solve.
>
> Creating the process around the topics, eliminating the factors that cause complexity, formalizing, knowing where the complexity is and then dealing with it . . . .

Practitioners have different ways of dealing with complexity. Overall, however, there appears to be a lack of project management procedures, processes and tools for dealing with project complexity.

8.6.8 Project Complexity during the Project Execution Lifecycle

It was important to learn, from the practitioner point of view, the various complexity scenarios over the lifecycle of a project's execution.

The quality of a project will decrease, which leads to higher project cost, if we do not deal with complexity. The level of complexity increases with the introduction of several new people into the project; this is associated with integration, and it increases the interfaces.

These practitioners emphasize that strategic changes increase complexity, for example, the business strategy, or possibly the country strategy.

> Situations change, increasing complexity. General experience: it's quite difficult to find what a company's strategy is because it's not easily filtered down. The link is not really there: the business divisions' strategy, the country strategy, it doesn't bother me very much.

There is a substantial body of opinion and sufficient experience to lead us to believe that complexity begins with the bidding phase, increases during the project phase and decreases after the beginning of operations.

The level of complexity in a project depends on factors such as size, the scope of research and development, interfaces between subsystems, political sensitivity and the involvement of multiple subject areas, all of which can increase complexity.

Practitioners gave further definitions in accordance with their experiences:

> A complex project is one with a high degree of one or more of the key project attributes—size, amount of development, interfaces between subsystems, political sensitivity, and so on. The more complex projects have a higher occurrence of multiple areas.

> There are many reasons the technical content of a project can cause complexity, such as technology, significant systems engineering, large development of complex software, multiple integrated interfaces, and interfacing with multiple complementary projects, programs, systems and users.

> High expectations, multiple stakeholders, no comparable baselines. . . .

> A combination of unclear or contradicting requirements, as well as stakeholder expectations, cultural differences, contractual ambiguities, a high-risk profile, and high numbers of parallel work packages that influence each other.

The experiences and opinions expressed are very strongly aligned concerning the definition of project complexity.

Interestingly, many of the respondents observed that there is a difference between complex projects and complicated projects. Execution of a project with inexperienced people is a complicated project. The implementation of a prototype project, on the other hand, is complex. For the complicated project, a set of measures, at least theoretically, is possible; such measures, however, cannot be applied to complex projects.

The definition of project complexity is given as keywords by interviewees. The most relevant keywords are summarized below:

8.6.9 Individual Perceptions of Project Complexity

- Project size
- Amount of development
- Interfaces between subsystems
- Political sensitivity
- High degree of multiple areas
- Technical content
- Technology
- Significant systems engineering
- Large complex software development
- Multiple integrated interfaces

- Interfacing with multiple complementary projects, programs, systems and users
- High expectations
- Multiple stakeholders
- No comparable baselines
- A combination of unclear or contradicting requirements, along with stakeholder expectations, cultural differences, contractual ambiguities, a high-risk profile and a high number of parallel work packages that influence each other
- Combination of unclear or contradicting requirements
- Stakeholder expectations
- Cultural differences
- Contractual ambiguities
- High-risk profile—many parallel work packages that influence each other

8.6.10 Practitioner Knowledge of Complexity

The level of knowledge of practitioners concerning complexity is shown using four characteristics of complexity: technological, organizational, environmental and process, described below.

8.6.11 Technological Complexity

In this section, a quantitative analysis of the technological elements contributing to project complexity is presented, along with a thematic analysis.

Here, all the participants agreed that the number of detailed technical requirements contributes to project complexity, and it was made clear that a high number of requirements means more interactions between the parties involved, in particular special technical solutions and change requirements, all of which leads to project complexity.

> On the one hand, more interaction is needed between the parties for clarification and understanding of details to avoid any contradictions or misunderstanding. On the other, special technical solutions and change requirements lead to project complexity. Within the project portfolio, the first project may be complex; however, those involved learn how to deal with this complexity, and apply what they have learned to further projects within that portfolio.

A high number of requirements is somewhat confusing, very detailed and very difficult to track and requires a lot of extra meetings and alignment, making the project more difficult and more complex, according to some practitioners.

> Special technical solutions or required technical changes...increase project complexity.

> ... then it's very confusing, very detailed, very difficult to track, and requires a lot of extra meetings and alignment, making the project more difficult and more complex.

The practitioners strongly agreed that complex requirements lead to project complexity; it was noted, however, that a recurring project is usually easier than a first project.

The experiences and opinions expressed are consistent with each other that the number of different branches (areas of expertise) and the number of different technical experts increases the complexity of a project.

Practitioners also report that the division of engineering and a greater number of interfaces enhances complexity; however, they say, there are also benefits, such as the fact that expert know-how can increase project value significantly.

> . . .with an increase in the number of technical experts and a growing number of departments and, increasingly, the dismantling of engineering in several departments and areas, it has become more difficult to manage projects. On the other hand, the technical experts have greatly helped us increase our know-how and made it easier to handle projects to customer satisfaction. I place a lot of value on the experts, even where the organisational difficulties have grown immensely.

There are, on the other hand, different opinions among practitioners as to whether uncertainties in project goals and strategy can lead to project complexity.

Uncertainty in project goals and strategy increase project non-conformance cost and risks. Some practitioners report that uncertainty in goals and strategy can increase the risks in, but not necessarily the complexity of, a project. Furthermore, they tell us that uncertainty exists only in the absence of a correct project strategy.

> I would even say ‘Strongly agree’, because if there is uncertainty about what its goal is and what strategy the project is pursuing, then there are lots of loops, and any amount of non-conformance costs, usually.

> Uncertainties should not be there; a project should have a strategy. One should assume that the project has the right strategy, therefore no uncertainties.

Project goals and project strategies influence the behaviour of a project’s team and of the stakeholders involved. Experiences and opinions are very much in line with the idea that poor communication within and/or between the project team and stakeholders about a project’s goals and strategies leads to project complexity.

Practitioners have highlighted the importance of communicating the goals of a project.

> Each project has a goal, and when this is not communicated, that affects project complexity.

However, some practitioners are of the opinion that the non-communication of strategy does not have an impact on project complexity, but it can easily increase the risks and difficulties.

> It does not increase complexity; it increases other things, like risks, or if you work in an unknown environment, it does not make things easier. However, I would not necessarily call it complexity now. Neither agree nor disagree!

In addition, some practitioners claim that complexity can be avoided or at least reduced, but that also there is a residual complexity that can be neither, which must, therefore, be managed.

> I have my own theory: you can avoid complexity. That's the first step: how do I avoid complexity? Failing that, the second step is that I try to reduce complexity. The third step is that when I cannot avoid or reduce it, I must manage complexity. There is a residual complexity that I cannot avoid or reduce, and so I must manage it.

Practitioners' opinions differ somewhat as to whether uncertainties in the scope of a project can contribute to its complexity. The general view, however, is that while the scope of a project must be clear, the number of requirements and the relationships and interconnectivity between those requirements can contribute to project complexity.

> Agree! Project scope must always be clear. The number of requirements can be problematic – that is, the relationships and interconnectivity of requirements.

Another opinion is that uncertainties in a project's scope can increase the risks but not complexity as such.

> If it is not clear what the customer requires, then of course that can hinder project delivery.

On the question of whether strict quality requirements might contribute to project complexity, we can see some diversity among practitioners' opinions. Indeed, many practitioners tell us that a strict quality requirement is almost inevitable and unavoidable. While this does not in itself increase a project's complexity, it does increase the formal effort and processes that make a project complex.

> The customer says, 'I want exactly this type of screw'. The strict quality requirement, I can understand. We deliver quality, we meet the requirements and standards, we deliver a safe vehicle. I do understand what is meant by 'quality'. In my opinion, a strict quality requirement does not increase the complexity of a project but, for me, would be something quite normal and a core principle of the culture of the company dealing with projects . . . Now, it does get complicated, and the formal effort is greatly increased. It is this increase in formal effort that naturally leads to an increase in project complexity.

> I'd say a strict quality requirement has no bearing on project complexity at all and is a matter of course. On the other hand, I'd say the formal processes involved increase the effort and that can make it more complex.

A further opinion expressed is that quality requirements not being clear increases complexity.

> If the quality requirements are not clear, then project complexity increases.

Opposed to this are opinions that the quality requirement helps those involved to understand a project in greater detail, thus serving to avoid complexity.

> I strongly disagree... I do not see that at all. Quality requirements do not increase complexity.

Experiences and opinions overall are consistent that uncertainties in applied technical methods contribute to a project's complexity.

> Agree it is so. If there are uncertainties, for example technology, then a project gets more complex.

Practitioners believe that uncertainty is part of innovation and new technology, and unproven solutions and unknown technology require an effort that increases complexity.

> Yes, of course, they increase project complexity...because if the technology and technical base and the innovation that should be a part of a product, together with the attendant uncertainties, are included, then this can have a significant impact on the project. Incidentally, this is rarely the case with our rail vehicles. Because we are always very close to what we already have, we do not make such strong technical changes. When I think of wind-power plants and offshore plants, where a connection must be sought from sea to land, there are still quite different uncertainties regarding the technical solutions in it. New, unproven solutions increase project complexity.

> I agree that if you do not know something, you have to put effort into it and that can increase complexity.

However, such complexity is manageable with platform technology simultaneity with product development.

> A platform is what we do to reduce complexity, because a project becomes more complex if I have management and, at the same time, product development.

Experiences and opinions are aligned that conflicting design standards and country-specific norms in a project contribute to complexity. Practitioners claim that, in their experience, the contradiction of standards can affect complexity.

> ... there are examples where standards contradict each other, where, for example, English standards contradict European standards.

However, there is another school of thought that besides contradictions in standards, these are often unknown to the processors and engineering personnel handling the project, and not knowing the standards can cause complexity.

> Conflicts usually arise from the fact that, for example, the BSI is defined in UK while there are other international rules in Europe, that there are certain deviations, or that, for example, the BSI demands one thing but there is a safety case and a claim that contradicts the BSI. Let's take an example where the doors should be locked so that no one can enter the train when it is turned off. What if, in the case of an emergency, someone still must come in? This could lead to a contradiction in requirements. However, these country-specific norms, the

national technical rules, only contribute to project complexity if they are unknown to the processors and engineering personnel handling the project. This means that it is not the standards themselves or the requirements that cause project complexity; it is the fact that the staff and the engineers handling the project do not know them. That is, in fact, the problem.

The experiences and opinions expressed are very much aligned that new technology is a complexity factor. Practitioners strongly agree that non-proven technology such as new vehicles and new platforms can lead to considerable complexity.

Yes, in any case that contributes; I think you could even strongly agree.

Strongly agree; when a new vehicle has a new platform, it is more complex.

Strongly agree, because the new is more problematic. There are often errors that were not known previously if you use something new. This then leads to problems. Everything new is untested and that's why it gets complex.

There are differing views among practitioners regarding whether poor experience of technology among a project's team can contribute to its complexity. Opinions vary about whether the (lack of) experience of technology on the part of a project's team can contribute to complexity; however, there is a perception that apart from technological know-how, other kinds of knowledge, about areas such as market, product and standards as well as personal and cultural issues, are also extremely important. Complexity, therefore, increases along with greater involvement of people and parts.

I fully agree. I would imagine that the question goes even further, and that also product knowledge, and market knowledge of the location, are included, not just the raw technology. For me, technology is the engineering-based knowledge as well as the technical solution stock. So, I would include market, product, and national standards in addition to technology.

The whole culture that prevails in the country is crucial since I deal with it. It's not just technology – it's the personal and cultural. In some countries, these are very difficult to negotiate with.

The more people and the more parts involved, the more complexity results.

It is also believed by some that an experienced team can better deal with complexity, but not be able to reduce it as such.

I think complexity remains, but it depends on how one deals with it. An experienced team can handle this better, but complexity remains.

8.6.12 Summary of Technological Complexity

The experiences and opinions expressed are, overall, consistent in that identified technological elements constitute complexity factors.

8.6.13 Organizational Complexity

There is a variety of experiences and opinions among practitioners on the question of whether the duration of a project's execution is a complexity factor. Duration is certainly an important factor, and it can increase the project's cost, but the consensus is it does not normally contribute to project complexity per se.

> This is hard to predict for me; if it takes longer, it is more expensive but not necessarily more complex.

> It is an important factor, but the complexity is less affected.

Experiences and opinions are strongly aligned with the view that incompatibility among project management methodologies or project management tools contributes to a project's complexity, particularly in relation to important stakeholders such as customers, consortium partners and sub-suppliers.

> It certainly has an impact, because I have to adapt to the customer.

> With proper methods and tools, it helps in coping with project complexity.

> If I have to use different tools that are not consistent with each other, of course, then I create more unnecessary complexity, and data is lost, or I have to translate into other tools.

There is also consistency in experiences and opinions that the financial objective of minimizing engineering expenses can contribute to project complexity (i.e. fewer engineering hours in a project contributes to its complexity).

> I really only see the effect when the engineering is put under pressure. . .in principle, with too little time, too little work to realize the project, then that contributes to its complexity – there is less engineering time. . .it becomes all the more complex.

> If programs can be carried out and you have fewer human resources on a project to save costs, it can be problematic. When fewer human resources are involved in the project to save engineering costs, it is often problematic. Complexity then becomes higher. Individuals then must do more and cover more topics.

> Saving at the beginning, in the design phase, is usually a big mistake and leads to complexity. . .the budget being too short or too tight in the beginning. . .increases complexity.

There is strong alignment in the views that an increased number of production/ engineering locations being involved in a project is a complexity factor. Distance, for example, has an impact on communication, resulting in longer travel times, and increases the interfaces, although in different locations one can expect to encounter different cultures. In general, all things being in one location results in less complexity.

> In many places, it leads to the fact that colleagues do not talk to each other, that contact is difficult, that many business trips are needed, and that has considerable impact on project complexity.

> More factories mean more interfaces, which leads to project complexity.

> The more units involved, the more complex it becomes. If different cultures come into play, then it is clear: complexity becomes much greater.

> Of course, if I have everything in one location, it's easier ....

There is, however, variation among the experiences and opinions of respondents that project delivery criteria, such as target cost, quality and schedule, contribute to complexity.

> When it comes to the requirements of customers, it can be very complex.

> ... already discussed schedule and quality, and if we limit the question to cost, then target cost influences project complexity.

> Of course, if the schedule is tight, it will be difficult and complex. Then you have to stretch dates, for example, or run in parallel.

Practitioners also differ on the question of whether, at the start of the actual project—as opposed to the bidding phase—and during a project's lifecycle, the level of resources required in that project, namely, material, human and skills, can have an impact on its complexity.

The experience of team members can help in managing complexity. Any change in the project can affect project complexity, in particular cost saving through human resources. Other opinions expressed by practitioners on the resources required in the project refer to the level of risk, without any effect on complexity.

> If you want to manage complexity, you must try to keep your team together during your project. If you cannot do that, you increase the level of complexity. New employees simply make new mistakes that older ones would not have made.

> You have changes in every project, that's normal life for me. If there are big changes, then it will be more complex.

> Cost saving through human resources leads to project complexity.

> This is not complexity, but risk.

On the question of whether an awareness of health, safety, security and the environment on the part of personnel in a project can have a bearing on the level of complexity, views differ somewhat. Practitioners have alluded to unknown requirements and legal consequences being a complexity factor.

When I report on the high amount of safety issues with legal consequences, that has an influence on the project's complexity.

If the safety requirements are not known and therefore not taken into account, then it can lead to problems and thus the project can become more complex.

Other opinions hold that international business involves greater stakeholder regulation that can have an impact on project complexity.

It is true; the number of stakeholders involved in international business is of course not only increasing European regulations, but also has an impact on regulations in each member state, which makes it more complex.

On the other hand, there is an opinion among practitioners that employing quality-related procedures helps to avoid project issues, with, consequently, no effect on complexity.

It does not add to complexity ... if you must follow quality guidelines anyway, then not. I see no problem for health, safety, security, and environment; you are required do these anyway as a company. If it's neatly organized within the company, it's not an additional problem for the project.

Broadly speaking, practitioners' experiences and opinions agree with each other that the interfaces between different disciplines (e.g. mechanical, electrical, chemical, civil, finance, legal, communication and accounting) involved in a project can lead to complexity.

When you set up a project team and have a lot of different work divisions, it increases complexity and means more to manage.

... more partners, and that not only brings you an interface, but your own legal matters, own engineering, own accounting. These many interfaces make it more complex. Therefore, joint projects are always much more complex.

Experiences and opinions are also strongly aligned that the number of financial resources (e.g. own investment, bank financing, JV parties, subsidies) in a project is a complexity factor.

Especially in England, it is true that we sell trains to leasing companies, but the operator has an impact on the project ... We have from the customer's side additional financial stakeholders...the bank that finances the trains when it re-values its residual value, which of course makes it complex.

It can be incredibly complex if you have multiple stakeholders who always make decisions.

There is strong alignment in opinions that the number of different main contract types involved contributes to a project's complexity. Practitioners are of the opinion that dealing with a high number of multiple requirements can affect complexity.

> I remember in one of my projects, we had hundreds of orders/requirements on contracts in English and then again in Greek. If mistakes are made somewhere, it can cost a lot of money. . .that makes it more complex.

However, extensions to the scope of the project, such as receiving extra product and service contracts, can benefit the business.

> . . . that makes it more complex . . . It is advantageous if, at the same time, you conclude a supply contract and maintenance contract and perhaps even sell the depot, which is much better and much cheaper than a project where we deliver only trains . . . Of course, complexity increases, the influence increases, but that is in fact more attractive and better, because this contradiction does arise. Complexity increases the need for work but that is not a bad thing as such.

Experiences and opinions among the respondents were fully consistent that the number of different locations, teams and engineering departments involved in a project contributes to its complexity. Practitioners argue that various experts distributed in different locations contributes to complexity, particularly due to work culture and using different tools.

> . . . the more various experts, the more complex . . . .

> One of my projects was distributed throughout Europe. . .extremely complex.

> For example, the production facility when the wrong parts are ordered and not everything comes from one location . . . We have examples where some parts are built in one of our production facilities located in a neighbouring country, and some from here in a domestic company. They are working in different ways . . . For instance, you would like to do plant drawings in one locale, and the review and correction in another location. This is more work because the works have different types of documents, tools, and so on, which makes the project complex.

The opinions among practitioners differ on the question of whether the number of different nationalities involved in a project contributes to its complexity. Practitioners argue that language barriers and the culture of people can contribute to project complexity.

> It is not the nationalities, but the language barriers.

> . . . when working across different countries or continents, it makes a difference. So, my domestic team, whether it's made up of one or five countries, it does not matter, but if I must work with three different countries that are really stuck in their culture, that adds complexity. . .so if a team works under one umbrella, then it's not that complex, but if they sit elsewhere (other cultures) then it leads to complexity.

On the other hand, some hold the opinion that the number of different nationalities involved in a project is not a problem and does not increase complexity.

> We can now work quite well with different nationalities.

We can also see different experiences and opinions among practitioners regarding whether the number of different languages used in a project contributes to complexity. Practitioners argue that a project needs a common language, particularly in global business. However, there are misunderstandings due to the different languages that mean a greater level of attention being required, without any effect on complexity. Others hold that the more languages, the more attention is required, and this can lead to complexity.

> In our projects, the business language is English. If it wasn't just one major language, I imagine it would be chaos.

> In all our projects we have. . .more and more people who are multilingual, but that is not the big problem in the company. We are global players. Of course, there are also people who can only speak one or two languages and then sometimes there are misunderstandings . . . If the project team is bilingual, then you have no problem.

> If I have more languages, then it gets more complex because you have to pay much more attention.

> . . . may make it an issue because of misunderstandings but it does not really add to complexity.

Practitioners differ in their views as to whether the issue of trust between different disciplines involved in a project—for example, between project team members on the deliverables, or between contractors and project teams—creates complexity.

> The project leader must form the team that works together with trust. And, wherever that does not work, the level of complexity increases and so does the risk of failure.

> Of course, if you have a client who trusts you, it's not that hard. In one of our projects, we had that (a client who didn't trust us), so many more documents and much more information were required.

There are different experiences and opinions among practitioners on the question of whether uncertainty in project organization constitutes a complexity factor. Some argue that missing resources and organizational changes can lead to complexity.

> If any roles are not occupied or changed, it will be complex.

> . . . absolutely clear, but it does not make the project more complex. . . .

8.6.14 Summary of Organizational Complexity

In general, the experiences and opinions expressed are consistent in that identified organizational elements contribute to complexity.

8.6.15 Environmental Complexity

In this section, a quantitative analysis of the environmental elements contributing to project complexity is given, together with a thematic analysis.

The experiences and opinions of respondent practitioners are very much in line with each other that the number of stakeholders involved in a project (internal, external suppliers, contractors, governments and so forth) is a complexity factor.

> The more stakeholders, the more complex.

> We have just seen this in one of our projects - where many stakeholders contribute highly to project complexity.

> The more stakeholders there are, the more complex; for example, communication and other requirements contribute to project complexity.

Experiences and opinions are also highly consistent that the existence of different objectives for different stakeholders contributes to complexity.

> If I have stakeholders with different goals. . .it gets very complex.

> For example, in one of our projects, the banks bought the object [the trains] and pursued the goal that they are universal and can run everywhere [on every track]. Then you have the operator of the object, for whom it must be tailored as perfectly as possible and, also, on the track. These different stakeholders have different goals and that does not make things any easier.

There is similar alignment of views that the degree of dependence on different stakeholders contributes to complexity. Practitioners point out that the interaction of different decision-makers and the responsibility of stakeholders can contribute to project complexity.

> If you understand that I have a conversation partner sitting across from me, who officially represents stakeholders, but then fails to answer my questions, either with unambiguous answers or decisions, because he must reinsure himself with his client . . . this happens when I hire consultants. As a rule, the consultant does not make any decisions, he always puts himself on the safe side, or he takes a decision that his client cannot negatively accept. . .this means dependencies that contribute to project complexity.

> A lack of power-of-authority makes it more complex.

Experiences and opinions are likewise consistent that the influence of a political situation on a project is a complexity factor.

> Of course, it doesn't help if project management does not know exactly what to do from the political situation. . .then it is difficult to do. We are experienced . . . The influence that some countries exercise is tremendous. If suddenly there is an embargo policy, that contributes to project complexity.

> . . . we have that in some countries only by political consent . . . .

The experiences and opinions of respondents are somewhat aligned that the impact of management support on project deliverables can lead to project complexity.

> Management support. . .may already have an impact on complexity.

> Of course, management support has an influence on the project. But that does not mean that the project can become more complex. It is an influence but only very weak.

Experiences and opinions are also in agreement that coordinating a project remotely can lead to complexity. Practitioners argue that distance makes communication difficult, especially scattered teams in different localities, and this can lead to complexity.

> If you are in one city or country and the others are all in other cities or countries . . . I understand that. . .it makes it more complex. . .if the team is not together.

> Basically, it's good if everyone is in a place where everything is going on. The more branched, the more complex.

Practitioners' experiences and opinions are broadly in line with one another that the experience and knowledge of a team about the countries in which the project is to be delivered can influence complexity. There is quite strong opinion that the involvement of locals in a project is vital. They allude to the language, culture and mentality, and they explain that absence of knowledge about regulation and standards, particularly in a new market, can contribute to project complexity.

> That's what I had already told them in the technical solutions, that knowledge of standards has an influence on project complexity.

> You have to have locals on board. . .without locals who know the language and the usual circumstances, it will not work.

> If you move into a new market, then it may be that it is more complex.

> If I want to sell the train abroad, I need to know about the circumstances. If I do not know that, then I must figure this out and that creates complexity.

> You have to know a bit about the mentality, norms and standards.

There are, however, different experiences and opinions among practitioners regarding whether pressure from internal business strategies contributes to complexity. Several of them claimed that current running projects affect decision-makers because of the different objectives of different stakeholders in the market, and this creates complexity. There are some opinions that after winning the project, internal business strategy does not affect project complexity.

> ... for example, if you want to conquer the market but still have side projects, it can affect complexity.

> It depends on whether they speak up or go in one direction. If they understand each other and everything is clear, it's not a problem, no. If there are different interests, different directions, then it becomes difficult and there is additional complexity, yes....

> When we do the project, there is no more discussion.

There are also different experiences and opinions expressed by practitioners regarding whether the stability of the project environment (e.g. exchange rates, raw material pricing) affects complexity.

> There are examples of not winning the project because exchange rates—sometimes overnight—would have been double-digit more expensive.

> The more stable the environment, the less complexity.

There are differences among practitioners' points of view as to whether the level of competition (in relation to market conditions, for example) can lead to project complexity. Practitioners explain that both the requirements and decisions of customers can contribute to complexity. Nevertheless, although it is a factor during the bidding stage, competition has much less of an effect on complexity after the project has been awarded.

> ... since the customer has given very early on to understand that he does not want a vehicle from abroad. In principle, it is not a real chance to win a project.

> If you are already in on the project, no matter what the competition does...it has little influence before the project starts.

> That is important in the bidding phase only ... In the bidding phase, we will win or lose the project. After winning the project, it does not matter what competitors do. I just deliver the project.

There is complete agreement (100% of all respondent practitioners) that uncertainty and risks in the project environment can contribute to complexity.

> Any kind of risk can add complexity, I must deal with a risk and take action. The degree of complexity can then become strong.

> If we submit an offer with little depth of technical clarification, then the risk is great that we might misjudge things. That reveals higher costs or higher complexity.

8.6.16 Summary of Environmental Complexity

The experiences and opinions expressed by respondent practitioners are consistent that identified environmental elements contribute to project complexity.

8.6.17 Process Complexity

There are different experiences and opinions on the part of practitioners that the (poor) communication of business management processes (e.g. strategy, financial, planning and control) and their links to project management processes can lead to complexity.

> If something is not communicated, then of course it can affect . . . .

> It produces work but not complexity.

Practitioners concur that the customer relationship management processes and their links to the project management process can lead to complexity.

> The relationship with the customer is unencumbered, and then you will quickly find solutions. If the trust is not there, it is more difficult – and complex.

> . . . from the experience of others, saying how we want to inform the customer, how we want to contact him, how we want to treat him, long or short term? What is the process of formal or informal customer relationship?

Experiences and opinions are, by the same token, very much aligned that the supply-chain management process practised in a project, and its links to the project management process, can lead to complexity.

> They have to be coordinated. If they are not aligned, then it affects the complexity.

The views and experiences of respondents are also in line that the product-lifecycle management process practised in a project, and its links to the management process, is a complexity factor.

> If there is a conflict, then it increases the complexity.

Likewise, the experiences and opinions expressed very much agree that the support processes (such as quality management, environment, health and safety, HR management, finance and accounting, procurement, IT, communication, export control/

customs) in a project and their links to the project management process can lead to complexity.

> If the necessary support processes do not work, then the project becomes very complex.

> Standard parts [small and mid-size parts, e.g. screws] ... There are often problems because the parts you need are not available on time or do not fit, and then you need to have the parts approved ... On the one hand, it is extremely important for a company to always use the same parts [standard], because the part fits the product and/or saves money. On the other hand, if it does not fit, you have extra effort, which can lead to project complexity.

8.6.18 Summary of Process Complexity

The experiences and opinions expressed are consistent that identified process elements contribute to project complexity.

8.7 The POET Complexity Framework

The POET (Process, Organizational, Environmental and Technological) complexity framework can be subdivided into several sub-categories in order to determine the relationship that complexity categories have with each other, thereby ensuring that all complexity factors have been considered in their various aspects; this may be useful in the application of POET complexity, in both theory and practice.

The category, Process complexity, can be subdivided into the sub-categories shown in Table 8.1.

Table 8.1 Sub-categories of Process complexity

Process complexity	Sub-category of process complexity
Communication of business management processes (e.g. strategy, financial, planning and control) and their links to project management processes	Process/communication
Customer relationship management processes and their links to the project management process	Process/relationship
Supply-chain management process as practised in the project and its links to the project management process	Process/stakeholder
Product-lifecycle management process as practised in the project and its links to the project management process	Process/risk
The support processes (e.g. quality management, environment, health and safety, human resources, intellectual management, financial management, accounting, procurement, IT management, communication, export control and customs, technical regulation and standardization) in a project and their links to the project management process	Process/uncertainty

Table 8.2 Sub-categories of Organizational complexity

Organizational complexity	Sub-category of organizational complexity
Duration of project execution	Risk
Non-compatibility of project management methodology	Process
Non-compatibility of project management tools	Process
Financial objective of minimizing engineering expenses	Finance
Number of production/engineering locations	Communication
Project delivery criteria: Target cost	Financial
Project delivery criteria: Quality	Risk
Project delivery criteria: Schedule	Risk
Resources required in the project: Material	Risk
Resources required in the project: Human resources	People
Resources required in the project: Skills	People
Health, safety, security and the environment	Process
Interfaces between the different disciplines involved in a project	Communication
Number of financial resources in a project	Finance
Number of different main contract types	Risk
Number of different locations	Communication
Number of different teams	People
Number of different engineering departments	Communication
Number of different nationalities involved in a project	People
Number of different languages used in a project	People
Trust between different disciplines involved in a project	People
Uncertainty in project organization	Uncertainty

The category, Organizational complexity, can be subdivided into the sub-categories shown in Table 8.2.

The category, Environmental complexity, can be subdivided into the sub-categories shown in Table 8.3.

The category, Technological complexity, can be subdivided into the sub-categories shown in Table 8.4.

The sub-categories of POET complexity are clustered in terms of the 'What?', 'Who?' and 'How?' in the responses of respondent practitioners.

The 'What?' cluster refers to interrelations within POET complexity such as technology, people and processes. The 'Who?' cluster refers to parties within POET complexity such as people, customers and other stakeholders, as well as their perspectives, while the 'How?' cluster refers to structure, methods and behaviour within POET complexity, such as organization, tools, human skills and trust.

Risk, uncertainty and communication relate to the logic and nature of POET complexity, and so these are considered not to fall within any of the above-described clusters of sub-categories. The categories of POET complexity are analysed for

Table 8.3 Sub-categories of Environmental complexity

Environmental complexity	Sub-category of environmental complexity
Number of stakeholders involved in a project	Stakeholder
Different objectives for different stakeholders	Stakeholder
Number of interdependencies among different stakeholders	Stakeholder
The influence of a political situation on a project	Stakeholder
Impact of management support on project deliverables	Stakeholder
Remote coordination of a project	Communication
Experience and knowledge of the team about the countries in which a project is to be delivered	People
Pressure from internal business strategies	Risk
Level of stability of the project environment	Risk
Level of competition (e.g. related to market conditions)	Stakeholder
Uncertainty and risks in the project environment	Uncertainty

Table 8.4 Sub-categories of Technological complexity

Technological complexity	Sub-category of technological complexity
Number of detailed technical requirements	Customer
Number of different branches (areas of expertise)	People
Number of different technical experts	People
Project goal and strategy	People
Communication	Communication
Uncertainty in the scope of a project	Uncertainty
Strict quality requirements	Customer
Uncertainties in applied technical methods	Uncertainty
Conflicting design standards and country-specific norms	Uncertainty
New technology, e.g. unproven technology	Risk
Experience of technology among the project team	People
Conflicts between customer requirements	Uncertainty
Conflicts between local customer safety standards	Uncertainty
Conflicts between the objectives of special-interest groups	Uncertainty
Conflicts between design standards	Uncertainty

determining the relationship that the various complexity categories have with each other.

The relationship between Environmental (E) and Technological (T) complexity can be determined by the complexity of the sub-category, Stakeholder.

E	Number of stakeholders involved in a project	Stakeholder
E	Different objectives for different stakeholders	
E	Number of interdependencies among different stakeholders	

(continued)

E	The influence of a political situation on a project	
E	Impact of management support on project deliverables	
E	Level of competition (e.g. related to market conditions)	
T	Number of detailed technical requirements	
T	Strict quality requirements	

The relationship between Organizational (O) and Environmental complexity can be determined by the complexity of the sub-category, Communication.

O	Number of production/engineering locations	Communication
O	Interfaces between the different disciplines involved in a project	
O	Number of different locations	
O	Number of different engineering departments	
E	Remote coordination of a project	

The relationship between Technological, Organizational and Environmental complexity can be determined by the complexity of the sub-category, People.

T	Number of different branches (areas of expertise)	People
T	Number of different technical experts	
T	Project goal and strategy	
T	Experience of technology among the project team	
O	Resources required in a project: Human resources	
O	Resources required in the project: Skills	
O	Number of different teams	
O	Number of different nationalities involved in a project	
O	Number of different languages used in a project	
O	Trust between different disciplines involved in a project	
E	Experience and knowledge of the team about the countries in which a project is to be delivered	

The relationship between Technological, Organizational and Environmental complexity can be determined by the domain, Uncertainty.

T	Uncertainty in the scope of a project	Uncertainty
T	Uncertainties in applied technical methods	
T	Conflicting design standards and country-specific norms	
T	Conflicts between customer requirements	
T	Conflicts between local customer safety standards	
T	Conflicts between the objectives of special-interest groups	
T	Conflicts between design standards	
O	Uncertainty in project organization	
E	Uncertainty and risks within the project environment	

The relationship between Technological, Organizational and Environmental complexity can be determined by the domain, Risk.

T	New technology, e.g. unproven technology	Risk
O	Duration of project execution	
O	Project delivery criteria: Quality	
O	Project delivery criteria: Schedule	
O	Resources required in a project: Material	
O	Number of different main contract types	
E	Pressure from internal business strategies	
E	Stability of the project environment	

The Process (P) complexity category is related to Organizational complexity.

O	Non-compatibility of project management methodology	Process
O	Non-compatibility of project management tools	
O	Health, safety, security and the environment	
P	Communication of business management processes (e.g. strategy, financial, planning and control) and their links to the project management processes	
P	Customer-relationship management processes and their links to the project management process	
P	Supply-chain management process as practised in a project and its links to the project management process	
P	Product-lifecycle management process as practised in a project and its links to the project management process	
P	The support processes (e.g. quality management, environment, health and safety, human resources, intellectual management, financial management, accounting, procurement, IT management, communication, export control and custom, technical regulation and standardization) within the project and their links to the project management process	

The complexity sub-category, Finance, is related to Organizational complexity.

O	Financial objective of minimizing engineering expenses	Finance
O	Project delivery criteria: target cost	
O	The number of financial resources in a project	

Within the POET complexity framework, there are interdependencies and interactions in terms of communication, people, stakeholders, uncertainty, processes, risk and finance, as seen in the presented analysis. The sub-categories process and finance are associated with the organization only. Communication is associated with both the organization and the environment. Uncertainty/risk and people are associated with the organization, the environment and technology. The sub-category, stakeholders, is associated with the environment and technology. The POET complexity framework provides the possibility of assessing further aspects of the organization, such as organizational resilience.

Reference

Dindarian, K. (2019). *Exploring enterprise resilience through the theoretical lens of complexity: A case study situated in the high value-manufacturing sector*. The University of Manchester.

Case Study II Enterprise Risk Management 9

This section describes an in-depth interview with an ERM practitioner at senior management level at a large high-tech engineering enterprise.

For any organization to be able to succeed, rules and practices are needed, and the structure of these rules and practices is what we call governance. This structure involves an extended variety of activities and procedures including the way senior executives direct and control their organization, using a combination of information applied for management purposes together with structure-control methods. Because vital management information is used for decision-making and for providing control mechanisms for strategies, guidelines and directions, it should be adequately comprehensive, precise and timely.

Governance has numerous roles, including the development of a comprehensive communication strategy, the provision of messages concerning the main topics of concern to the company, and managing the various incidents and events related to it. By defining structures, guidelines and procedures and endorsing their performance, it creates a global schema for communications. The organization's management is efficiently supported by communications and government affairs departments. On the other hand, governance ensures the transparency of consequences and procedures for creating added value for those working in the field of communication.

9.1 The ERM General Governance Process

We will now consider the process of general governance in enterprise risk management terms, within the organization the subject of this study.

There is a corresponding management board mandate, a Management Board Circular that regulates the process and structure of 'risk management' within the organization, which has the approval of the body of the organization's executive committee, with quasi-governance sovereignty. This is done in the form of corporate finance, risk management and internal control, all of which are the 'governance

K. Dindarian, *Embracing the Black Swan*, Future of Business and Finance,
https://doi.org/10.1007/978-3-031-29344-3_9

owners' on behalf of the Executive Board in the matter of 'risk management and internal control systems'.

In the words of the respondent senior manager:

> Of course, we work very closely with the other governance owners such as IT, Human Resources, Legal, Compliance, and Supply Chain, but we are the ultimate risk process owner, who must make sure we have a working system in which a risk-management system can be implemented . . . We communicate, train, periodically benchmark, keep updated and, if necessary, make adjustment; we are also reviewed by external auditors. How do we do that? We have a quasi-established ERM module as an ERM tool, an IT interface. This ensures worldwide accessibility. We are a globally functioning organisation in such areas as ERM. I have my contact persons in all lead countries and in all divisions, with whom I ultimately operate in an ERM network where it is possible to obtain, analyse and report risk information from every part of our organisation worldwide. We have created various training programs. . .where we keep this global ERM community up to date so that they remain in the spirit of training, with a sense of awareness and being able to perceive this professional task. Last, we are also in regular communication with the other governing bodies when it comes to identifying new risks to ensure that themes fit together . . . So, that's all in the context of the task. As a Governance Owner, we understand all this . . . Once a year, there is a so-called self-evaluation, together with the Executive Board, where the extent of our role as governance owner is determined. The extent to which we have succeeded in our mission is also evaluated.

Risks are identified at all levels of the subject organization from the bottom-up, through the various business divisions, to the top-down level, through the so-called vertical reporting process. At country level, the Assigned Countries and Lead Countries identify risks. Any risks perceived in the country are reported to the central risk team, which is run according to the bottom-up and global risk reporting concepts. In addition, there is a vertical reporting process in place. The divisional colleagues who sit in the lead countries look at what is relevant to their parent companies and what they perceive in those countries.

The Corporate Risk Committee at the top organizational level takes a decision on the order of precedence, meaning and scope of these respective topics and the organization's own risk prioritization. The membership of the Corporate Risk Committee is comprised of the members of the organization's Board of Management together with the organization's main departments.

The Division Risk Committee and Lead Country Risk Committee make the decision for divisional and country risks, which are discussed by the Central Organizational Risk Committee. As the respondent points out,

> The results of this self-evaluation from the Risk Committee and the Lead Country Risk Committee are to be reported to the Corporate Risk Committee.

There is a risk owner for every risk. The risk owner is a member of senior management who makes decisions and determines the risk strategies as appropriate and decides whether to accept the risk, reduce it, avoid it or transfer it.

> The risk owner ultimately has the responsibility for determining how he wants to handle this risk, and which response strategy of the risk is chosen. There are four strategies: Accept, Reduce, Avoid and Transfer.

Emergent risk is a top-down process. Emergent risk trends are part of the risk management standard process. Although emergent risks are considered globally in a systematic way, they are not part of the bottom-up risk register.

> It goes into the so-called top-down process. Otherwise, if new risk trends develop, then of course we react very quickly. Apart from that, there is a standard process that we go through once a year – typically at the beginning of the fiscal year – where we consider, in a systematic way, what new emerging risk trends we are seeing globally and to what extent these are already included in the bottom-up risk register or not. Typically, these topics are preferably not considered in the bottom-up register.

Emergent risks are addressed and discussed by the governance owners, who are all relevant functional departments such as strategy, corporate technology or legal/ compliance. Ultimately, the Corporate Risk Committee mandates the emerging risk trends and discusses them with the Lead Country Committee, which, in turn, provides feedback to the Executive Board on the extent to which the identified top-down topics are relevant for the divisions and Lead Countries.

Emergent risks are either opportunities or risks. Emergent risk trends can influence the business considerably. It is, therefore, important to handle and make concrete decisions regarding these as soon as possible.

> There can be both opportunities and risks. This is a topic that you can see more in the medium- or long term. It does not matter the first time. It's about reflecting on how important emerging-risk trends can be for our future business, and to get them on the agenda as early as possible. To decide as early as possible, how do we handle this?

The process for dealing with emergent risks can be established, operated and monitored in a systematic way, which can be broken down and addressed at the bottom level of the enterprise.

> I think that that is well established so far. It has been practiced in this form for several years now, and there is a systematic process where we look closely once a year at any new topics we see and to what extent they have already been broken down and discussed at the bottom level of the company.

The decision on project portfolios involves a top-down process that considers the assessment and evaluation of the number of business risk aspects such as legal and compliance, commercial and various technical areas. The result is communicated to the responsible business line management. This process is not part of the ERM system, but it has an interface to ERM as part of operational risk management. The decision process on project portfolio runs until the end of the bidding phase. Once a project has been won, there is a project risk management system in place with a well-defined interface to ERM. Project risk management handles the risks at project level;

however, ERM considers the relevant project risks such as major country risks, major technical risks and, perhaps most importantly, compliance risks, which are addressed to the business division and business units. Business unit management and divisional management are responsible for big issues. Thus, ERM is not actually focused on small operational issues.

Financial risk contingency is part of bid calculation or project ongoing calculation. This means that identified risks at project level are covered by risk contingency. Financial risk contingency takes place at project management level, and it is an integrated process within the project management process. The project risk management process is an ongoing one. It links to ERM as part of operational risk management, and the reconciliation must be made regularly.

Organizational resilience is about emerging risk trends. The term 'resilience' is not systematically in place; however, the various aspects of resilience and their diversity are considered, and the organization deals with elements of resilience. The elements of a resilient organization are regional settings, different portfolio settings, an intelligent property portfolio, employees, interaction with non-government organizations and fostering a variety of partnerships with universities, suppliers and other companies. It is important to identify alternatives for the resilience process in the short term and to avert greater harm to the company through suitable alternative solutions. It would, nonetheless, appear that there is a need for the development of organizational resilience, as pointed out during the interview.

> We have a resilient organisation. It is fortuitousness rather than strategy as such, but the result is the same. There is perhaps more potential for development in this area. That we are a resilient organisation whatever negative events may occur is, I think, illustrated by the fact that recent crises, such as the Japan earthquake, the Thailand flooding disaster, sanctions against Iran, the current situation in Russia, and so on, failed to have any noticeable effect on us and we weathered all those storms, so to speak, very well. None of these crises have so far led to the endangerment of the company. Instead, we were usually able to pinpoint alternatives in the short term and to avert greater harm to the company through appropriate alternative solutions.

There are different interests at every level of the organization, such as the Audit Committee of the Supervisory Board, the Board itself, the Executive Board, the Corporate Risk Committee, the divisional lines, the business unit lines, the country lines and, finally, middle and lower management. The expectations are different: for example, the Board of Directors will certainly provide a functioning ERM system that will not overlook any major issues that could harm the business. Rather, top management would like to ensure the security of the company with a functioning ERM system. Project managers, meanwhile, have an interest in a functioning project risk management system. However, at the various levels, a project risk management system is not accepted, so there is no one-size-fits-all type of solution. Nevertheless, the risks are regularly discussed at each level to get the best out of the risk management system. It is understood that there are no systems for aligning the different expectations of stakeholders within the various level of the organization.

> A board of directors wants to ensure a functioning ERM system where no major issues are overlooked, and that we have a functioning state-of-the-art accepted system that prevents harm to the company and, of course, provides security in matters of corporate liability from the point of view of top management. This is, of course, a very different interest from, for example, that of a project manager, who wants to have a working project risk management system with which he can manage his project. Now, we can see exactly this on the different levels where a project risk management system is not accepted. There is no one-size-fits-all solution. . . . We have not developed a system for measuring this concretely, but this is now more about different setups, of different rounds . . . We discuss this with the Board of Management via the Corporate Risk Committee on a quarterly basis. The same happens at divisional and lead-country level. We discuss projects regularly as part of our project discussions. Every stakeholder, every management level, must find an optimum for themselves to get the best out of the risk management system.

The next chapter presents, based on empirical data and data analysis, an enterprise risk framework suitable for the purposes of establishing enterprise resilience, which can ultimately ensure competitive advantage and business continuity and protect both stakeholder interests and shareholder value. The discussion examines the complexity theory mindset within a multi-project environment, culminating in an exploration of practitioners' perceptions of complexity in a large railway engineering program.

Development of Enterprise Resilience Framework (ERF) 10

The ERF has been developed using the four knowledge areas of strategy, resilience, complexity and ERM. Resilience and complexity constitute the core, to which strategy and ERM are of very high relevance in terms of the aims and objectives of this book.

The basic model of our study is built around an exploration of enterprise resilience through the lens of the complexity theory, and for this reason, the study has been designed to show how organizations can apply a holistic view, presented as complexity thinking, to their ERM processes. It should be noted at this point that the knowledge area of risk and uncertainty was considered during this author's research.

The author's study and research are concentrated in two strands: the first of these, the theoretical background covering the specific fields relevant to the key issues, has in the process identified the data sources other researchers have used and, more importantly, has exposed the remaining gaps in the body of theoretical knowledge. This part of the research was designed to support the three objectives of the study: (1) to show how effective emergent strategies are characterized by resilience; (2) to address the fact that resilience is concerned with emergence, a characteristic of complexity; and (3) to illustrate how complexity thinking (the holistic view) might be embedded into ERM processes.

The second strand is an empirical study covering the exploration of enterprise resilience in practice, which has taken into consideration both the top-down and bottom-up management perspectives.

Following is a discussion of the results and findings of this research study of the second strand, using as its basis the theoretical fundamentals in the first strand and the semi-structured and in-depth interviews with practitioners, of the second.

10.1 Theoretical Background

At this juncture, it might be useful to briefly review the theory discussed in detail earlier in our review of the literature.

K. Dindarian, *Embracing the Black Swan*, Future of Business and Finance,
https://doi.org/10.1007/978-3-031-29344-3_10

This review has given us a better insight into the theory of the four knowledge areas of strategy, resilience, complexity and enterprise risk management (ERM). Resilience and complexity constitute the core, to which strategy and ERM are of high relevance in terms of our aims and objectives. The literature review, therefore, considers three prominent notions: first, resilience is a strategic objective; second, ERM is a strategic decision-making property; third, resilience is a governance process of complexity.

10.1.1 Effective Emergent Strategies, Characterized by Resilience

Emergent strategy is researched based on the definition of the best-known strategy theorist, Alfred D. Chandler, and two other leading strategy theorists, Henry Mintzberg and Michael Porter. Further definitions are used, such as that found in Exploring Corporate Strategy, to explore the strategy knowledge domain. Strategy-and-structure and strategy formulation both fall within the main scope of the strategy domain in this book. Strategic thinking and three levels of strategic decision-making have been developed, based on extensive literature review and desk study.

Understanding the dynamics of macro-environmental change at the global business level is a growing concern both for scholars and for economics practitioners. Effective decision-making strategy is an organizational capability that enables an organization to cope with changes in its macro-environment, such as changes that impact the organization. Consequently, corporate, business and operations units are adapting their strategy to be able to cope with those changes. The present uncertain conditions require a resilient strategy, the so-called emergent strategy, that can adjust to vulnerability and change.

Based on its findings, this study challenges the currently perceived parameters of strategic management and decision-making, using a SWOT analysis, and it notes that a more holistic view can increase the ability of enterprises to cope with uncertainty, unpredictability and complex environmental changes and, therefore, with emergent risks. For this reason, we argue in favour of building a resilience strategy and point out the need to understand the characteristics of strategic thinking and decision-making, which can be related to the creation of a resilience strategy. Based on a theoretical study (Dindarian, 2019), the most important strategic factors are clustered into seven sub-categories: processes, organization, environment, technology, finance, resources and leadership. This has enabled the author to develop a better understanding of the characteristics of strategic thinking and decision-making, and it clarifies their relationship with further aspects of enterprise resilience, which has been empirically researched. The conclusion is that the level of decision-making is an important factor in strategic thinking and decision-making, and the levels described in the literature have been modified according to the various categories of strategic management.

10.1.2 Emergence: A Characteristic of Complexity

The application of different aspects of the definition of resilience suited to this research study has been considered—such as David Chandler's definition. In addition, the British Standards Institute's definition of organizational resilience is applied. BSI provides a framework for organizational resilience (BSI, 2014; Chandler, 2014).

Based on a theoretical study (Dindarian, 2019), the powerful resilience factors are clustered into nine sub-categories: organization, technology, people, process, information, supply chain, operations, environment and leadership. This has allowed me to develop a better understanding of the characteristics of resilience, and it clarifies their relationship with further aspects of enterprise resilience.

Strategy and Resilience: The relationship between strategy and resilience has been researched from the literature. From these studies, it is argued that resilience is an emergent strategic objective, characterized by complexity, which is essential for the development of an enterprise risk framework (ERF) (BSI, 2014; Davies, 2009; Everson et al., 2012; Lampel et al., 2014; Kerr, 2016).

Strategy and ERM: From the theoretical and empirical study of the relationship between strategy and ERM, it is argued that ERM is a strategic property. The management of strategic risks has a greater impact on the realization of strategic objectives; it has, in the same vein, been said that ERM as a strategic instrument can bring competitive advantages. ERM is a strategic approach that can be seen from both the top-down and bottom-up perspectives and, as confirmed by both empirical study and data analysis, it can be employed at both the micro and macro levels.

Whereas traditional ERM tends to be static in its design, the actual business environment is dynamic and ever-changing. It is, therefore, not enough—at least not in its current form—for dealing with an uncertain environment, and there is a need for enterprises to develop strong risk resilience if they wish to ensure survival and success in the world of today. Risk resilience allows an organization to recognize, to anticipate and to rapidly and effectively adapt to changes and resulting risk. This study, therefore, has set out to find possible theoretical and empirical solutions based on a holistic view.

Resilience and ERM: The differences between conventional ERM, on the one hand, and enterprise resilience, on the other hand, need to be clearly understood. For this reason, this author's research has explored the relationship between ERM and enterprise resilience and, based on its findings, argues that business continuity can best be ensured with an integrated approach, such as the ERF presented in this book, combining business strategy with business resilience and contingency planning. Furthermore, the assessment of organizational resilience and risk management can—and indeed should—be aligned in order to close the breach in the resilience profile of an enterprise.

Complexity: In this book, there is a very strong focus on the application of the complexity theory in practice, on the science of complexly interacting systems and, on an operational level, on how the complexity theory provides a basis for understanding the delivery of a project—especially of a complex global portfolio—which is characterized by the number of different elements involved, by their interconnection and mutual dependencies and by how these elements interact. In more recent times, research on complexity and projects has considered many aspects and several viewpoints have emerged, some of which are concerned with complex projects per se, whereas others are more interested in the management of project complexity.

Various aspects of the complexity domain have been explored to give us a better understanding of both its theory and its application in practice.

One important distinction is that between 'complicated' and 'complex'. No matter how many interacting parts there may be in a complicated system, it is still an independently functioning system, and its behaviour is therefore predictable. In a complex system, on the other hand, each part or subsystem functions independently of the others, but because of the system's interconnected nature, any changes in that part or subsystem caused by internal or external forces can greatly affect the whole system's behaviour, thereby making it highly unpredictable. One example of complicated is a jet engine, which is an independently functioning machine, whereas the flying of the actual plane, with all the variable factors (such as weather or human behaviour) that can have a bearing on the process, is complex.

In a modern train system, such as the subject of the main case study of this research, the train—with its intricate, state-of-the-art machinery and workings—can be described as complicated. The delivery of such a train, on the other hand, is complex, because of the myriad factors at play that can affect it, such as changing customer requirements, sudden increases in labour costs or energy or unexpected supply-chain interruptions. This is because the different elements and factors involved are variable, as are the relationships between them. Nothing can be said to be predictable. There are many stakeholders in such a project, including shareholders, the government, end users, designers, engineers, workers and environmental groups and considerations.

10.2 Governing Complexity and Building Resilience

The contention of this book, based on the theoretical and empirical findings, is that while the train itself, in terms of its workings, is complicated, the delivery of that train is highly complex.

In fact, the diversity of customer requirements is very high. Generally, requirements include the reduction of journey times, high capacities and quality of service, safety and security, low lifecycle cost, keeping up with technology trends, environmental considerations and sustainability. UK railway regulations had been changed shortly before the announcement of the project, resulting in few or no references for new requirements being available. The number of units and stakeholders involved was high, as was the extent of their links to and interaction with each other, with considerable variability in actions and relationships. The contractual, technical and other specifications for train design were extensive. A train is a complicated system composed of small and large parts, comprising mechanical, hydraulic, pneumatic and electrical components, equipment, devices, systems and subsystems. All these systems are engineered and integrated as a complete, unitary system that we know as 'the train'. There are necessary stable and approved processes for issuing concepts for initial ideas and design and production specifications. These specifications are strictly applied to highly detailed systems that must adhere to contract requirements, with the result being a high-performance train as required and fully adaptable to the particular railway operational system, known as an integrated system. The train specifications form the basis for its design and build. Although the order received by Siemens was for the design and manufacture of a complicated machine, its true brief was the delivery of a highly complex project without any compromise in terms of meeting requirements. Within a very short time, managing the requirements from design process to commissioning phases became the primary challenge.

There was broad agreement among the respondent practitioners that process, organizational, environmental and technological complexity contributes to the complexity of a project. Evidently, an understanding of complexity and the ability to deal with it can help to build enterprise resilience from the bottom-up perspective, or the micro level.

The opinions expressed are very strongly aligned concerning the definition of project complexity. However, one of the definitions differs from the others. The respondent practitioners observed that there is a difference between complex projects and complicated projects. Execution of a project per se with inexperienced people makes it complicated rather than complex. The implementation of a prototype project, on the other hand, is complex. For the complicated project, a set of measures, at least theoretically, is possible; such measures, however, cannot be applied to complex projects.

Project process complexity, in the view of this author, assumes the interrelations between organizational behaviour, management and organizational processes are all absent. The relationship between complexity theory and the delivery of complex portfolios, which has resulted in deficiencies in the perceptions of complexity practitioners in multi-project environments, is highlighted. The above points are explored using as a case study a large railway engineering program, to contribute to the available body of knowledge. The characteristics of process complexity have been identified and then compared with empirical data from the case study, and the experiences and opinions expressed within the latter are consistent that identified process elements contribute to project complexity.

Project organizational complexity refers to organizational elements such as organizational structure and stakeholders and involved parties. In general, participant practitioners in the case study are consistent in the view that identified organizational elements contribute to complexity.

Project environmental complexity includes knowing and involving the project environment in project planning, control and monitoring, especially stakeholders' behaviour and their influence on the project. However, there is limited practical knowledge about the implications of the complexity theory mindset within that environment. The characteristics of environmental complexity were determined from the literature and are in line with the empirical data from the case study.

The experiences and opinions expressed by respondent practitioners are agreed that identified environmental elements contribute to project complexity.

Project technological complexity can be seen as a range of technology delivery processes, including—among other things—delivery requirements, design, engineering, purchasing, logistics and manufacturing, collectively an important transformation process of operations. It can also refer to material characteristics and, moreover, can be seen as knowledge and skills. The complexity theory applied to the research of organizational behaviour, management and organizational processes and to the economic system has been classified as a complex adaptive system (CAS). CAS is a vehicle for understanding the complexities of socio-technical systems and provides an assessment of the holistic view, which leads to a better understanding of projects in the context of their environment. The characteristics of technological complexity as in the literature is compared with the empirical data from the case study. The experiences and opinions expressed in the case study are, overall, consistent that identified technological elements constitute complexity factors.

The POET (process, organizational, environmental and technological) complexity framework is now presented. The major difference between this framework and those from the literature is that the POET framework is developed from an enterprise resilience perspective. Other frameworks provide for an assessment of the complexity of projects and for the management of projects. Thus, the complexity factors are described without considering the behaviour or action of practitioners in the face of complexity.

In this book, on the other hand, we attempt to examine the impact of complexity on organizational ability while exploring the 'reality' of delivering complex portfolios into global markets and, in the process, to understand the organization's capability and possibly measure the implementation of effective complex projects. Furthermore, we address at some length the category of process complexity, which is missing from existing frameworks. This will, hopefully, allow the possibility of assessing further aspects of the organization, such as governing complexity, and provide support to organizations in establishing enterprise resilience, which can ultimately ensure competitive advantage and business continuity, while at the same time protecting both stakeholder interests and shareholder value.

10.3 Building Resilience at Strategic Level

It has been suggested by researchers on risk management that the concept of ERM is a holistic one, which can help in solving important practical problems.

An analysis has led this author to determine risk identification, the quality of which depends on the scope of the information that has been obtained. The presented risk factors resulting from the literature research (Dindarian, 2019), which can be considered as important risk indicators, are clustered into nine categories: compliance, environmental-and-social, financial, information technology, information-and-communication, operational risks, process, strategic and technological.

Based on the research findings, it would be feasible for an organization to consider a limited fusion of the macro- and micro-risk approaches. The researchers and, especially, the COSO framework have elaborated appropriate measures that might be considered for the development of an enterprise risk framework.

There is no need for another type of ERM to overcome the dynamic business environment as such; however, there is a need to ensure the dynamic of an operation, along with the ability to deal with unexpected risks and handle confrontation with the more extensive business environment. A set of questions ought to be considered, for the improvement of conventional ERM.

- Who owns risk?
- How effective is the board in overseeing risk management?
- How proactively is risk managed?
- What is the return on risk management?

What these all come down to, however, is just one question: Is the organization ready for 'black swan' risks?

10.3.1 Risk Ownership and Overseeing Risk Management

The risk owner in the engineering company the subject of our research, is a member of senior management who makes decisions and determines the appropriate risk strategies, and it is they who decide whether to accept, reduce, avoid or transfer the risk. The decision on project portfolios involves a top-down process, where after assessing and evaluating various risk aspects such as legal and compliance, commercial and various technical areas, the result is communicated to the responsible business line management. This process is not part of ERM as such, but it has an interface to ERM as part of operational risk management. The decision process on project portfolio runs until the end of the bidding phase.

10.3.2 Dealing with 'Black Swan' Risks

Emergent risk is a top-down process. Emergent risk trends are part of the risk management standard process and are considered globally in a systematic way. However, they are not part of the bottom-up risk register. The governance owner, who may be a functional department such as strategy, corporate technology or legal/compliance, involves and discusses emergent risks. Ultimately, the Corporate Risk Committee mandates emerging risk trends and discusses them with the Lead Country Committee, which, in turn, provides feedback to the Executive Board on the extent to which the identified top-down topics are relevant for the divisions and lead countries.

Emergent risks are either opportunities or risks, and trends can influence the business considerably. It is, therefore, important to handle and make concrete decisions regarding those as soon as possible. The process for dealing with emergent risks can be established, operated and monitored in a systematic way, which can be broken down and considered at the bottom level of the enterprise.

10.3.3 Organizational Resilience

Organizational resilience is about emerging risk trends. The term 'resilience' is not systematically in place; however, the various aspects of resilience and their diversity are considered, and the organization deals with elements of resilience. The elements of a resilient organization are, as we have already seen, regional settings, different portfolio settings, an intelligent property portfolio, employees, interaction with non-government organizations and fostering a variety of partnerships with universities, suppliers and other companies.

It is important to identify alternatives for the resilience process in the short term and to avert greater harm to the company through suitable alternative solutions.

This book presents an enterprise risk framework (ERF) suitable for the purposes of establishing organizational resilience, designed to counter the risks that can affect business activities to such an extent that a business or organization suffers considerable damage or even has its existence threatened.

10.4 Resilience Framework

It is fervently hoped that the author's research will serve to enhance the current BSI resilience framework as illustrated in Table 10.1. The BSI areas of basic components, the qualities of a resilient organization (resilience benefit) and critical resilience are all covered by information from the literature. Current research

Table 10.1 The most important factors of the enterprise resilience framework

Resilience Framework	Basic components	Resilience benefits	Critical resilience area
Component of BSI framework	Product excellence	Strategic adaptability	Operational resilience
	Process reliability	Agile leadership	Supply-chain resilience
	People behaviour	Robust governance	Information resilience
Enhancement of BSI Framework (Dindarian, 2019)	Organization flexibility	Financial credibility	Environmental resilience
	Resource availability	Economic sustainability	
	Innovative technology		
	Social integrity		

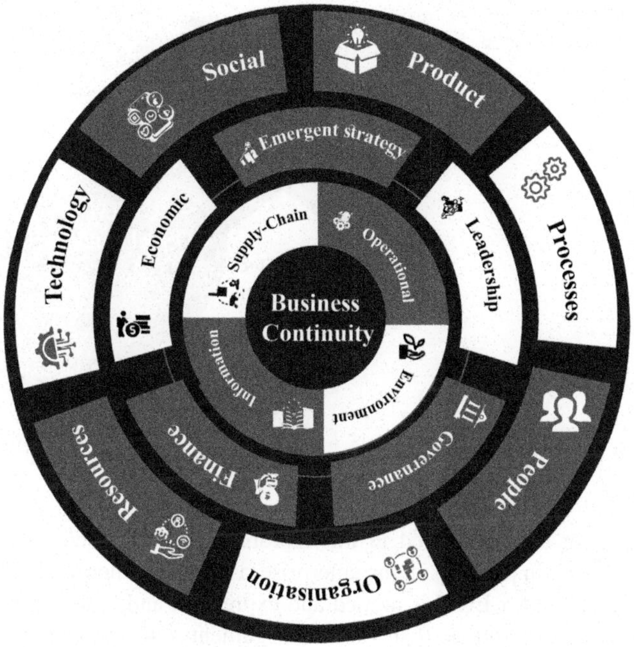

Fig. 10.1 The enterprise resilience framework

contributes with additional components such as organizational flexibility, resource availability, innovative technology and social integrity. Furthermore, the benefit of resilience is extended into financial credibility and economic sustainability. Finally, the critical resilience area is supplemented with environmental resilience.

Furthermore, the mechanisms by which uncertainties and emergent risks take place within ERM processes are explored, and how this relates to business continuity is addressed.

Figure 10.1 shows the enterprise resilience framework. The focus is on the business continuity that surrounds the crisis sector with the group of critical factors. In the third section are the factors that make up the advantages of a resilient organization. In the outer part is the group of fundamental factors in the assessment of enterprise resilience.

10.5 Embedding Complexity Thinking into ERM Processes

A total of 42 risk factors resulting from literature research—which risks can be considered as important risk indicators—is being ordered into nine clusters: compliance, environmental-and-social, financial, information technology, information-and-communication, operational risks, process, strategic and technological. These clusters have been created according to risk category. The definition of enterprise

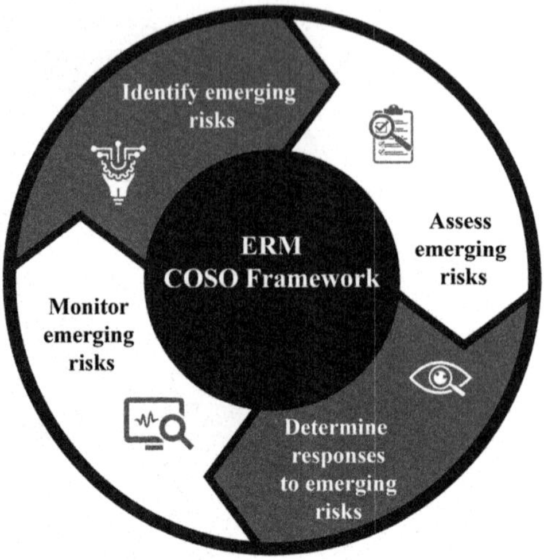

Fig. 10.2 Embedding emergent risks into enterprise risk management

risk management that is applied in this research study is based on the generally accepted one used, in practice, in the enterprise risk management COSO framework, Fig. 10.2. The need for ERM is argued and expressed, and based on data analysis, this research study argues that risk management and governance are major challenges for companies, and the ability to identify and manage risks in a highly uncertain environment—the so-called emerging risks—can change the strategic direction of a company.

References

BSI. (2014). *Guidance on organizational resilience, in BS 65000:2014* (p. 16). © The British Standards Institution.

Chandler, D. (2014). *Resilience: The governance of complexity*. Routledge.

Davies, W. (2009). *Reinventing the firm*. Demos.

Dindarian, K. (2019). *Exploring enterprise resilience through the theoretical lens of complexity: A case study situated in the high value-manufacturing sector*. The University of Manchester.

Everson, M., et al. (2012). *Resilience: Winning with risk* (Vol. 1, p. 1). PWC.

Kerr, H. (2016). Organizational Resilience. *Quality, 55*(7), 40.

Lampel, J., Bhalla, A., & Jha, P. P. (2014). Does governance confer organisational resilience? Evidence from UK employee owned businesses. *European Management Journal, 32*(1), 66–72.

Conclusions

11

In today's business environment, the unprecedented rapid rate of change, coupled with revolutionary improvements in the speed of information flow, has greatly increased the range of risks and uncertainty to which organizations are constantly exposed, and this drives new threats. Consequently, corporate, business and operation units are adapting their strategy to cope with those changes. Effective emergent strategy is an organizational capability that enables an organization to cope with changes for ensuring business continuity.

This book argues, based on the author's research findings, that in any organization, the most effective emergent strategies are characterized by resilience, which in turn is concerned with emergence, a characteristic of complexity.

In the light of this, organizations can apply a holistic view, called complexity thinking, to their enterprise risk management (ERM) processes. This will, hopefully, close the gap that complexity thinking by itself has not hitherto been able to fill. This combined holistic approach has been developed to foster a higher level of resilience in organizations from a strategic point of view, and it is strongly recommended that enterprise resilience be integrated into this approach. Based on the results of our study, it becomes clear that complexity thinking is at the heart of holism, a key term in ERM processes.

The benefits of using a novel enterprise risk framework (ERF), suitable for the purposes of establishing organizational resilience, are pointed out. This will hopefully serve to counteract the risks that can affect business activities to such an extent that a company suffers considerable damage or even has its existence threatened. The ERF is developed from the concept of the complex adaptive system, resulting in the POET complexity framework. This way, it can be ensured that the ERF applies to both the macro (top-down) and micro (bottom-up) levels of an organization.

The proper implementation of ERF can, hopefully, ensure business continuity, improve company performance and allow competitive advantage to be maintained, even after ordinarily destructive incidents have occurred, in turn protecting stakeholder interests and the corporate reputation and brand, thereby retaining—or even increasing—shareholder value.

K. Dindarian, *Embracing the Black Swan*, Future of Business and Finance,
https://doi.org/10.1007/978-3-031-29344-3_11

The purpose of this book is to provide mechanisms by which uncertainties and emergent risks take place within ERM processes and to examine how this relates to business continuity.

In particular, the study started with three research objectives, which are addressed substantially and summarized below.

Firstly, the research study has highlighted that effective emergent strategies are characterized by resilience, as well as by the relationship between strategy and resilience and that between strategy and ERM. It has concluded that strategic management is a framework for analysing the environment, for integrating enterprise activities, for learning and for adapting to change. This ensures business continuity, thus creating added value both in the present and into the future for shareholder and stakeholder alike, even in times of complex environmental change.

The conclusion is that resilience is a strategic objective, so called because effective emergent strategies are characterized by resilience, and ERM is a property of strategic thinking and decision-making.

In a nutshell, strategic thinking and decision-making are necessary in any environmental conditions, even in the face of complexity and uncertainty. It is, therefore, pointed out that resilience is an emergent property, a characteristic of complexity, and it is an adaptive process that concerns a system's ability to deal with high levels of uncertainty and the ability of that system to adapt to a threat.

Secondly, this study has argued, based on the characteristics of a resilient organization and the relationship between resilience and complexity, that resilience can be regarded as a process that responds to adversity. In general, there is a strong consensus that resilience relates to disaster, crisis, disruptions and unexpected change. Indeed, it is evident from both the literature and our research that resilience is increasingly seen as a strategic objective that should help an organization to survive and, indeed, to thrive.

Furthermore, this study contends that resilience is about the ability of an organization to self-organize because of both negative and positive feedback generated by its interaction with the macro-economic environment. Self-organization is a characteristic of a complex system and, we argue, there is a case for a complexity theory-based approach to an understanding of resilience, especially in high-tech multinational organizations in areas such as engineering and manufacturing.

The result is the POET complexity framework, an appropriate methodology that recognizes the interconnectedness of risks and can enable practitioners to interrelate emerging risks through robust analytical methods. This framework allows for the possibility of assessing further aspects of the organization, such as organizational resilience. The study also emphasizes the impact of cultivating a complexity theory mindset within a multi-project environment, as can be seen from our exploration of practitioners' perceptions of complexity in a large railway engineering program.

Thirdly, this study argues, based on the research results, that there are differences between conventional ERM and enterprise resilience. Complexity thinking is applied, therefore, to enterprise risk management processes as a holistic tool that can be used to assess the extent of complexity and which can also help determine the way in which complexity thinking may be incorporated into ERM processes.

In addition, it is argued that an organization can better deal with emerging risk through the embedding of complexity thinking into its ERM, to ensure survival and success in this increasingly uncertain global environment.

Finally, the research on which this book is based contributes to the existing gap through the creation of a novel enterprise risk framework that is suitable for the purposes of establishing organizational resilience, which can ultimately ensure competitive advantage and business continuity, and protect both stakeholder interests and shareholder value; for this reason, a pragmatic approach is taken.

In the view of this author, all organizations are exposed to—and exhibit varying degrees of—complexity; it is contended in this book that this complexity should be embraced in the context of fostering greater degrees of resilience within the organization. The assessment of organizational resilience and risk management can—and indeed should—be aligned, so as to close the gap in the resilience profile of an enterprise.

11.1 Research Contribution to Academic Knowledge and to Practice

This book is primarily intended to contribute to both theory and practice, and to the body of academic knowledge, with some significant implications for the research fields of strategy, resilience, complexity and enterprise risk management.

From the study has emerged the POET (process, organizational, environmental and technological) complexity framework, which can be used to assess people's knowledge of complexity and its application in practice. Practitioners and academics alike can use POET to better understand the impact of risk and uncertainty on an operational level such as in a multi project environment, thus enabling the formulation of an effective operational emergent strategy. It is an appropriate methodology that recognizes the interconnectedness of risks and which can enable practitioners to interrelate emerging risks through robust analytical methods. The POET complexity framework provides the possibility of assessing further aspects of the organization, such as organizational resilience. This is argued as a bottom-up approach, with decision-making being at micro level.

Furthermore, the study outlines nine organizational resilience categories in proposing an organizational resilience framework that expands on the BSI resilience model. It is hoped that both academics and practitioners can benefit in terms of assessment of organizational resilience in practical terms. On top of that, the application of the proposed frameworks can provide responses to unexpected incidents through the sharing of strategic thinking, thereby aligning the top-down and bottom-up approaches and the sharing of decision-making authority throughout the organization.

Finally, this research highlights the fact that the provided enterprise resilience framework, designed to make sense of complexity thinking, lies at the heart of 'holism', a key concept in ERM processes, which expands on the COSO enterprise risk framework, and can be used to support the executive decision-making process in practice.

12 How Recognizable Is the Black Swan?

The Black Swan notion, according to Nassim Nicolas Taleb in his book, The Black Swan (Taleb, 2007), is ultimately about ignorance. The whole Black Swan concept is based on the structure of randomness in empirical reality. Black Swan events are wholly unexpected occurrences that happen outside the normal range of predictability, with potentially disastrous consequences. A severe blizzard in Europe in January may be unexpected and extremely disruptive, but it is not beyond what can be reasonably predicted for such a place and time of year and would therefore not be considered a Black Swan. An equally severe blizzard in May, on the other hand, would be a Black Swan, because of its utterly unpredictable nature. There are two types of rare events that fall into the Black Swan definition. There are those Black Swans that exist through narratives and are present in contemporary discourse, about which we may hear on television; such Black Swans are generally overestimated. Then, there are the Black Swans that cannot be captured by models and which no one dares to talk about in public simply because they are not plausible. This second kind is, by and large, mostly underestimated.

Taleb sees a Black Swan event as having three essential attributes: it is, first of all, an outlier, being outside the realm of regular expectations, since nothing in the past can convincingly point to its possibility. Secondly, it has enormous implications. Thirdly, despite its status as an outlier, human nature leads us to construct explanations for its occurrence after the fact, to make it explainable and predictable. So, the three attributes are rarity, massive impact and predictability in retrospect, but not in foresight (Taleb, 2021a, 2021b).

The logic of the Black Swan makes what we do not know much more meaningful than what we do know. Indeed, such events are often greatly exacerbated by the fact that they come unexpectedly. A Black Swan event can happen precisely because nobody expects it to happen or expects the consequences. Epidemics occur according to Black Swan dynamics. Wars are completely unpredictable and, since we do not understand the causal chains between politics and trade, they can easily trigger Black Swans because of our aggressive ignorance.

K. Dindarian, *Embracing the Black Swan*, Future of Business and Finance,
https://doi.org/10.1007/978-3-031-29344-3_12

This begs the question of how to defend ourselves against such occurrences. Since Black Swans cannot be predicted, we must be prepared for their coming into existence. If we focus on the 'anti-knowledge'—on what we do not know—we can really do a lot in terms of preparing for the occurrence of Black Swans. What defines Black Swans, after all, is their utter unpredictability. To illustrate his point, Nassim uses the analogy of shooting a movie: unlike with a movie script, where the cast and crew know exactly what is going to happen, we as experts cannot tell the time or nature of the next Black Swan.

What we do know cannot hurt. This holds especially true for the worlds of economics and business. The more unexpected the success of a project, the smaller the number of competitors and the more successful the entrepreneur behind it will become. Experts and entrepreneurs should, therefore, focus less on top-down planning in their strategy and more on maximum trial and error and spotting the opportunities that come their way. The best stratagem, then, is to try to plan as much as we can and seize as many opportunities as possible from which Black Swans can emerge. One can feed the phenomenon in two ways. The first is to exclude the extraordinary and concentrate on the 'normal'. In other words, leave aside the 'outliers' and deal with the usual cases. The second method is based on the belief that phenomena can only be understood by dealing with the extreme cases first—especially if, like Black Swans, they have an enormous cumulative effect.

Healthcare, for example, can only be understood if we also deal with serious illnesses and epidemics. The normal is often meaningless. The problem is that, on the one hand, we do not have prior knowledge (only retrospect) of where the map is wrong, while on the other hand, mistakes can have serious consequences. The gap between what we know and what we think we know is dangerously wide. This is precisely where Black Swans are produced. The combination of low predictability and high impact makes the Black Swan a great mystery. The central theme of this book, however, is not to discuss the theory of Black Swans, but ways in which we can be prepared for their occurrence so we can not only neutralize their impact, but even—ideally, anyway—capitalize on it.

A Black Swan is understood here as an unexpected event that can be assigned to one of three categories: (1) unknown unknowns (we do not know what we do not know), (2) unknown knowers (we do not have the knowledge, but others do) and (3) events whose probability of occurrence is considered negligible and therefore not assumed to occur. There is some scientific research in this context.

After World Wars I and II, arguably the third biggest event in terms of global impact occurred in 2020, when the world was faced with one of the most adverse events in modern human history, the COVID-19 pandemic. It was not the first of its kind, but it was arguably the worst in terms of social and economic impact. The still-lingering global epidemic has not only cost millions of lives but has wrought havoc on our social, political, healthcare and economic systems. We have had similar issues in the last two decades, such as the SARS, Swine Flu and Ebola epidemics, the Lehmann Brothers crash and terrorist attacks in Europe, Africa and the Middle East. Political upheaval, military conflicts such as the Ukraine war, natural disasters and economic recessions have all had massive negative impacts on private lives, governments and organizations.

All of these were unexpected events, so-called interrelated emerging risks, created by man, nature or a combination of both. Such unexpected events can and do disrupt the global dynamic system and its behaviour. It is in this light that the area of resilience is considered. Despite the utterly unforeseeable nature of such events, however, governments and organizations applying the principles that are described in this book would arguably have been better prepared to deal with them as soon as they started and to prevent the negative outcomes we witnessed. The first question, therefore, on which we must focus, is how we can identify those emerging risks. From there, we need to ask ourselves, how can we assess those risks and then embed the findings of our assessment within strategic management and decision-making processes?

References

Taleb, N. N. (2007). *The black swan: The impact of the highly improbable* (Vol. 2). Random House.

Taleb, N. N. (2021a). *Der Schwarze Schwan: Die Macht höchst unwahrscheinlicher Ereignisse.- Der Klassiker erstmals vollständig überarbeitet und in einem Band*. Penguin Verlag.

Taleb, N. N. (2021b). *INCERTO: Fooled by Randomness, the Black Swan, the Bed of Procrustes, Antifragile, Skin in the Game*. Random House Trade.

Part III

Geopolitical and Macroeconomic Systems

Introduction

Our world is inherently complex and highly dynamic, its change rapid and volatile. Two man-made systems, namely, geopolitics and macroeconomics, are the main drivers of global world system change. The structure and behaviour of the global world are changing because of both systems and their inseparable interconnectedness, which we understand by the term 'complex system'[1]. This part takes a closer look at the complexity of both systems and the structural and behavioural changes that occur within them because of the dynamics and volatility of their elements, such as geopolitical power and decision-making. These elements, in turn, are determined by factors that include population size and changes, the availability of and access to natural resources and raw materials, levels of technology, and the import and export of goods and services measured by a country's GDP. In addition, geopolitical power is determined by the military resources and levels of military spending of individual countries and regions of the world. Moreover, demography and globalization strongly influence geopolitical power to a large extent.

Geopolitics and macroeconomics are inextricably linked. In 2022, just before the completion of the first draft for this book, Europe faced unexpected change arising from another crisis, this time in the form of a military conflict, the Ukraine war. This raises more questions about geopolitics and macroeconomics.

The structure of the geopolitical system is shaped by human society, which in turn is made up of almost eight billion individuals. On the one hand, these societies form the social units that need and use technology, an increasing and ongoing need that drives innovation. On the other hand, this innovation cannot happen without the resources of the macroeconomic system, comprised of technology, business and financial organizations whose main goal is to make a profit and whose functioning is necessarily supported by political systems. Private interests wishing to earn a profit

[1] Refer to chapter on complexity theory.

are linked to macroeconomics by the need for energy which, as we already know, comes from natural resources. All of these are intrinsically linked to, and dependent on, each other. This broad complexity deserves to be looked at very seriously, since it is essentially about geographical boundaries that are, in their turn, mainly decided by politics. The goal of politics is and must be the public interest, and therefore, it must regulate and constrain private profit-making enterprises when they are not in the public interest. Otherwise, there would be a return to the Middle Ages and its monarchies, where the state (i.e. monarch) was the private owner of all land, people and resources.

The core of geographical boundaries is closely tied to the structure of a world that covers continents from Europe to Asia and Oceania, from Africa to North and South America. The borders of countries, regions and continents determine the geographical map. Most social, economic and political activities take place within some territory established by borders. Although the aim of this book is not to philosophize about the general knowledge of geography, it is important to be aware of the value of such observations and studies to help us understand the structure and the behaviour of the global system and its changes. In this context, the importance of the location of mineral resources and their connection to geographic boundaries and, thus, their impact both by and on political decisions cannot be emphasized strongly enough. We must consider the risks and uncertainties of natural and man-made changes, such as disproportionate deforestation and forest fires caused by climate change. Similarly, the impact of drought on agricultural and food production cannot be ignored. Essentially, however, the main factors affecting the geopolitical and macroeconomic systems are (1) an increasing world population and changing demographics, (2) a disproportionate use of natural resources, (3) rapidly increasing energy demand and (4) a disproportionate use of water and food resources and of land use for agricultural production and its impact on health. Related to this is the unequal ratio of the global agricultural labour force to the total population and the disproportionate consumption of what is produced. Other important factors include (5) the professional world and healthcare, (6) education, (7) industry, (8) economy and commerce, (9) finance and, last but not least, (10) world politics.

In the following pages, the key drivers of global system change in terms of the geopolitical and macroeconomic systems, including their risks and uncertainties, are described. It is sincerely hoped that this opens the door for further reflection on how, with the correct knowledge, to limit and minimize the risks and clarify the uncertainties of global system change and its positive and negative impacts on our lives. The focus is on demonstrating the interrelationships between the above factors (1-10) and thus the causes of change and its complexity. This will lead to consideration of their structural and behaviour changes in order to cast light on the possible impacts of global world system change. This will, hopefully, throw open the discussion on the importance of making the global world system in which we live more resilient.

Demographics, Education and Employment Dynamics 13

13.1 World Population and Demographics

Over the course of the last 50 years, the world's demographics have changed beyond recognition. There are twice as many people living on our planet today as there were in the 1960s, and a far higher proportion of those now live in urban areas. Those changes are, obviously, of great interest to sociologists, demographers and social scientists. They are, however, equally interesting to politicians, environmentalists, economists and business planners, and virtually all non-linear global system changes are linked to demography. The population of the earth is the most important element influencing global systems. Due to the planet's rapidly growing population, which is unevenly distributed, the ownership of the earth's surface has become more important than ever. There is no unknown earth surface and no surface without an owner. The story of current demographic change is simple: the earth had never experienced the rates of population growth that it has in the last few decades. This book considers demographic changes on two strategic levels: continental migration and international migration. Changes on each of those levels exert strong positive and negative socio-demographic, geopolitical and macroeconomic influences. For this reason, the effects of demographic change on the development of organizational resilience in the last three decades have been immense, with enormous implications for the future in the world of business and finance.

13.1.1 Motives for Migration

People relocating from one place to another can be divided into two main categories. The first group is people who do not go into exile voluntarily, but have moved because of expulsion, banishment, expropriation, expatriation, forced resettlement, religious or political persecution, natural disasters, war, violence or other 'push' factors. This group is of special importance to me, personally. Exiles and asylum seekers, along with their causes, are very important topics for political scientists,

K. Dindarian, *Embracing the Black Swan*, Future of Business and Finance,
https://doi.org/10.1007/978-3-031-29344-3_13

sociologists and other scientific groups, which topics cannot be dealt with in this book. The second group are those emigrants who voluntarily seek a new country to live in, for myriad reasons, such as better work prospects, a particularly attractive job opportunity, a better business environment, closer proximity to family or friends or even a more attractive climate or lifestyle. These reasons are commonly referred to as pull factors. Both groups create change, particularly within the socio-economic system; language, mindset, ethnicity, customs and traditions and different cultures all drive the complexity that gives rise to a need for resilience.

There are significant changes involved for not just the migrant and the host country, but also his/her country of origin, and a range of complexities to be coped with and managed. This has been, in recent years, the case more than ever before, given the vast increase in migration over the last three decades. It is, however, not at all surprising, given that the world population has exploded over the last two decades. There are simply more people to move around. There are many organizations, both governmental and NGOs, that conduct migration research and produce statistics. Academics make many attempts at discourse on the topic of migration, and they recommend frameworks, standards and important indicators. This topic is discussed in this book in the context of the global system and its complexity, and about coping and dealing with such complexity, in the hope of finding further solutions for building global system resilience.

13.1.2 Regional Migration

In many if not most countries, people have a strong tendency to move from rural to urban areas in search of a better life. Usually this means work, but it can also have to do with marriage, education, curiosity about the 'bright lights' or even just a desire to get away from home or parents. This accelerates the process of the socio-technological system, which is a complex one. Also, ever more domestic migrations are now forced onto people, driven by armed conflicts, loss of livelihood and climate disasters. This domestic migration has been responsible for massive urban expansion, which shapes the structure of cities and megacities, with the result that a new socio-technological system has evolved, which has directly affected economic growth. It has also had a significant impact on quality of life. Beyond the essential elements that spring to mind, such as safety, access to water, food, housing, quality of education and healthcare and realistic employment opportunities, a broader concept of quality of life might also include intangibles such as job security, political stability, individual freedom and environmental quality.

Whatever one's idea of what makes for a high quality of life, one thing most social scientists agree on is that material wealth is not the most important factor in assessing how well a life is lived, and this has been reflected in surveys. Such statistical figures are mostly influenced by sponsors who apply arbitrary benchmarks to achieve their goals, one example being the use of GDP scales as opposed to reality. It is important that most statistical targets focus on important elements such as personal security, political stability and a well-developed public healthcare system. There is, of course, the reality that in many countries it is difficult or even impossible to conduct such surveys. These, therefore, are not considered in this book, and the UN figures are recommended to the reader instead.

While quality-of-life rankings are based more on urban life, rural life is also undergoing significant changes, with new and unknown structures. Relatively wealthy migrants from the city move in, seeking a quieter life. Severe depopulation has, not unexpectedly, occurred in many areas, leaving whole villages standing as ghost towns. Investment by domestic and foreign investors has also taken place, however, a recent case in point being Tesla's investment in the Brandenburg region of Germany. Here, the village landscape, nature and infrastructure have all changed massively within a short period. At the same time, economic growth has been boosted by the influx of people into the region. The newcomers demand living infrastructure, and this influences the behaviour of the socio-technological system. This system behaviour is the reverse face of urbanization and is the new shape of rural areas with, just as in the big cities, a major impact on economic growth.

The future of an organization's strategy depends to a great extent on how it copes and deals with the increasingly complex socio-technological world that is emerging from the interaction of people and nature, which is shaping the structure of social and technological systems. These systems require natural resources, and how these are used demands a whole rethink about strategic and decision-making processes concerning the environment and sustainability, along with an understanding of the diversity and psychology of human resources, taking into consideration vision, purpose and cultural behaviour.

Civil society, local governments and the private sector all have opportunities to be part of this mega-trend and to serve the needs of megacities. For domestic migration to take place and to run smoothly, a sort of 'governance bridge' is required between civil society, local government and the private sector. Politicians and city councillors are under obligation to revise laws and even introduce new ones, to regulate domestic immigration issues, to be prepared for developing threats and to exploit new opportunities in a fundamental and legal way. The time has come to rethink conventional frameworks for civil society, local governments and the private sector, with the aim of ultimately increasing and strengthening their resilience.

13.1.3 International Migration

Emigration to a nearby country has long been part of human behaviour, and it makes solid sense. Countries in close proximity to each other within a given region offer many of the advantages of home: cultural familiarity, perhaps the same language or one with similar roots (such as Romanian and Italian), relative proximity to relatives and friends for regular visits home and often—especially for those migrating for non-economic reasons—similar economic conditions.

Immigration within Europe, particularly internal migration whether permanent, temporary or circular within the European Union (EU), has significantly increased over the last three decades. The main reason for this is the free movement of persons, one of the fundamental freedoms of the EU, which allows citizens of member states unrestricted migration opportunities within the EU area. In effect, citizens of EU countries can cross the borders between individual member states unhindered and unnoticed thanks to the lack of border controls, and they fly between European countries without identity checks—a privilege that is not enjoyed by people from non-EU member states.

The modern internal migration of European citizens has a darker side too, however, namely, the expulsion policies of some European countries during the twentieth century. The total number of victims of ethnically motivated forced migration was around 60 million people during the 1940s alone. When we consider that there were also mass victims of violent population displacements outside Europe at that time, including 22 million forced migrants in the cases of India/Pakistan and Israel/Palestine alone, the global historical significance of the 1940s as the dark climax of 'ethnic cleansing' is indeed stark. For those readers wishing to delve deeper into this topic, the newly opened Documentation Centre for Flight, Expulsion, Reconciliation, in Berlin, is recommended. The centre provides information on the causes, dimensions and consequences of expulsion, resettlement and forced migration in twentieth-century Europe and beyond. The primary focus, however, is on the expulsion and resettlement of Germans caused by Germany itself at the end of the Second World War.[1]

Even short-distance migration, whether intercontinental or intracontinental, does not come without its challenges. Thanks to EU regulations, modern (and future) intracontinental migration has assumed a new shape in terms of structure and processes that differs significantly from other continents. Any migration issues within the EU pale compared to, for example, the experience of the United States and Mexico. By the same token, migration experiences even within the EU at different times in history have differed fundamentally. The immigration of workers from former Eastern Bloc countries such as Romania and Poland into Germany and Britain differed somewhat from the migration from Ireland to the UK (then an EU member state) and to other EU countries during the 1980s and even a previous Irish wave of immigration to Britain during the 1940s–1960s period.

The Irish emigration situation is an interesting one. Although the country has suffered a continuous flow of its citizens to the (historically) economically stronger Britain since its independence in 1922, two periods stand out where the constant bleed turned into a haemorrhage. The first of these was during the two decades from 1945 to 1965, when a vast number of workers, mostly unskilled, emigrated to British cities to take advantage of the post-war construction boom. Although those workers experienced a good deal of discrimination and homesickness, the majority benefited from the experience, being able to earn paycheques that those back home could only dream about. A country suffering from the destruction of war and the depletion of its male workforce had a ready-made army of 'Paddies' (as the Irish were known) to take their place. The families in Ireland gained the economic benefits, which paved

[1] There were very little organized population movements by Germans at that time.

the way for the economic boom of the 1960s, which saw not only emigrant numbers dwindle but many of those who had left now returning home. Those returning emigrants brought considerable benefits in terms of small-scale investment, such as new houses and businesses, new technical knowledge and consumerist ideas and expectations, all fuelling the boom that continued through the 1970s.

That boom that started in the late 1960s proved, however, to be rather short-lived, and another recession, arguably resulting from economic and financial mismanagement at government level, hit the country in the mid-1980s. Emigration returned with a vengeance, but this time, the typical emigrant profile was different, with different expectations and ambitions and the higher education and qualifications that would enable them to enjoy considerable financial and career success. As with the last wave of emigration a few decades before, the main destination was Britain, but this time, many young migrants also relocated to continental Europe.

The greatest difference, however, was that the benefits this time around were more one-sided. While the host countries got all the gain in the form of an infusion of highly educated young professionals, the country of origin experienced all the pain. Apart from the broken-up families and social desolation we expect from mass emigration, Ireland suffered economically through the massive 'brain drain', the depletion of a highly educated and skilled human resource that was the product of an expensive taxpayer-funded education system.

Things took another unexpected turn in the 1990s. The so-called Celtic Tiger boom started to attract many of the 1980s emigrants back home. Here again, the experience differed from the earlier emigrant return. Although those older and wiser middle-class professionals brought back a new level of skills and ideas, especially in the fields of science and technology, they found themselves experiencing a massive barrier, that of rapidly rising housing costs. Although they were often in a better position to obtain mortgage loans, the increase in residential demand in Ireland created a corresponding surge in property prices and flaws in the whole borrowing system that have not, to this day, been fully resolved, with disproportionate (to income) residential purchase and rental prices in the country. The net result was the near collapse of the banking system in 2008, a severe housing crisis despite a surplus of (empty) recently built residential units and an economic recession that, despite being strongly connected with the international crisis, seemed more pronounced in Ireland because of the housing and banking issues.

Ireland was not unique in such difficulties, however. The deregulated financial markets (after repeal of the Glass-Steagall Act in the United States by a neoliberal government and similar measures elsewhere) embarked on a never-before-seen lending spree. The lending of money with high default probability and imaginary collateral (the so-called sub-primes) exploded, just to be derivatized immediately and resold to uninformed buyers all over the world. Then, in 2007–2008, oil prices hit a multi-decade record high, the overheated economy slowed down and the sub-primes defaulted. It was definitively not the still-growing demand for houses that triggered the financial crisis, let alone migration, but an unregulated banking system and the beginning of the end of oil (conventional oil peaked in 2008, according to the IEA[2]).

There was another reason why stronger immigration, and the resulting increased housing demand, could not possibly have been the trigger for the 2008 crash, let alone its origin: for as long as real estate stays in high demand, there cannot be a burst of the housing bubble. There was no obvious reason why demand and prices would suddenly fall. Had all those immigrants gone back home? Or did they all simultaneously decide to abandon their real estate projects? Very unlikely. The burst of the housing bubble in 2008 that triggered the financial crisis was, in fact, due to over-indebted house owners defaulting on their loans. When their overpriced properties were put on sale, nobody wanted to buy them at the high prices that would have been required to cancel the vendors' loan indebtedness. This in turn drove down house prices in general, and the collaterals of even intact loans collapsed in value, plunging a great many mortgaged homeowners—prime as well as sub-prime borrowers—into negative equity. The holders of those subprime derivates suffered huge book losses that often resulted in their bankruptcy. What followed—banks too big to fail and governments bailing them out—is now generally seen as the end of the neoliberal era. The all-powerful, all-knowing 'invisible hand of the free markets' was more invisible than ever simply because it had never existed in the first place.

More recently, the main source of intracontinental migration in Europe has been the former communist states, notably Poland, Romania and Bulgaria. Through the course of the 1990s, after the fall of the communist system had failed to bring about the economic advances that many had expected, millions of young Eastern Europeans flooded the more affluent western states, particularly Germany, Italy, France and UK. Very often, whole families emigrated. At first, western European countries were glad of the influx of badly needed labour, with the large number of Polish skilled tradesmen arriving in UK in the late 1990s—just in time to fill the gaping skills gap—being a case in point. After Romania and Bulgaria joined the EU in 2007, however, a considerable number of unskilled workers headed west, many of whom failed to find employment, often ending up in impoverished ghettoes or even becoming homeless. Law enforcement services reported a disproportionate share of crimes being committed by Eastern Europeans.[3]

Despite these problems, the host countries got the better end of the bargain, while the benefits to the home countries were questionable, although the cash remissions home of many agricultural workers provided considerable relief to older family members who remained in the rural areas from which most had come. Overall, it could be argued that the loss suffered by the East was the greater by far. Whole villages in Bulgaria and Romania still lie almost deserted, thus diminishing the justification for rural infrastructural development. Given the wide chasm between

[2]https://www.engineeringnews.co.za/article/conventional-oil-peaked-in-2008-iea-2013-01-18

[3]https://www.researchgate.net/figure/Total-police-recorded-crime-rate-per-1-000-head-England-and-Wales-1950-2012-Data_fig 1_325894271

wages in those countries and in affluent countries such as Germany, skilled tradesmen and even semi-skilled workers are hard to find in Eastern Europe, with a heavy impact especially on the construction, hospitality and tech sectors.

Whatever the experience, modern migration to neighbouring countries can become a resilient process through balancing the economic performance of the respective states involved, such as wage differentials for the same work in neighbouring countries, taking into consideration the differing standards of infrastructure in both countries and even considering the relative population density. For example, a migration from Portugal into Spain would not have the same effect on the host country as would a large influx of people going the opposite way. Strong economies ensure high employment, and states are therefore obliged to create a labour-wage balance between themselves and neighbouring countries. It is important to balance work and housing for internal migration. Other areas of balance include security, health, education, technology and finance. Essentially, it is about the relative quality of life in neighbouring countries, and so resilience within the above areas becomes critical for states. There are many indices that measure quality of life; although many gaps remain, there are also solutions for filling them when it comes to quality-of-life resilience. There are no one-size-fits-all solutions, nor can we even attempt to quantify and anticipate individual risks, and no single preventative measures for individual risks. It is only by introducing a broad range of measures designed to protect against all possible risks—the unexpected even more than the expected—that we can truly build resilience into the systems that allow and facilitate migration. It is the task of states, political leaders and governments and organizations—both private and NGOs—to redesign the processes now, not after unexpected events happen. The future of business and finance depends on ensuring the resilience of human migration to neighbouring countries. The ideal would be to control migration by political means such as immigration laws and quotas, as opposed to letting it run loose driven only by free market demand, in the interest of minimising emergent risks and creating more positive outcomes.

The considerations relevant to domestic migration can also be said to apply to international migration, but there are other factors at play that create distinctions. To begin with, the range of reasons for migration between continents tends to be greater, and there also appears to be a greater presence of the 'push factor', such as persecution, extreme economic hardship or civil strife. There is also mass migration, with people seeking a new home because of changes in the natural and human ecosystems. Natural environmental changes, such as drought, floods and wildfires, are increasing in both degree and frequency, especially with climate change becoming more of a driver.

It is estimated that by 2050, around 200 million refugees (both domestic and international) will be leaving their homes for climate-related reasons alone, a figure that today is not taken into account when planning for future population growth and trends.

For comparison: according to UNHCR, there are 84 million refugees in total today from all causes combined.[4] Similarly, natural disasters such as earthquakes can cause sudden surges in mass migration. Shortages of water and food due to erosion and other natural disasters have increased the hunger figures that have forced masses of people abroad in recent decades. Human ecosystem changes include political conflicts, which have increased massively in all parts of the world in the last three decades, along with, albeit to a lesser extent at least in terms of numbers, political and religious persecution of minorities and ethnic groups. A major potential cause for alarm with serious implications for international migration over the coming years is the change within the geo-economic system in which the gap between rich and poor is growing wider.

The experiences of Southeast Asia, sub-Saharan Africa, post-communist Eastern Europe and Great Britain all serve as evidence of the effect of demographic change on economic growth (or lack thereof). In many countries, outdated technology and methods of production, political instability, natural factors such as climate change and desertification, and severe financial and economic problems are all cause for international migration, and they serve as a significant push factor. The worst effect of this for such countries is the loss of what is arguably the greatest of all resources, the human resource. Resilient countries find a balance between the absorption of demographic resources, on the one hand, and the export of technology to emigrant countries, on the other hand. Political relations and diplomatic actions are the most important democratic methods to be used in difficult times as a means of maintaining this balance. Resilient countries offer their organizations the best opportunities for establishing sustainable organizational and business relations with other countries in difficult times and beyond.

Key elements of rapidly changing demographics are safety and security, water and food, healthcare, mobility and logistics, ICT, digitalization, education, energy (electric power generation, transmission and distribution), economic and financial solutions and rapidly developing technology. Although for the most part beneficial, such rapid technological advancements are not without their drawbacks, contributing to the collapse of the global ecology and, potentially as a result, of human society. Linked to these, infrastructure for more and better living and working spaces is becoming an increasingly critical issue. Developing, expanding and protecting all of these will become a matter of resilience.

13.1.4 Safety and Security

Some researchers report on the approach of policymakers to security in cities around the world, and it has divided the broad security problem into four security categories: digital, healthcare, infrastructure and personal. Although the results of the survey highlight the problem, they do not provide any guidelines for improving the

[4] https://www.unhcr.org/refugee-statistics/

resilience of cities. As mentioned earlier, such statistical figures are mostly influenced by sponsors who apply arbitrary benchmarks to achieving their goals. All those points have one thing in common—they can be easily turned into a profit. The crucial 'security problems' of cities are food security (food riots, hunger), political security (riots, war), environmental security (heatwaves, floods, tornadoes) and social security (poverty, inequality). Indeed, although neoliberalism sees potential profit in everything, it also holds that this is not necessarily for everyone. Potential security problems give rise to emergent risks that might be from nature, from humans or from a combination of both, such as pandemics and natural disasters striking developing countries already suffering from political and/or economic instability. The importance of having clear early monitoring and warning systems in place in anticipation of such events—coupled with an assumption that they could happen at any time—cannot be stressed strongly enough if we are to ensure the resilience of urban areas. The result of effective security systems in cities will be a visible feel-good factor and a sustainable quality of life.

13.1.5 Personal Security

Natural disasters and man-made accidents, or a combination of both, are multifaceted and can appear with a high degree of complexity. Daily accidents on our roads, railways, waterways and airways are clear examples of this, which are already partly considered through prevailing measures, namely, traditional risk management. Environmental health and safety (EHS) is an important pillar of personal workplace security in just about all developed countries. This is secured through legal, civil, governmental and industry standards and regulations and enhanced by organizations' internal policies. In this book, EHS is examined in considerable depth from several perspectives, such as sustainability.

Personal security and safety is a further important pillar of personal life in cities. Coping with the complexity of new emergent social life in an urban environment is, of itself, a growing challenge. When we speak about people's personal security, we immediately think in terms of crime. Criminal activity can take many shapes and forms, such as homicide, physical assault, burglaries, robbery, sex offences, pickpocketing or, especially in recent years, cybercrime.

In every city, local authorities are responsible for the safety of citizens. People want to feel safe, whether in their homes, on the streets, in parks or in the shopping centres. Failure to protect them creates a sense of danger and threat, and trust in—never mind support for—the authorities will dwindle rapidly. It is therefore important that the authorities be able to protect citizens by building, funding and maintaining police forces and security services. The prevailing level of crime determines the demands on policing, and the actual capacity and resourcing of police and security services in turn determine their effectiveness. These ways are tied in with neoliberal thinking, which is based on impoverishing large parts of the population through exploitation. After large numbers of people have fallen through the cracks of the demolished social system and become criminals, as substantial numbers do, certain businesses see their way to making even more profit out of the problem through private security services, private prisons (such as in the United States), forced labour camps and other means; this writer, on the other hand, believes in preventing crime in the first place by providing a decent living to as many as possible together with a functioning social support system.

The problems may not end there. A depressed urban economy will negatively affect growth in areas such as education, healthcare and commercial services, with the resulting lack of both education and proper healthcare, along with the various related social issues, leading to even higher crime rates. This phenomenon could easily be seen in major American cities during the 1970s and in Britain in the 1980s, when a vicious circle of unemployment, lack of opportunity, economic hardship and crime laid waste to many large urban and suburban areas of the Midlands and East London.

Education is arguably the most important factor in ensuring a high quality of life in cities. The infrastructure of education begins at home, running through kindergarten and school and culminating in college or university. In many countries around the world, especially less developed ones, a more traditional model of education is used, involving a great deal of rote learning and acquisition of mere facts,[5] without necessarily the same level of cognitive development that is emphasized in more developed nations. This means that, in effect, people are not trained to be able to migrate and are not made aware of the implications and practical challenges involved even in domestic migration to larger urban centres. Education at all levels must be fostered and well-protected, and this also includes resilience.

The infrastructure of living and working spaces comes under the umbrella of personal security. Inevitably, the cultural mindset of newcomers influences the form and shape of these spaces, for which the design of infrastructure becomes a kind of instrument of prestige and power. This infrastructure, complex by its very nature, needs to be resilient. It is, of course, a major question as to how such complex infrastructures can be protected against unexpected events that would normally result in loss of life, economic losses and interference with the ecosystem. Accompanying problems would include insufficient supplies of food and clean water, poor waste disposal and inadequate energy supply. This begs a serious question: can trust in technology ensure the resilience of infrastructures for living and working spaces?

13.1.6 Digital Security

It is not so much the case that digitalization will be an integral part of our future, as that it is already a huge feature of our present. As cities grow, they require more infrastructures, including transport, water and sewage, energy and communications. Schools, hospitals and leisure facilities need to be built, and there will be an

[5] https://www.youtube.com/watch?v=_yAPDjYuzrY

increased need for local retail shopping, clinics, pharmacies and various services. The construction, installation and maintenance of these infrastructures and facilities will have to be planned, managed and monitored, with procedures for obtaining permits, regulations for safeguarding the natural environment, and public health-and-safety processes all put in place. The requisite legal and regulatory systems, urban authorities and public administrations—all of which make up an extremely complex human ecosystem—will, if they are to properly meet twenty-first-century demands, need to be fully digitalized. The levels of digitalization that we realistically envisage will inevitably be subject to a range of threats: hacking, sabotage, online fraud and technical malfunctions. The ransomware cyberattack on Ireland's Health Service Executive's computerized records and appointments system in May 2021 left patient records and appointments in disarray, resulting in considerable setbacks and exposure to liability, including the publication online of confidential information on over 500 patients.[6] The consequences could have been much worse, and in similar attacks in the future, will be, unless there is adequate protection. What is noteworthy about this attack was not the damage itself, but the ease with which it was carried out (reputedly by Russia-based hackers) and the level of exposure that was revealed. Digitalization demands security in the highest degree. This security is linked to digital reality, so working efficiently in digital environments can become inefficient and almost impossible, depending on the behaviour of the network. It will not be enough to cover the gaps in technologies with new and innovative technological solutions. Installing expensive cyber protection software, for instance, will not be an adequate solution if that software slows up or renders inefficient computer systems and functions that rely on speed.

Digitalization considers the security of infrastructure and technology more than ever before. Smart infrastructure needs to be secured against any crime, terrorist acts and other damage, whether intentional or not. One possible solution is to decentralize critical computer infrastructures by isolating them and taking them off the network. Networking has many advantages, of course, but with smaller events it can cause greater damage. In this regard, decentralization reduces the intelligence of networked computers, but increases security. To put it very simply, the 'dumber' a computer is, the less likely it is to be hacked!

13.1.7 Healthcare and Medical Solutions

The growing population of the world is undoubtedly grateful for the medical advances and solutions of the last 150 years, in particular the range of vaccinations against infectious diseases and the significant reduction in the infant mortality rate, among others, although these remain very unequally distributed between developing and industrialized countries. Advanced medicine has not reached all parts of the

[6] https://en.wikipedia.org/wiki/Health_Service_Executive_ransomware_attack#Hospital_disruptions

world, large numbers of people are still suffering from chronic diseases, and many children in Africa are dying from minor illnesses, with inadequate medical infrastructures in place in developing countries. The numbers of doctors, hospital beds and nursing staff are not nearly sufficient in relation to the number of inhabitants. On the other hand, there are clearly diseases whose causes are associated with affluence, such as circulatory system illnesses, tumours and cancer of the respiratory tract, which is associated with smoking, not to mention the mortality rate from acute myocardial infarction (basically, heart attacks). All of these happen despite new medicines and advanced medical solutions. Further deaths are due to advanced technologies and infrastructure, such as traffic accidents.

Truly accurate statistics are hard to come by since population growth and mortality rates and even their causes are recorded differently by continent and region. Overall, however, it can be safely said that life expectancy is higher in industrialized countries than in less developed regions. We also know that population growth is higher in Africa, South America and Asia than in Europe—especially the western part of the continent—and North America. These factors are all changing the structure of global systems, with the result that regulating social and healthcare spending is overwhelming governments and policymakers. With population growth, the complexity of the whole network of global systems increases, which cannot be handled by conventional processes.

13.1.8 Resilience in Healthcare

The healthcare and medical sectors are important pillars of any resilient city. Given the non-linear nature of domestic migration, a complete rethink is in order regarding the development of healthcare systems and the provision of medical solutions.

In 2020, the world was faced with one of the most adverse medical events of recent history, the COVID-19 pandemic. It was not the first such event, but it was arguably one of the worst. We have had to face similarly dangerous and potentially disastrous issues in the last two decades, such as the SARS, swine flu and Ebola epidemics. This pandemic—which is far from completely over—has not only claimed the lives of millions of people around the world, but has also wreaked havoc on our social, political, economic and healthcare systems, and it bears stark witness to how well any given healthcare system can or cannot deal with such unexpected events.

The economic system has made two things clear: on the one hand, industrialized countries were able to support their economic systems with financial injections when the pandemic hit, thereby maintaining the strength of industry and exports to developing and third-world countries. The economic systems of the developed world even had the opportunity to develop anew during the pandemic period, such as by placing digitalization in the foreground. New gaps were discovered in old technologies, and new systems of work and business became commonplace, with the swing to remote working and the growth in online retail shopping being cases in point. The world economic and financial systems rediscovered their strength, but this could not have been done without being stabilized and sustained by taxpayers' finances, in which support has been good against factory closures and unemployment. On the other hand, many small entrepreneurs and self-employed people were not so lucky. The vulnerability of certain sectors became evident, most notably the hospitality, travel and entertainment industries, with many businesses closing and large numbers of people becoming unemployed.

This book has considered some important aspects of healthcare and the relationship between healthcare systems and demographic changes, especially the cultural changes associated with migration. When it comes to personal health risks, modern medical science considers resilience in relation to people and to their behavioural changes resulting from unexpected events, such as illness, war, persecution and the loss of family members. During some inspiring conversations that I had with Prof. Dr. Jalid Sehouli (Sehouli, 2019) and Prof. Dr. Ulrich-Wilhelm Thomale, I learned much about the growing importance of resilience and complexity in the field of medicine in recent years. The content of this valuable discourse is something I am very keen to share with readers.

According to Prof. Dr. Sehouli, speaking from a medical perspective, resilience is the ability to tolerate toxicities and complications arising during medical interventions such as surgery or cancer therapies. Resilience can greatly help in overcoming the side effects of medical procedures. For instance, even in the case of very minor surgery (5 to 10 min), a patient can lose at least 15% of his muscle weight. An effort is made, therefore, to implement what is known in medicine as 'pre-rehabilitation', as opposed to post-intervention measures, for training the patient in a variety of ways, since health—according to the WHO definition—includes psychological, physical and social dimensions. If, therefore, we wish to 'pre-habilitate' the patient, we must work on three levels: increased physical activity, education and information for empowerment. The first mentioned of those is self-explanatory. Education is necessary because by being informed about the medical procedure, the patient can endeavour to improve his healthcare status, including psychologically. Information empowerment is part of the so-called treatment decision-making process because there must be a participation aspect so that the patient and doctor can agree on the nature of therapy, thus creating a feeling of identification with the proposed approach.

Such a multidimensional approach even extends to breaking particularly distressing news in a worst-case scenario. If, for example, there is a diagnosis of advanced-stage cancer, which of course must be communicated in an extremely sensitive and tactful way to the patient, the doctor must remind themselves of previous experiences with life-threatening or complex situations in different contexts. Sudden unemployment, changes in one's social environment or the loss of a partner are, among others, all situations that can be drawn upon to put oneself in the patient's shoes, so as to be better prepared for the task of breaking the bad news. Perhaps one patient needs music to help him to overcome the bad news and to find a dialogue with himself. In other cases, the help of a partner may be required. Resilience, as Prof. Sehouli sees it, means being prepared for carrying out such a task and knowing how to best prepare the patient.

13.1.9 Complexity in Specialized Healthcare Systems

Prof. Dr. Thomale, in giving us the benefit of his expertise and insights, points out that from a medical perspective, sub-specialization in all medical fields has become—and will increasingly be in the future—one of the key aspects of progress in the quality of medical treatment over recent decades. This is brought about by two major factors. First of all, medical diagnostic capabilities have evolved in a highly complicated manner, leading to more complex disease categorizations. Secondly, treatment options and protocols have become extremely sophisticated and are often linked to a high level of expertise in implementing modern treatment strategies. This has been supported by technical developments such as molecular genetic sequencing and ongoing digital transformation. For example, technical developments in various surgical fields are leading more and more towards computer-aided surgery or even robotics, which includes the need for professionals who can handle technical solutions at a higher level of expertise. In effect, providing expertise at this level will require not only sufficient routine exposure for the individual professional, but the development of training models for younger generations for the sustainable availability of expert knowledge and its execution.

Let us take a realistic scenario. Brain tumours are the most common solid cancer diagnosis in childhood, with about 500–600 new patients per year in Germany, presenting highly heterogenous sub-entities in terms of originating cell types, age distribution and anatomical localization. Recent developments in brain imaging and molecular genetic diagnostics have revolutionized the understanding of this disease and greatly extended possibilities in terms of new treatment strategies. Nevertheless, surgery is still the most important treatment modality next to chemotherapy, newly developed targeted therapy or radiation.

Mutual decision-making among the involved disciplines is the mainstay of the optimal treatment protocol in individual cases, which is based on experience-oriented protocols developed on a national and international basis over the last few decades. Surgery is already necessary for acquiring tissue specimens for diagnostic purposes; it usually becomes necessary also for eliminating or significantly reducing the tumour load to a safe level, in order to maintain the functional integrity of the patients and ensure a decent quality of life for long-term survivors, which will be more than 80% of patients.

The application of surgery is based on digital-oriented preoperative planning, with the application of the surgical plan being carried out by computer-assisted measures or robotics and microsurgical techniques. Mastering these techniques in an effective and efficient way requires the knowledge and experience of not just the surgeon but the entire team. Surgery includes not only manual and anatomical skills in relation to the regular internal condition of the patient but also the correct application of digitally assisted guiding and executing techniques. Continuous navigation data is presented to the surgeon, for example, by an additional screen or augmented reality, together with interpretation of the magnification of the surgical field through the microscope in the spatially complex anatomical environment. Collating this information for correct decision-making to balance the risk and achieve the best therapeutic effect for the patient is the routine challenge facing any responsible surgeon. Making the correct surgical strategic decision during the intervention ultimately relies on a skillset related to the predefined goal of the intervention within an increasingly complex framework of ongoing sophisticated technical and technological advances.

Further challenges in this scenario, such as low blood volumes in small children, need to be safely handled in bigger tumour surgeries, not only by the neurosurgeon but also by the entire intraoperative team including nurse specialists and anaesthesiologists, all of which is achieved by close communication during surgical interventions. The basis for this scenario is mutual respect among all the expert professionals involved, along with a high level of combined experience on the part of the whole team. Since this scenario might also apply to emergency situations, where patients have been diagnosed too late and surgery has become necessary for patients sent to the hospital in a severely impaired neurological state, there must be a high level of multidisciplinary expertise available 24/7.

These preconditions warrant solutions that involve expert resources and appropriate investment within the institution for future developments. Human resources are one of the main pillars for guaranteeing sustainable care, which can best be achieved through the centralization of high-expertise tertiary care centres, smart recruiting and continuous education, as well as through an effective policy of keeping highly educated staff in the system through reward, motivation and identification programs within the institution.

In the future, it is likely that only the larger medical centres will be able to keep up with the pace of development, making the necessary investment and applying continuing and sustainable training and research structures at a high level of sophistication. On the other hand, large-sized medical centres will face even bigger challenges in dealing with complexity. Since sub-specialization is one of the basic preconditions in healthcare development, structures are needed to enable fruitful and effective interdisciplinary care, in which sub-special disciplines cooperate on content- and context-oriented bases without any loss of resources through interdepartmental competition or issues related to the distribution of power within the institution.

In the abovementioned scenario, when a child with a brain tumour arrives at the medical centre, the decision-making process will include detailed consideration of the relevant treatment strategies so as to determine which protocol can be best applied in the individual case. Required surgery will be performed using a diagnosis based on imaging, histopathology[7] and all molecular genetic diagnostics. This information needs to be classified for further optimal treatment protocols to be applied. It will be part of a continued process involving follow-up on the patient, since it is not so rare for multiple steps of treatment to become necessary in this often-chronic disease. By far, the best approach to this task is mutual

[7] Histopathology means using a microscope to look at human tissue to see if it has signs of diseases, damage or other abnormalities.

multidisciplinary decision-making at each step of the way in a highly developed culture of experience, problem-oriented knowledge and skills, and fruitful collegiate respect during interactions.

The optimal framework for this interaction requires the delegation of resources determined purely by patient needs rather than by considerations such as political structures within the institution. Monitoring patient needs and making appropriate decisions from an objective point of view is one of the major challenges in the allocation of human resources. Enabling a culture of fruitful interaction among the various experts is a continuous challenge, but it does guarantee the most efficient use of expert knowledge within the institution. Positive identification with the centre by the personnel is a parallel benefit which may further evolve and it will increase the chances of retaining high-quality experts in the system and avoiding a 'brain drain' to competing employers. In addition, future-oriented investment in new technologies is another key factor in implementing new and sophisticated treatment strategies, and this will automatically drive centralization in the system as a whole since not all institutions will be able to afford high-level outlay and expenses.

To further develop and maintain very large institutions, on the other hand, the guidance of high expertise towards modern treatment strategies is an ongoing challenge. A finely tuned network, as illustrated in Fig. 13.1, will be the basis for future development, which presents as a mutual cycle in healthcare towards centralization. The adaptation of decision-making towards this cycle is required for developing and sustaining a high level of centralized care both at supra-regional level as a complex system of itself and also within the environment of basic caregivers at regional level.

As we can see from Fig. 13.1, a mutual cycle in the complexity of the healthcare system is leading towards centralization. This starts with research, which lead us into a comprehensive knowledge of sophisticated diagnostic and treatment technologies and will further define new classification of heterogenous diseases and treatments available, using the appropriate technology. It then becomes necessary to provide relevant personnel working within the system with the requisite knowledge and expertise gained from new insights, through suitable education and training programs. Although each healthcare professional will already have their specialized qualifications, skillset and expertise, the supplementary expertise and detailed knowledge will, logically, determine new fields of sub-specializations for most of them. While such sub-specializations will be a major boost in creating resilience in an increasingly complex world of healthcare, it will also, of course, necessarily mean an intricate interrelationship between them, involving an ethos of cooperation, coordination and unity that will serve to create a strong culture of interdisciplinary care. The increasingly centralized healthcare system will, in due course, use the accumulated knowledge and continuously reinforced culture of expertise to drive further research and thereby continue the cycle.

The greatest emergent risks in today's troubled world are arguably related to further pandemics. Organizations need more support than ever to be able to cope with such emerging risks, to improve strategic direction and to ensure business continuity. Ultimately, only resilient companies will overcome the uncertainty in

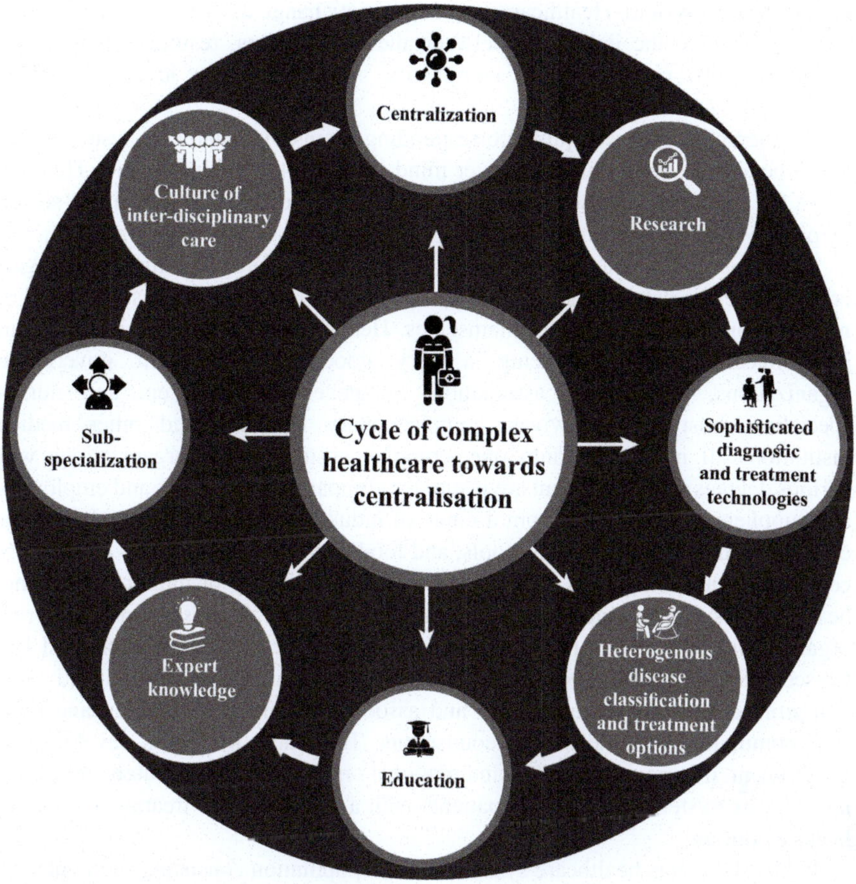

Fig. 13.1 Cycle of complex healthcare towards centralization

today's global complex system and survive pandemics—such as COVID-19—with relatively minor losses; some will even benefit from it. It is, therefore, of critical importance to make resilience a part of our strategic plans and incorporate consideration of the emerging risks in our strategic decision-making process.

Clearly, one of the most important elements—indeed one of core relevance—in resilient systems is a well-functioning healthcare and medical solution framework. Without this, the complexity of the global environment and the fast pace of demographic change merely serve to create a great deal of potentially dangerous uncertainty that can have an extremely negative impact on quality of life, at all political, social and economic levels. We are still recovering from the residual negative effects of COVID-19 all over the world. The functioning of a healthcare system depends on its organizational structures and decision-making processes, and whether a system is controlled in a centralized or decentralized way can make an enormous difference. Demographic changes arising from urbanization can strongly influence the structure of a healthcare system. Healthcare systems do not change as fast as cities do, which tends to increase the imbalance between the two systems, resulting in increased complexity. To overcome this complexity, some important levers should be considered.

Demographic change requires corresponding changes in healthcare systems, if we are to be able to even maintain, never mind improve, the quality of life. This then poses the question: how should local authorities, governments and private sectors prepare to make healthcare systems more resilient?

To answer that question, it is important to look at the healthcare infrastructure generally in greater detail. Organizations and societies function like a system and so must be considered systems in themselves. Healthcare systems or subsystems are interconnected, Germany being a very good example, with government organizations, bodies and associations of general practitioners and nurses, specialists, hospitals, midwives, complementary medicine and other medical institutions all interwoven into one, complex system. Other organizations with various degrees of involvement are insurance companies, employers and employees, and suppliers and providers from a range of industries (such as chemical, pharmaceutical, medical equipment and tools, and food and catering), medical distributors, consultants and pharmacies. Organizations that can directly or indirectly influence healthcare systems include universities, research centres and non-profit organizations such as the fire brigade and rescue services, the Red Cross and Red Crescent Societies, the Federal Agency for Technical Relief (THW) and other non-profit emergency organizations and associations such as Christian and other faith communities and telephone counsellors. This entire system is developed by government, non-government and international organizations. Ultimately, the aim of a healthcare system is to provide patients with a wide range of treatment, care and healing options.

In Germany, this healthcare system serves a population consisting of people that are officially registered with the local authorities in 16 German Länder or have a right of residence in Germany. This includes people who are only temporarily in Germany, such as visitors, tourists and other groups who self-insure. The local authorities are state organizations linked to the healthcare system. Each patient may choose his or her own family doctor, specialist, complementary doctor, midwife and so on. There is no obligation to do so, however, and the patient can see a doctor or specialist or use medical facilities. Referrals to hospitals, specialists and other medical facilities are usually made by family doctors, but it is also possible to go directly to a specialist. Hospitals are divided into three categories, public, private or non-profit, and for medical care, everyone can choose which hospital they wish to go to. Every person in Germany is legally or privately insured in a health insurance fund, which is an independent subsystem directly linked to the healthcare system. Employers and employees are obliged to make contributions to health- and long-term care insurance based on an index set by law. The medical services of both publicly and privately insured are subsequently billed to and paid for by the insurance companies. Other patients, such as persons with restricted or temporary stay in the country, pay the doctors and other providers directly and then forward their bills, as appropriate, to their own insurance companies for settlement. Pharmacies cooperate with the insurance companies as described above, although for medicines, the insured pay a small part themselves, except for children and certain social groups who are exempt from co-payment. In emergencies, various organizations are involved, such as the rescue services of the fire brigade, the Red Cross or Red Crescent Societies and the Technical Relief Agency. These organizations operate independently of each other, but they work together in emergencies ranging from rescue situations to epidemics and natural disasters. The healthcare system is further influenced by other organizations that are not directly connected to it, but where there is a clear relationship nonetheless, such as the meteorological services.

State organizations, societies, institutions and so on are linked to the healthcare system. These are assigned differently from one state to another, but they all have an impact on the healthcare system in some way and are thus part of the overall health ecosystem. In the Federal Republic of Germany, the important state organizations are, among others, the Ministries of Health, Finance, Labour and Economics, which legally represent the interests of the German population and business entities, including employers and employees, in conjunction with other organizations, such as insurance companies. All 16 German Länder have ministries, who work together with the Federation to retain the support of the German population. Since 2020, cooperation between different organizations has been significant due to the COVID-19 pandemic. Cooperation is expanding with other ordinations such as universities, research and development centres and other government institutions such as the Robert Koch Institute (RKI). The RKI is the government's central scientific institution in the field of biomedicine and is one of the most important institutions in terms of safeguarding public health in Germany. This includes the Standing Commission on Vaccination (STIKO) as another organization. In Germany, the STIKO develops national recommendations for the use of licensed vaccines.

The function of a healthcare system makes it a complex one; it is assumed that the interaction of one system or subsystem with other systems and subsystems operates in a negative/positive feedback loop that can change the behaviour of the entire system. In such a case, the outcome is unknown, thus increasing uncertainty. The extent to which healthcare systems are interconnected depends on the structures of the countries or societies in which they operate, which are governed and managed by governments and by non-government and private organizations. Decision-making processes and procedures are in turn based on the rule of law, including political decision-making, which is rooted in cultural and religious beliefs as well as human and social will. The question thus arises: how can a resilient structure be built for a healthcare system?

To answer this question, I will draw upon my own experience and discussions with various organizations in Germany that are directly or indirectly involved in the ongoing COVID-19 pandemic and are part of the German healthcare system. This in turn leads us to consider another question: how resilient, in fact, is the German healthcare system itself? Although Germany is but an example, it is, I believe, a highly relevant and important one that will, hopefully, become a door opener for academics, scientists, politicians and various organizations working in different regions and countries of the world.

13.1.10 The Case of Germany: How Resilient Is the Healthcare System?

In Germany, everyone has access to all levels of care. Every patient has the right to go directly to any specialist without the need of a referral from a family doctor, or so-called general practitioner. The drawback with such a system is that a great deal of valuable specialist time may be wasted by unnecessary consultations, when perhaps more deserving cases are forced to wait. In this respect, a primary-doctor system would make more sense, in that the family doctor decides whether the patient even needs to see a specialist and, if so, which one and when. In the case of privately insured persons, the doctor does not have to look at the criteria set down by law but can decide freely with the insured person which services are to be provided. It goes without saying that privately insured patients naturally bring in more money for the doctor, with the result that those patients usually also get appointments more quickly, particularly with specialists.

In terms of more general structure, the healthcare system is undoubtedly efficient, but it is also very rigid. This can be said to apply across the board, but it is especially the case in the outpatient sector, where there are general practitioners and specialists who are in direct competition with each other. Whether within the Association of Statutory Health Insurance Physicians, the Association of Statutory Health Insurance Physicians of the Länder or the Federal Association of Statutory Health Insurance Physicians, doctors obviously wish to defend their power to ensure that the outpatient sector is not left behind. In the inpatient sector, however, there is a great financial need right now, because intensive care beds need to be kept free due to the still-lingering COVID-19 crisis, with state support being vital. In this era of pandemics, when further waves of viruses threaten to cause sudden surges in demand, capacities must be maintained also in non-intensive-care beds.

Of course, it is not just in relation to inpatient care that capacities must be maintained, and within the outpatient sector also, at both general practitioner and specialist levels, care mandates must be fluid and not so divided and separated. Although the healthcare system in Germany is undeniably a modern, highly effective one, the overall rigidity remains because of the separation of inpatient and outpatient care. The German system has unquestionably coped better with the COVID-19 pandemic than other countries, but the experiences of individual doctors were often different. At the beginning of the pandemic in 2020, medical practices were avoided by patients with minor illnesses, but in time it became clear that treatments for various illnesses could no longer be postponed, so that at present there are patients with chronic illnesses as well as patients with acute infections, not to mention vaccinations. The problem with patients with acute infections is that doctors have no way of knowing beforehand whether it is COVID-19 or a simple cold or flu and, ideally, they would like to clarify matters by phone beforehand. Unfortunately, patients no longer follow the instructions, and it has been the experience of many doctors that many patients come to their practice unvaccinated and without a mask showing cold symptoms and want to sit in the waiting room. Doctors, it goes without saying, try to prevent this. There were also other experiences during the pandemic that doctors found unsettling, and some have complained about insufficient support for protective measures such as masks. From the point of view of many in the medical profession in Germany, their healthcare system has been dehumanized for a long time; on the other hand, the precise number of inpatient cases and the situation regarding increased privatization of clinics and outpatient services remain unclear. Many now see the system as being too expensive, particularly for those who pay contributions; the state itself does not pay for healthcare as such, and state subsidies are not available in all areas of treatment.

Hospital financing is a significant part of the healthcare system, so it is very important to prepare it for unexpected events such as the COVID-19 pandemic. By international comparison, the numbers of hospitals and hospital beds in Germany are excessive. It should be possible to shorten the length of stay, despite some physicians considering a longer stay to be essential since patients who are not yet completely healthy must be cared for at home, whether by relatives or professional caregivers. At the end of the day, many feel it is sometimes better to leave the patient in the hospital, but this presents a difficulty for the hospitals, since they are billed in accordance with diagnosis-related groups. For gallbladder operations, for example, there is sufficient money for even 2 or 3 days. In a time of pandemics, hospitals have become highly bureaucratized. They are also overburdened, with the added complication that patients were tested on admission to hospital but not after discharge, with the result that they became infected in hospital and then passed the infection on to their relatives at home. Furthermore, results of COVID-19 PCR[8] tests were often not waited for, with infected patients (until the test result) being grouped together with non-infected patients. Procurement of hygiene and safety equipment, such as protective clothing and disinfectants, is the responsibility of hospitals. During the pandemic, it was a question of not only providing equipment to hospitals but also of equipping practices with protective clothing, disinfectants and gloves. This was especially the case at the beginning of the pandemic that practices were poorly supplied, simply because the free market was unable to provide protective clothing, disinfectants and masks. Since then, however, the situation has improved, and all the required materials are currently available.

Since the onset of the pandemic, many organizations have been working together, which in Germany means the Federal Ministry of Health, the state Ministries of Health and, at municipal level, the health authorities, including hospitals, as the most important organizations. It also includes the Robert Koch Institute and the Standing Commission on Vaccination. The reality is that there is considerable room for improvement between those organizations. For example, some health ministers

[8]A polymerase chain reaction (PCR) test is performed to detect genetic material from a specific organism, such as a virus.

said everyone should be provided with a third booster vaccination, 6 months after the second vaccination. The Standing Commission on Vaccination, on the other hand, said at the beginning that only people over the age of 70 or hospital staff and immunocompromised people should be vaccinated. This left doctors in a considerable quandary, having to work with different sets of guidelines, not an easy task in practices where patients still had high expectations. This clear case of inefficient cooperation is likely due to the lack of digitalization.

In Germany, the first point of contact for those seeking medical treatment is normally either a family doctor or a private practice. In the earlier part of the COVID-19 pandemic, many of the latter refrained from providing COVID-19 treatment, while some family doctors were not sufficiently informed about the recommendations of the STIKO or the Robert Koch Institute and thus refused to make a vaccination appointment when the vaccines became available. Instead, they referred patients to vaccination centres, which were equally uninformed about booster vaccination and timing. Two issues are apparent here: firstly, GP practices had difficulties in obtaining materials and, secondly, although they had few patients at first when the pandemic started, they later experienced confusion when they were expected to administer vaccinations in addition to treating regular patients, a situation that was compounded by the necessity for endless discussion with vaccine opponents. Clear notices were posted at entrance doors and messages were left on answering machines that patients with cold symptoms should not come to the practice without an appointment and that mandatory masks and social distancing would be the rule in practices, including waiting rooms. Every effort was made to get the patients out of the practice quickly so that lines of patients would not accumulate like in public transport. Some of the practices were seen as competent and motivated, while others were perceived as overwhelmed and dominated by fear. Some doctors' surgeries even closed because they did not want to treat COVID-19 patients. On the other hand, many doctors continued to treat patients in outpatient and inpatient clinics throughout the pandemic, which they have been fighting with all their strength and resources, including psychological stabilization and placement of post-COVID-19 patients in rehabilitation clinics.

Digitalization can be a solution in relieving the healthcare system in difficult times, and it can play a major role in combating unexpected events such as a pandemic. However, it is difficult to introduce digitization during such a turbulent time, with the 'Electronic Sick Leave' introduced in early October 2021 being a case in point, where a very large administrative burden was placed on practices in addition to a financial one. The initiative failed to work because the health insurance companies had yet (at time of writing) to receive claims electronically. In addition, doctors were supposed to write e-prescriptions and create electronic patient files—all a bit difficult in the middle of a pandemic that had already started. This is a rather clear case of politics not having really taken the role of doctors into account, with decisions being made over their heads instead, as if everything had been in a normal state. Wordy guidelines, tight schedules and hastily drawn-up rules do not work, and even the introduction of telemedicine with its backup of all patient data in the Cloud failed because of resistance and disagreements between different organizations. That there is an urgent need to make greater use of digitalization, such as the networking of the health authorities and between hospitals, doctors' surgeries and nursing homes, is beyond doubt. Some of the actors involved, however, such as nursing homes, do not consider digitalization to be necessary, or are attempting to delay its implementation for as long as they can. Digitalization is both a blessing and a curse, because while it facilitates processes and makes many things easier, at the same time it leads to changes in relationship terms, which some find difficult. Some see the use of robots as a solution for relieving nursing staff, whereas others make the argument that a robot can never replace interpersonal contact. Perhaps the greatest need for digitalization, to start with, is in continuing medical education.

A healthcare system is resilient if it can cope with the consequences of unexpected events, such as a pandemic, and avoid negative effects. Yes, the German system was able to react flexibly and prudently despite the situation being a difficult one, and Germany is certainly not finished with COVID-19. Nevertheless, we can indeed say that the healthcare system in Germany is resilient, but whether it will continue to hold out is a question that cannot be answered too easily. Doctors believe that there is still room for improvement in terms of resilience and that now politicians must pledge themselves to supporting them accordingly. Any healthcare system can only react as quickly as politicians make decisions. The latter process often took far too long during the pandemic and, in such future scenarios, could lead to the collapse of the system.

A truly resilient healthcare system is one in which the requisite resources are available, where, for example, pandemic plans do not disappear into drawers but are implemented and where the different actors are given appropriate attention and funding. Sadly, that has not been the case in Germany in the past and certainly not as far as the outpatient sector is concerned. Other factors in resilience are reliability, good structures, flexibility, creativity, sufficient medical and nursing staff and adequate intensive-care bed numbers. Information and communication technology is a vital pillar of a modern resilient healthcare system.

Demographic changes and migration cause complexity in social systems, including healthcare, and resilience encompasses and manages such systems. Or not, which is more likely at this moment! Our socio-economic system has been stretched too far, largely thanks to decades of neoliberal economic policies that saw redundancies as a necessary evil, and resilience has thus been sacrificed on the altar of quick profit. This is at least one of the most important takeaways from the COVID-19 crisis, visible to anyone who dares to look. It is about a system in which everyone is involved. The ability to deal with complexity within such a system and the issues to which it gives rise is fundamentally what gives it its resilience.

13.2 Work and Employment

People look for work so they can better manage their lives and pursue their desires. This does not just include a wish to increase material standards, although this is, of course, a very significant factor. As well as poverty, people may wish to flee other negative factors such as persecution, physical danger or discrimination, or might be attracted to positives such as better healthcare and services, a more attractive climate or—especially in the case of young people—the 'bright lights' excitement of large cities. At this juncture, it might be appropriate to remind ourselves of the interconnection between geopolitics, demographics, macroeconomics and globalization and how the human desire for a better life permeates all these areas. Having first looked at the critical role of migration in shaping geopolitics and macroeconomics, we then saw how it also related to the issues of resources and food and water supply. This desire of humans to improve their lot has inevitably created challenges that affect the structure of the dynamic global system. Political events such as war, ethnic persecution, forced migration, deportation and religious intolerance and persecution are all reasons for migration.

Since the beginning of the sixteenth century, massive structural changes have taken place in the global dynamic system. The United States, for example, was founded upon immigration from Europe to North America. The geopolitical landscape is heavily influenced by migration, and the impacts on the host/receiving country can be considerable. However, while the situation can be tense for the resident population of the receiving country, it can be quite traumatic for the immigrants.

Immigrant people, whatever their reason for migrating, usually need work and bread in the receiving countries. The situation in those host countries can therefore become tense, especially in economically weak ones such as Pakistan, where there are large numbers of Afghan refugees. All too often, this tension rebounds on the immigrants, where they get blamed for a situation that is not of their making.

Immigrants face myriad problems. Chief among the fears pervading many immigrant communities—bearing in mind that people who flee to another country often do so illegally (without visa or official immigration status)—is that of being expelled or deported, often back to extreme poverty, political or religious persecution, or life under oppressive regimes. In Africa, millions leave their home country every year, mainly for European countries; all too often, these migrants pay what to them are vast amounts of money to traffickers, only to then end up risking life and limb to get to a country where their expectations and hopes will be greatly disappointed. Sadly, the laws and processes of the receiving countries are inadequate, and loopholes and unrealistic bureaucratic requirements allow unscrupulous and corrupt middlemen to run what are, effectively, modern slave businesses. The impact on the receiving country is also considerable, with shelters and processing centres needing to be built, accommodation and food to be provided and incidences of social tension increasing and manifesting themselves as xenophobia, racism and sometimes even physical violence.

Other issues arise especially in relation to Gulf countries. A considerable deal of international attention has lately been focused on countries such as Saudi Arabia, Qatar, Kuwait and United Arab Emirates, who have extremely high numbers of foreign workers relative to their native populations. Most of those workers, most of whom enjoy legal status, come from India, Bangladesh, Pakistan, Nepal and other economically weak countries. Their own economic situation often exposes them to exploitation and poor working conditions, including unpaid overtime, lack of workplace H&S protection and overcrowded and unhygienic living quarters. Human rights organizations and labour rights activists regularly complain about unfair treatment of migrant workers. Of course, such problems are not by any means confined to the Gulf Region, and the international community must also remain vigilant in relation to the rights of migrant workers in Europe, the more affluent Asian countries and the Americas.

Another difficulty facing immigrants is that very often, they are seasonal. Rather than wishing to migrate permanently, they move abroad for seasonal work in areas such as agriculture and tourism. Within Europe there are labour markets where workers only work seasonally, a case in point being workers from Romania and Poland who come to Germany at harvest time. The same applies to North America, where Mexicans work across borders as seasonal workers who have a permanent residence in their home country. Criticism is merited here regarding working conditions and wage payments. The housing of seasonal workers is all too often not up to standard and the health-and-safety regulations and various workplace rules are often not respected, according to critics, human rights activists and NGOs. Another less obvious problem faces these migrants, too. Because of the temporary nature of their stay, they have neither the time nor motive to assimilate into the host culture, which is often interpreted by the natives as unwillingness to respect the host country.

This author's own personal experience shows that such guest workers do not always count as part of the social and societal systems of host countries. The hierarchies are visible, even though these people are strenuously committed to the welfare of the host country. Further criticism is levelled at the procedures by which migrant workers are recruited from their home countries.

Employment and unemployment have a strong influence on demography and thus on the changes in the dynamic global system structure. Unemployment is a reality in almost all countries of the world, and while the extent of the problem can and does vary from one country and region to another, it is nonetheless an important topic that gets lots of discussion and media airtime. In the world of politics, unemployment assumes increased importance when it comes to elections. To complicate matters, the definition of 'unemployment' varies around the world. Statistical values are assessed differently between Western countries and Eastern and between developed, emergent and developing countries. In some countries, selling sweets or watermelons from a cart in the street or on the beach is counted as employment. In others, the number of unemployed is falsified below productivity. In many Western countries, certain types of black market work are tolerated because there is seen to be a need for the service, while at the same time undeclared work is publicly criticized. These are among the reasons why unemployment cannot be accurately recorded anywhere on earth in statistical terms. One thing is clear, nonetheless: there is not enough work for all the people in the world, and a great many of those employed are not decently paid. The rise in unemployment globally is accelerating the movement of people around the planet, and labour migration is increasing sharply.

Outside of the statistics, there is an opinion that the introduction of new technologies can destroy jobs. I would like to share with readers my own experience in this regard. My father, who owned a textile factory, told us how his business was forced to close. Textile machinery was imported into our area and new machinery created. Unsurprisingly, the price of textiles dropped within a short time due to the oversupply of textiles, while at the same time the quality of the traditional textile manufacturers' produce was called into question. The employees of the traditional manufacturers migrated to the mechanized textile factories. Low prices and the loss of a labour force forced my father to give up his factory.

This has no impact on the number of people employed in agriculture, however. Because agricultural workers moved to the cities for higher earnings and a new quality of life after developing economies were industrialized by the West, agriculture suffered a serious setback despite the tremendous technological advances over the previous century. While employment in industry and services was increasing, the shortage of labour in agriculture became more acute.

For new arrivals in urban areas, the downside is a scarcity of housing. In response, real estate markets have taken off, with high-rise apartment buildings being built for the new working population, while at the same time banks and private credit have become more attractive. Population increases have, in turn, driven higher demand for a variety of services, thus pushing up the level of employment in the service sector and a corresponding decline in the numbers employed in industry.

The world system is becoming more and more complex and volatile as a result of interrelationships between many different factors: migration of all kinds, population shifts especially after two world wars, employment and unemployment, unequal working hours between countries, male-female workplace inequality being the norm in some places and other, related developments in wages and prices. It is important to note here that one measure of the labour force is the breakdown by economic sector, including, for example, agriculture and forestry, fishing and mining, trade and services, and industry and manufacturing. Unemployment rates are mostly considered in the above clusters. The most important point to consider, however, is that the relationship between industry, real estate and the finance markets is still at the heart of economic, political and social debate and is influencing the structures of the global dynamic system.

13.3 Education

I remember my first day at school very well. It was a special day for me because we children were looking forward to learning the official language of our country. My country of birth is a multi-ethnic one, where different groups of people live and communicate in their mother tongue without learning to read and write, so everything is communicated orally. Even the exchange of knowledge is done orally, so trust is important, because those who can read and write now have a knowledge advantage; the common view is that we should always listen carefully to what these educated people have to say. Knowledge whose transmission is based on oral narratives, is at least partially forgotten in time, or its content is changed by new narratives. This is normal, since each one tells the story exactly as he has already heard it but covers the inevitable gaps with his own assumptions and experiences, so that the story loses its original meaning over time. This has been scientifically established around the world. Oral communication does not last and hinders education. The content of oral communication is always transformed into information with assumptions, so that that information loses its original meaning and accuracy.

In my time as a child, there was no means of recording oral languages, and a limited number of people had access to the modern technology of the time, in which the recordings of the language were stored in a recorder on a long magnetic roll. Yes, it was a special day for me and the other children on that first day of school, when we started to learn the country's national language using a big poster on which the teacher showed us pictures and asked us to name the pictures. Imagine a German native speaker in First Grade at school learning Spanish with pictures because the main language in Germany is Spanish, not German. Of course, the German language is not forbidden as such in that scenario but is spoken only for communication at home by you, your family and your community and with those who know German. In just about every country in the world, the official national language is the only language in which one learns to read and write, so formal education becomes possible only through the official national language, which is laid down by law and therefore obligatory. The disadvantage for non-native-speaking students is that they are essentially taught the reduced content of the subject matter. Language cannot always be translated directly, so there is considerable room for interpretation—and misinterpretation! On the other hand, people who know several languages can broaden their horizons and knowledge and better understand the world in which they communicate and form their own opinions of it. In an ideal world, the medium of education would be, first, one's mother tongue and then other languages. In most industrialized countries, schoolchildren learn other foreign languages at school; in Germany, for example, schoolchildren learn the country's official language first and then possibly second and even third foreign languages. Information reaches people through communication. For that, one needs at least one language, preferably one's mother tongue. The familiar expression, 'knowledge is power', expresses the value of information and education in society.

Today's modern communication systems are linked to various industrial revolutions: the first (1780–1850) in England, the second (around 1880–1930) in the United States and Germany and the third (roughly during the 1970s–1990s) in high-tech industrialized countries. Today, we are in the fourth industrial revolution. The third industrial revolution changed the world through electronic data processing in such a way that information could be transmitted in large quantities at an extremely high speed. In just a few short years, we moved from the typewritten letter, through the telex and fax machines, to email. At that time, information and communication systems were not equally distributed around the world. Until the end of the 1990s, the world news market was dominated by agencies—effectively news monopolies—such as the American, English, French and Soviet news agencies. The news was transmitted around the world by these agencies through modern communication systems. These determined the transmission strategy, volume and content of the message to be transmitted and, above all, the language of transmission. Information and communication systems are an important tool for social life, for business, for politics and, perhaps most importantly, for education. Today, attempts are being made to narrow the gaps in information exchange through modern technologies and especially social media, but this whole issue remains one of the most important arguments for change in the dynamic global system structure.

'Education is a human right and the key to individual and social development. It enables people to develop their personality and lead a fulfilled life. Education strengthens democracy and promotes tolerance and a cosmopolitan attitude. At the same time, education is a prerequisite for sustainability. It enables individuals to understand the impact of their own actions on the world, to deal with change and risk, and to make responsible decisions. For education to realize its potential, it must be high-quality, inclusive and offer equal opportunity. In their efforts to raise the level of education, developing countries are in a difficult position because the very high proportion of children and young people in the population requires a correspondingly large number of teachers, who are to be paid from tightly limited state budgets'. Press release, 6 September 2018: 'At least 750 million adults worldwide lack basic literacy skills. Two-thirds of these are women, and 102 million are young people between the ages of 15 and 24. This means the situation has barely improved compared to 2017. Many of the world's 192 million unemployed cannot find work because they lack basic skills'.[9]

Education enables socio-economic advancement and is a key to overcoming poverty. Over the past decade, great strides have been made in improving access to education and enrolment rates at all levels, especially for girls. In 2018, however, around 260 million children were still not in school—almost a fifth of the world's population in this age group. More than half of all children and adolescents worldwide do not reach the minimum requirements in reading and mathematics. In 2020, as the COVID-19 pandemic spread across the globe, a majority of countries announced the temporary closure of schools, impacting more than 91% of students worldwide. By April 2020, close to 1.6 billion children and youth were out of school, around 370 million of whom rely on school meals. Never have so many children been out of school at the same time, disrupting learning and upending lives, especially the most vulnerable and marginalized. The global pandemic has had far-reaching consequences that may jeopardize hard-won gains made in improving global education.

The international community reaffirms that education plays a key role in building sustainable and resilient societies and contributes to the achievement of all other sustainable development goals.

Specifically, the Global Education Coalition aims to:

[9] https://www.unesco.de/bildung

- Help countries in mobilizing resources and implementing innovative and context-appropriate solutions to provide education remotely, leveraging hi-tech, low-tech and no-tech approaches.
- Seek equitable solutions and universal access.
- Ensure coordinated responses and avoid overlapping efforts.

UNICEF has also scaled up its work in 145 low- and middle-income countries, to support governments and education partners in developing plans for a rapid, system-wide response including alternative learning programs and mental health support.

Some facts and figures

- Before the COVID-19 crisis, projections showed that more than 200 million children would be out of school, and only 60% of young people would be completing upper-secondary education, in 2030.
- Before the pandemic, the proportion of children and youth out of primary and secondary school had declined from 26% in 2000 to 19% in 2010 and 17% by 2018.
- More than half of those children who have not enrolled in school live in sub-Saharan Africa, and more than 85% of children in that region are not learning at the minimum level.
- Six hundred and seventeen million youth worldwide lack basic mathematics and literacy skills.
- Some 750 million adults—two-thirds of them women—remained illiterate in 2016. Half of the global illiterate population lives in South Asia, and a further quarter live in sub-Saharan Africa.
- In 10 low- and middle-income countries, children with disabilities were 19% less likely to achieve minimum proficiency in reading than those without disabilities.
- Four million refugee children were out of school in 2017.

13.3.1 Quality Education

'Education transforms lives and is at the heart of UNESCO's mission to build peace, eradicate poverty and drive sustainable development. It is a human right for all throughout life. The organization is the only United Nations agency with a mandate to cover all aspects of education. It has been entrusted to lead the Global Education 2030 Agenda through Sustainable Development Goal 4.'

'4.1. By 2030, ensure that all girls and boys complete free, equitable and quality primary and secondary education leading to relevant and Goal-4 effective learning outcomes.'

'4.2. By 2030, ensure that all girls and boys have access to quality early-childhood development care and pre-primary education so that they are ready for primary education.'

'4.3. By 2030, ensure equal access for all women and men to affordable and quality technical, vocational, and tertiary education, including university.'

'4.4. By 2030, substantially increase the number of youth and adults who have relevant skills, including technical and vocational skills, for employment, decent jobs, and entrepreneurship.'

'4.5. By 2030, eliminate gender disparities in education and ensure equal access to all levels of education and vocational training for the vulnerable, including persons with disabilities, indigenous peoples. And children in vulnerable situations.'

'4.6. By 2030, ensure that all youth and a substantial proportion of adults, both men and women, achieve literacy and numeracy.'

'4.7. By 2030, ensure that all learners acquire the knowledge and skills needed to promote sustainable development including, among others, through education for sustainable development and sustainable lifestyles, human rights, gender equality, promotion of a culture of peace and non-violence, global citizenship, and appreciation of cultural diversity and of culture's contribution to sustainable development.'

'4.8 Build and upgrade education facilities that are child-, disability- and gender sensitive and provide safe, nonviolent, inclusive, and effective learning environments for all.'

'4.9 By 2020, substantially expand globally the number of scholarships available to developing countries, particularly the least developed countries, small-island developing States, and African countries, for enrolment in higher education, including vocational training and information and communications technology, technical, engineering and scientific programs, in developed countries and other developing countries.'

'UNESCO provides global and regional leadership in education, strengthens education systems worldwide and responds to contemporary global challenges through education with gender equality as an underlying principle. Its work encompasses quality educational development from pre-school to higher education and beyond'.[10]

'A child's right to education entails the right to learn. Yet, for too many children across the globe, schooling does not lead to learning. Over 600 million children and adolescents worldwide are unable to attain minimum proficiency levels in reading and mathematics, even though two thirds of them are in school. For out-of-school children, foundational skills in literacy and numeracy are further from grasp. This learning crisis—the rift between the levels of learning that children receive and those they, their communities and entire economies need—hit a global scale even before the COVID-19 pandemic brought education systems to a halt. Around the world, children are deprived of education and learning for various reasons. Poverty remains one of the most obstinate barriers. Children living through economic fragility,

[10] https://www.un.org/sustainabledevelopment/education/

political instability, conflict, or natural disaster are more likely to be cut off from schooling—as are those with disabilities, or from ethnic minorities. In some countries, education opportunities for girls remain severely limited. Even in schools, a lack of trained teachers, inadequate education materials, and poor infrastructure make learning difficult for many students. Others come to class too hungry, ill, or exhausted from work or household tasks to benefit from their lessons. Compounding these inequities is a digital divide of growing concern: Some two thirds of the world's school-aged children do not have internet connection in their homes, restricting their opportunities to further their learning and skills development. Without quality education, children face considerable barriers to employment and earning potential later in life. They are more likely to suffer adverse health outcomes and less likely to participate in decisions that affect them—threatening their ability to shape a better future for themselves and their societies'.[11]

Communication systems are important for the exchange of information, but this only takes place in industrialized countries. The means of communication are technologically advanced, and even the traditional means of communication are in the transformational state of digitalization. Newspapers, telephones, radio and television in Europe, United States, Canada and Australia, to name but a few examples, are being digitized at great expense. The uneven pace of digitalization and the money being spent on it are not sufficient, so delays are inevitable. In many developing countries, this transition will take much longer.

Education depends heavily on the proportion of teachers in the total population, which is extremely low in many countries, especially developing countries. The big challenge is to equalize the level of education of the total population worldwide, and investment has to be made for this. Countries allocate little budget for education, and this is also measured by the GNP ratio.

Education is a core issue and greatly influences changes in the structure of global system dynamics.

Reference

Sehouli, J. (2019). *The art of breaking bad news well* (1st ed.). Routledge.

[11] https://www.unicef.org/education#how

Earth's Resources: The Challenges 14

14.1 Natural Resources

Mineral raw materials extracted from nature are limited. The most important and well-known reserves are gold, copper, bauxite (aluminium), iron ore, lead, tin and tungsten, just to mention a few examples from hundreds of mineral raw materials. It is noteworthy how quickly these resources are coming to an end, and the values of gold and copper will steadily increase due to their scarcity. Lead, tin and tungsten have already shown their limits. The reserves of iron ore and bauxite are probably greater than most others. It is obvious that such reserves are not infinite, and so the future focus must be on sustainability. Industrialized countries face fluctuating markets and prices for raw material deposits, which depend on the global political and economic situation. Commodity exports from developing countries under commodity agreements could help stabilize prices, for example, through the foreign exchange earnings on which they rely and which influence global economic, social and societal structures. All of this, of course, depends on countries' political positions and ideological attitudes.

In the following sections, we will examine the important role of energy sources and their impact on international politics, demographics and the various stages of technological development, from the coal- and gas-powered industrial revolution, through the electricity-driven transistor era and nuclear technology, to the development of ICT and the digital age. Last, but not least, we will consider renewable energy. Moreover, we will look at the link between macroeconomics and energy, together with further indicators such as GDP.

14.2 Energy Resources

Populations need energy; sources of energy are, therefore, a vitally important geographic element of the global system. It is increasingly clear that energy is at the centre of all change, giving rise to three critical considerations: where does the

K. Dindarian, *Embracing the Black Swan*, Future of Business and Finance,
https://doi.org/10.1007/978-3-031-29344-3_14

energy come from, who owns the sources and who gets to use that energy? Those questions bring us closer to the history of mankind, which has always involved a struggle for new geographical lines. It is important to note that natural energy sources are available free of charge, so it is clear that whoever owns or controls those sources, has the right to manage, donate and sell them. Natural resources in general are becoming increasingly scarce, and their consumption—unevenly distributed among the world's population—is proving to be highly damaging to nature and the environment. These human-induced changes influence natural phenomena, such as climate, which puts additional pressure on natural changes such as in the ocean floor and even in the earth's plates, and their all-too-familiar consequences such as earthquakes, volcanic eruptions, tsunamis and soil erosion in turn trigger further geopolitical, demographic and economic changes. Such changes are interconnected within the global complex system and create new dynamics, the negative consequences of which are not always so visible or communicated to the earth's population at large. Population is distributed unevenly over the earth's surface, with varying values being calculated by different institutions. As a reference, the UN's evaluation is used for this book. What has become clear from the many changes is that most people on the planet want to live in cities. So, urban areas are growing rapidly, and this in turn influences the elements of the global system and its structural changes.

Although energy sources and supply lie at the heart of global system structure, there are critical social, societal, economic and political elements also in play. Energy availability, however, remains largely the measure of all things and shapes the present and future of the global system structure and its behaviour. The future of peace and prosperity on the earth depends crucially on an adequate and secure energy supply. Changes in the global system structure began during the late nineteenth century when the main energy source was coal, and they continued throughout the twentieth century as we moved to hydroelectric power, then through the oil and gas and nuclear power stages. Now, in the twenty-first century, we are witnessing further changes as we turn to energy obtained from wind, solar radiation and other renewable sources.

Energy sources and supply have been setting the rules for important elements of prosperity in industrialized countries, poverty in developing countries and, above all, global power over energy sources and supply. It is obvious that these sources are unevenly distributed across the world, such as oil production, which is still the most important source of energy. OPEC countries have played an important role in changing the global system structure, as was clearly observed in 1973–74. Natural gas as a source of energy for production has assumed enormous importance in industrialized countries that want to move away from coal production. The current war in Ukraine shows us just how much European countries, especially Germany, depend on gas. For many economies, it has now largely become a matter of maintaining prosperity and avoiding a weakening of their industrial export strength.

Rising world population is not proportional to energy use and consumption. The use and consumption of world energy are determined by technical and economic strength, with North America and Western Europe in the lead and Africa in last place. In the future, this situation will change, and with it the future energy production, use and consumption of the world will be reshaped. As to why, the answer is simple. Oil and natural gas, as fossil fuels, have their limits and will run out sooner rather than later. The task now facing mankind is to replace these missing future sources of energy production. Important factors coming into play in this equation will include technology, financial strength for investment in new energy production and the ideological and political positions of various countries. Although substantial coal reserves remain, the phasing out of coal is an already-decided issue in Western industrialized countries for mostly environmental reasons, which increases the space for investment in renewable energy. Uranium reserves supply nuclear power plants, especially the energy sources of the United States, France, Japan, Russia, Germany, UK and Canada. Many Western countries have already taken the political decision to abandon nuclear energy, although uranium reserves are still sufficient for some time to come. For the future of energy production, few options remain but to invest in alternative, renewable energy sources (such as wind power, solar radiation or the gasification of biomass), and in many cases this will require ideological change and political will. Developing a mentality of renewable energy use and reduced consumption is, therefore, another important task facing us for the future. One example of this might be the development and use of hydro technology for passenger and freight transport.

Energy is the most important element—the core—of resilient systems in shaping demographic structure. The transformation from fossil fuel power generation, with its attendant problems of cost, pollution and increasing scarcity, into more environmentally friendly renewable energies, with a focus on sustainability and non-pollution, is a must-win strategy about whose adoption we have very little choice, for the sake of the future of mankind; this will become a core element of resilience.

The importance of a reliable and effective power supply was highlighted by the power outage in New York City in 2003. Although control and risk management are an ongoing process in the operation of such power systems, the question arises as to why the failure was not detected at an early stage. Quite simply, the energy supply of countries and, more especially, megacities is centralized. This has the disadvantage that was so vividly demonstrated in the NYC power failure: centralized systems are vulnerable to complete shutdown and are not sufficiently resilient. All complex systems, even decentralized ones, are prone to failure, but while decentralized systems only fail locally, centralized ones can fail totally, with a much greater impact.

Two critically important issues facing the energy industry today are the generation of power and its transmission and distribution. The predominant traditional sources of power generation have long since reached their limits, especially in terms of their carbon footprint and environmental damage to the planet. Scientific research shows that fossil fuels are a major cause of pollution; however, it ought to be mentioned that there is a distinction between pollutants (such as soot, particulate matter, NOx, SO_2) and greenhouse gases (CO_2, NH_4, N_2O). The latter were for a long time not classed as pollutants, because they were seen as not directly harmful to the environment since they only exist in traces in the atmosphere and have no direct impact on human health. Whatever the case, there is an urgent need for change, so that people can be provided with safe and environmentally friendly energy. Immediate changes would certainly be timely and most welcome, but even these may be already too late to undo all of the damage, although technological advances show that reversal is achievable. Such techno-optimism, however, is counterbalanced by another school of thought, which holds that such technologies are demonstrably not scalable to the extent needed to make an impact. The latter opinion holds that these technologies are wishful thinking at best and delay and distraction strategies at worst. The point here is to show complexity and to open doors for further action. Hopefully, this topic of discussion will find a place in practical research and development as well as in scientific research in universities.

In the past, three technological advances were responsible for energy production, but the reverse is also true: energy in abundance enabled new technologies, and there is a positive feedback loop between technology and energy, both of which were needed for the development of the modern technological society. These energy sources were hydroelectricity, steam and coal. Steam engines and coal mining have driven major change and revolutionized people's lives, enabling new production methods, processes and procedures, including mechanical engineering, mass production lines, the manufacture of chemical-based products and, perhaps most importantly, new technologies and processes for iron production. The benefits were massive, and so we witnessed the first industrial revolution in human history. Densely populated settlements developed around factories, cities expanded very quickly and people's quality of life improved over time. People also benefited from the machine production of textiles and greatly increased agricultural output.

There was, however, also a dark side to this industrial development. Life expectancy remained short, with many people dying at the age of 40–50 years because of dust from coal mines; over the longer term, the increase in pollution levels affected the whole planet. These changes would continue well into the twentieth century, affecting the development of the whole socio-technological system in both positive and negative ways.

At this point I would like to emphasize that this book is not an account of the history of the industrial revolution, nor is it an exploration of the different opinions and theories surrounding when or why pollution began, or what were the causes of major unexpected events. It is, however, important to keep in mind the root causes of today's changes so we can better understand the links between technological development and our society and the complexity from which the socio-technical system evolves.

The second industrial revolution owed much to the use of oil for energy production and the electrification of industry. The harnessing of hydroelectric power was quickly followed by the invention of the internal combustion engines. An important result of this development was mass production, along with transport infrastructures that shortened distances and speeded up communication, which eventually opened the door for modern globalization through international trade. At the same time, oil refining gave rise to the chemical and modern metal industries, leading to rapid rail, air and ocean cargo transport, which were a key factor in the rise of the modern financial world. Another cause-to-effect, the so-called 'modern' financial system (e.g. debt-based fiat money, fractional reserve lending and central banks), had in fact been invented centuries before the industrial revolution,[1] and indeed fiat money and fractional reserve lending are even older. However, given that the material flow was limited, mainly due to a lack of abundant energy, there was no need for mass-volume, high-performance financial transactions until the twentieth century. It is clear, in any event, that finance and economics form a reinforcing positive feedback loop that co-evolved over centuries.

Technological advances in the last three decades of the twentieth century led to further automation, the rapid development of information technology and, eventually, the digital age, collectively known as the third industrial revolution. Automated systems increased the efficiency of production, bringing about a massive expansion in global business. Electronics and information technology accelerated the rate of exchange of information and data and provided the possibility of data storage, thus allowing machines to take over human tasks. Unlike in the second industrial revolution, where functions were still carried out by humans, automation and information systems have made technological systems intelligent through computation and data processing. Such technological progress has made it possible to control the energy systems and increase their efficiency, while at the same time increasing the safety of power generation networks, including their transmission and distribution, through control automation and diagnostic systems.

Computer science and technological developments in both hardware and software have altered the functions of global systems in a range of areas, in which we can see the connectivity of man, nature and machine, particularly since the 1990s. This development has led to the so-called fourth Industrial Revolution—more commonly referred to as the digital age—where cyber-physics has gained enormous importance.

In effect, over the last 200 years, industrial revolutions have had a powerful influence on social structures. This has, in turn, had both positive and negative impacts on more global social structures, in tandem with political and economic interests. It is worth bearing in mind that the production and use of energy will greatly determine the future of technological development and, therefore, of economy and finance.

Energy production and the exploitation of natural resources have always played an important role in environmental changes and the behaviour of socio-technical systems. The complexity of these systems is increasing in the context of the four industrial revolutions mentioned above. Migration is also related to this complexity, and it can even be argued that migration has slowed down considerably in the course of human history. Twenty thousand years ago—long before the advent of agriculture—practically all of humanity, as hunter gatherers, was on the move, all the time! It was only agriculture that allowed nomadic societies to become sedentary.

[1] https://www.riksbank.se/en-gb/about-the-riksbank/history/

As social systems evolved thanks to the interaction of cultural backgrounds, and diversity increased among people migrating from one place to another, this in turn affected the way energy was used.

The whole structure of urban areas is changing at an unprecedented pace. Populations are increasing steadily as more people move to cities in search of greater opportunities and adapt quickly to more mechanized and technologically grounded modern ways. This has already had a profound impact on natural resources, an impact that can only increase in the future. Urbanization and the accompanying human consumption have increased the pressure on those resources, further contributing to environmental deterioration such as pollution and the compaction and sealing of soil. An important part of this urban development has been the shortening of distances and an acceleration of the movement of people and goods through new developments and innovations in transport systems. How we manage those systems is a double-edged sword. At this point, it is worth raising important questions about energy that will directly affect almost everyone within the near future. Will there be enough energy to support a still-growing human population as projected by demographers (11 billion by the end of this century)? Can we decarbonize our current energy consumption, 80% of which is from fossil fuels, in the next 30 years? What are the best energy sources for the future: wind, solar, hydro, nuclear? And if this proves impossible, what are the biggest risks of runaway greenhouse effect and climate tipping points? What will be the consequences of the end of cheap oil, starting right now? Can our current growth-based economic paradigms be sustained if the availability of energy decreases?

Are you, dear reader, aware that the average human being today consumes 200 times more energy than his pre-industrial revolution ancestors did? In the case of Europeans, this increases to 500–600 times, and for Americans, 800–1000 times. What would it mean for our prosperity and well-being if we had to divide our energy consumption by a factor of 10 or more?

14.3 Water and Food Sources

Water and food sources are a highly relevant and important element of the global system. The land area of the earth is mainly used for economic purposes, which is always limited by geographic and climatic conditions: arid soil, extremes of temperature and stony ground that is not suitable for nutrient-poor farming. One major question is whether the food supply is generating enough globally.[2] The unequal distribution of food production between industrialized and developing countries causes people to suffer from hunger and deficiency diseases. Humans influence the natural food supply through disproportionate consumption, consuming more than is

[2]I do not address statistically due to permanent changes and the actuality of data; however, I refer to the available sources.

produced, one example being overfishing in oceans, lakes and rivers. This massively affects the global system.

Another worrying fact is that the migration of people from agricultural regions to cities is leading to a decline in agricultural production. One important reason for this migration is a rapid increase in urban industrialization. Industry requires mass movement, which people willingly do for work, lifestyle ambitions and prosperity. It is also responsible for the enlargement of cities and the shrinking of rural communities. The more industry there is in cities to attract them, the more the agricultural workforce declines. In the world, the ratio between the labour force in agriculture and the total population is changing dramatically, as becomes evident when comparing the ratio of total population with the number of people relying on agriculture for a livelihood. In this context, the supply chain and the import of food and beverages to industrialized countries play a major role, with massive exports of food and beverages from the tropics to Europe, thereby leading to a surplus of agricultural production in European countries. This global inequality is particularly visible in four agricultural production sectors: cereals, potatoes, cow's milk, and meat. The connection and interaction between industrialization and agricultural production is an important part of the global system.

Water and food are the most important elements for life on earth, and both types of commodities, therefore, have the greatest importance for the changes within the global system. Both hold great relevance for us in terms of the shaping of geopolitics and macroeconomics.

Natural changes affect the geography, and thus the structure, of the global system. Geological changes have been continually taking place over millions of years, such as plate tectonics, continental drift, rock formation and erosion, and volcanic activity. In recent decades, however, shorter-term geographical changes have become the focus of attention, primarily because of climate change. This is caused both by natural changes and by humans. The consequences of climate change look rather grim, as the changes brought about by wind, rain, storms, heat, drought, snow and ice affect other geographical areas and thus create further disadvantages for future life on Earth. In recent decades, it has been noted how quickly glaciers are melting due to climate change, creating a new geographical boundary. Agricultural land is shrinking thanks to the increasing frequency of floods, on the one hand, and to drought and desertification, on the other. This greatly affects the availability of clean, fresh water and of food products, thus creating additional changes in the global system structure.

We look at the changes and growing imbalance in wealth and poverty in the world with a standardized scale value, namely, gross national product (GNP) and per capita income, and what we might consider the 'wealth-poverty scale'. Not unexpectedly, the industrialized countries are at the upper end of this scale, followed by the emerging countries with a medium level of development, such as the Eastern European ex-communist economies and BRICS, considerably lower down the scale. At the lowest end are the developing countries, with the highest proportion of the world's population. Such scales are inaccurate in that the performance and production of some countries are close to zero, but they are nevertheless placed at the top of the scale, because they have free natural resources that they exploit and sell using foreign technologies, which can give them a very high GDP on paper. While the subject of GDP is not explored in depth in this book, it might be useful to remain aware of the inaccuracy and discrepancies in such scales and definitions. Such scales also affect the dynamics of the global system structure, these being due to, on the one hand, the unequal distribution of commodities, especially food, in the world and, on the other hand, the GDP indices that measure the gap between wealth and poverty, thereby creating geopolitical and macroeconomic tensions. This tension creates a great disadvantage for the people of the developing nations, who suffer from the most unequal distribution of food and scarcity of water and from geopolitical and macroeconomic decisions, although many industrialized countries, especially the European Union and some other Western countries, have development aid for the least developed countries on their agenda.

In addition, various non-government organizations (NGOs) and other international bodies and agencies are pursuing pragmatic approaches with a view to improving economic strength and living conditions in developing countries. People in poorer countries are suffering more than ever, despite development aid and support from international organizations and despite technological developments for the production and distribution of food and treatment of drinking water. The United Nations appeals to richer countries to provide aid to the developing countries, but there are no binding commitments involved. One reason financial aid does not achieve its goals is that funds and food often end up being used for emergency aid programs for famines and natural disasters. Furthermore, commodity prices fluctuate greatly due to global economic and financial recessions, which are directly linked to increased debts, so that interest piles up and cannot be paid. Although economic and financial recessions are global, it is the poorest countries that are hardest hit. As mentioned earlier, economic and financial recessions greatly affect food production, resulting in hunger, higher child mortality, unemployment and a plethora of political, ideological and national conflicts in most developing countries. The imbalance in food production—one of the major causes of hunger in much of the world—along with natural disasters and climate events causes havoc, including famine epidemics in many regions, especially Africa, and floods are having an increasingly devastating impact on some Asian countries. Certainly, the fight against hunger continues, food technology is improving, and famine relief is underway thanks to the efforts of various NGOs, but this does not alter the fact that there is less to eat in Africa today than there was a few decades ago. Families in Africa have learned to feed themselves and, if something remains to sell, they take it to market, but the markets are often controlled by states and by geopolitical influences, resulting in suppressed prices. Land ownership is another factor that hinders self-sufficiency. The necessary agricultural lands are frequently sacrificed to speculation by real-estate developers, so that for the growing population, there is less land available.

It has become clear that the current level of development aid is not sufficient, and the gap between rich and poor countries continues to widen. While the index of gross national product (GNP) is used as a measure of wealth and poverty, we must wonder whether it truly reflects such serious issues as infant mortality or the on-the-ground results of unmanageable debt. Food production is, as we have seen, insufficient in Africa, Latin America and parts of the Middle East and South and East Asia. Attempts at resolution are hampered by geopolitical and economic measures. If we are to get past this and avoid a worsening of an already dire situation, it will be necessary to formulate new approaches through the complex dynamics of the global system structure and to better master the interaction between geopolitics and macroeconomics.

Two critically important levers in a resilient system are sustainable water and food management. Clean, potable water resources in cities are at best limited and, in many cases, completely inadequate for meeting the high demand. It has, therefore, become necessary to set as a goal the daily water needs of cities, and this is best achieved using advanced technology such as the processing of wastewater, which increases the resilience of the city. In order to avoid problems with food distribution and to minimize the risk of surpluses, an efficient and reliable process can be ensured through the decentralization of production and distribution and through innovative logistics and transport technology. Transportation is the most critical factor in food management; a few days without transportation for whatever reason and modern city life will become chaotic and potentially violent. Today's just-in-time management has all but eliminated storage capacities and left big cities lethally vulnerable. Food and water supply security must become a strategic priority for the future of mankind. This is, therefore, a key element of resilience.

15 The Changing Nature of Politics, Globalization and Business

15.1 Politics

15.1.1 Geography and Politics

The global system, characterized by its myriad interconnected subsystems, is constantly being redefined by academia and other actors such as politicians, journalists and authors. The global system is often referred to in the context of the economic, political, natural and social systems. In today's rapidly changing world, unexpected events with negative and/or positive consequences occur more frequently than ever before. However, the emerging risks of the global system are still met with reductionist procedures, which need to be reconsidered in the light of the increasing complexity of that system. The complexity of global system increases is, to an important degree, related to the geographical and political systems. This connection becomes particularly visible today when we take a brief look back at the Berlin Wall. The division of a city into two parts (1961–1989) is a symbol of two very different political systems, and of the Cold War and the Iron Curtain. The two political systems formed a clear world order until the people of the East took to the streets and demanded change, which social movement ended in 1989 with the fall of the Berlin Wall. The 'fall of the Wall' reunited the city with the hope of a change of political system, which would be of great importance for Germany and Europe, especially for the Eastern European countries. With the end of the Berlin Wall, geographical borders changed in a short period of time, which until then had seemed unimaginable to most. We now look at these complexities through the lens of geography and politics, but with economics in mind.

Geography and politics cannot be separated. The relationship between geographical elements such as water and soil quality has brought people together; moreover, migration and settlement are important signs of the possession of land, water and natural resources. Immigrants from Europe used this privilege to build the new nation state that is now the United States. The Black Swan was already present at that time. The indigenous people were very aware of their own land and everything

K. Dindarian, *Embracing the Black Swan*, Future of Business and Finance,
https://doi.org/10.1007/978-3-031-29344-3_15

they needed to survive, but the European immigrants had no idea what was hidden in this new land. Parties were united by ethnicity, language, culture and faith. Political organizations emerged; many wars were fought to gain power and to own the water, land and various natural resources. This example is not intended to describe the historical discovery of the Americas, but to illustrate the geography and politics associated with the concept of the Black Swan. Geography and politics form a complex system. The possession of land is politically motivated, and whether that possession is accidental or deliberate, one thing is clear: this creates a complex system.

In 1989, the tearing down of the Berlin Wall caused the collapse of one system, which changed geographical boundaries, while the other system was changed by uncertainty. This change was neither peaceful—as evidenced by friction between the former Yugoslav Countries and by the Balkan war—nor compatible with the goals of the United Nations to protect human rights. Military power is claimed to be a guarantor for the protection of geographical borders. Historically, Europe was home to the two largest military pact systems, the North Atlantic Treaty Organisation (NATO) and the Warsaw Pact, which had divided up the continent between them. The two world superpowers, United States and the Soviet Union, held the central positions of power. Their respective allies shared political, social and economic beliefs with them. Another pact was the ANZUS Treaty (Pacific Pact), a defence alliance between the United States, Australia and New Zealand. The latter two countries are geographically isolated from the rest of the world, which made the threat of direct Japanese attack during WWII even more stark, but concerns about communism may already have outweighed the Japanese threat. In the 1980s, New Zealand declared itself a nuclear-free zone, which meant that no US nuclear submarines were stationed there. The ANZUS Treaty fell apart as a result of the United States unilaterally suspending its treaty obligations to New Zealand, with ANZUS, consequently, not being extended. Not all nation states adhere to military pacts. Many countries are part of non-aligned states, especially developing countries. The policies of such countries are to deliberately distance themselves and create opportunities for negotiations depending on how economic opportunities and world politics change.

In 2022, there remained only one military pact, NATO, whose goals, it is worth noting, have changed and adapted over the years. The main reason is most likely the disintegration of the communist systems in Eastern European countries. After the fall of the Berlin Wall, many former Warsaw Pact countries decided to join the West. The borders were redefined both because of the liberation of Eastern people from totalitarian communist governments and because of economic incentives. Western policies prepared for those changes in the Eastern countries. Globalization increased in importance, thus furthering Western politics and economy. The imperialist power of the Soviet Union surrendered in two different directions:

1. Economically to China and, later, partly to the BRICS countries.
2. Politically mainly to Western Europe.

Contrary to expectations, these changes have made the global system more complex than ever before. Networking is taking place everywhere and the participants of the network have different interests.

The economic systems of the East have been reshaped by China. A large part of the socialist system has accomplished the transition to a form of industrialization that is essentially a copy-and-paste from the West, including technology transfer and education and training. The first investors were the Western industrial countries, which wanted to sharpen their competition in the new emerging economies, especially by outsourcing to low-cost countries. Low labour costs, Chinese raw materials and low energy prices were other important elements for Western companies eager to expand or to relocate their production facilities to China. The global market was large enough, so re-localization was not an obstacle to investing in China. Production in China for Chinese markets created great price advantages for industry. Logistics and transport and the supply chain quickly found their way. China provided a great advantage to Western companies because of its geographical location and the ease of distribution of products and goods from there to the rest of the world, especially Asia, the Middle East and Australasia. The economic, political and social complexity of the newly globalized world started to increase, mainly thanks to China's growth and rapidly rising level of technological innovation. The 'Made in China' branding of products of low quality and low selling prices in Europe, the United States, Japan and other developed countries became ever more present. Today, however, products that are 'Made in China' tend to be qualitatively competitive in the global market because of China's technological progress.

Since the fall of the Berlin Wall, China's growth has accelerated considerably. China's economic growth in the world market has opened the door for its political ambitions. Political ambitions require military power, and China has accelerated the modernization of its military forces. Cooperation with countries on the Western sanctions list has given China more power to assert its ambitions in the global world, both economically and militarily.

By 2022, China was acting as a world power—politically, militarily and economically—with claims to determine the new frontiers. It invests in developing countries in the long term, especially in Africa, with financing in infrastructure projects as well as in food production, healthcare and energy.

15.1.2 Expansion in Western Europe: Growing Complexity through Geopolitics and Macroeconomics

The former Eastern bloc countries[1] have, for the most part, suffered quite severely in economic terms, experiencing poverty and, in some cases, even famine. The Soviet

[1] Eastern bloc countries: Soviet Union (Union of Soviet Socialist Republics), the People's Republic of Poland, the German Democratic Republic (GDR), the Czechoslovak Socialist Republic (ČSSR),

Union tried to open the doors to foreign aid and investment in the 1980s but without success. Two years after the Berlin Wall was torn down and East and West Germany started the reunification process in November 1989, the Soviet Union collapsed thanks to former Soviet leader Gorbachev, who carried out democratization and economic restructuring, thus ending the Eastern bloc, uniting the independent states and bringing Western aid to all independent states. Western European policy is directly related to the disintegration of the Eastern European Economic Community. Since 'the fall of the Wall', Western European states have been rethinking their geopolitical strategy. The EU states have been striving to clarify their geopolitical role after the failure of the Soviet superpower. Western economic and financial models were introduced into the Eastern bloc countries, leading to a systemic change that affected the structure of global economic and political alliances.

The greater the number of Eastern bloc countries that join the West, the more complex the global system structure becomes. In 2004, eight former communist states[2] joined the EU, followed 3 years later by another two Eastern European countries and another in 2013. The additional EU accession candidates from Eastern bloc countries,[3] among others, will strongly influence the geopolitical complexity. The new EU member states have guaranteed their own freedom and security both politically and militarily by joining NATO. Between its foundation in 1949 and the end of the Cold War in 1989–1991, NATO grew considerably, and this was strengthened by European reunification in 1991–2001. Since the 9/11 terrorist attacks in New York, NATO's strategic importance has become evident in crisis countries in the global world. After the fall of the Berlin Wall and the collapse of the Warsaw Pact, NATO found itself operating in a more complex international environment. One very important strategy was and is to defend the values of Western countries led by the United States outside the European border. From NATO's point of view, Russia is still a threat to the West even without the Warsaw Pact. From this writer's point of view, although the imperialist power of the Soviet Union is no longer there, the political leadership of Russia still operates militarily in the global world just as NATO does, particularly in conflict regions. Militarily, NATO and Russia did not reduce their operations after 1989, but rather, they found a new direction after the Cold War. The military factor is still of paramount interest and has made the global systemic structure more complex. The future outcome of ongoing crises remains unclear, especially considering proxy wars (particularly in the Middle East and Africa) and, now, the Ukraine War. These have changed geopolitical structures including demographics, thus making the world even more complex.

Over the last four decades, Western European countries have stayed out of military conflicts. However, they stand as partners in the strategic goals of the

the Hungarian People's Republic, the People's Republic of Bulgaria and the People's Republic or Socialist Republic of Romania (SRR), Albania and Yugoslavia

[2]Estonia, Latvia, Lithuania, Slovakia, Slovenia, Czech Republic, Hungary, Poland (2004)/Bulgaria, Romania (2007)/Croatia 2013

[3]Albania, Moldova, Montenegro, North Macedonia, Serbia, Bosnia and Herzegovina, Kosovo, Georgia and Ukraine

United States of establishing peace and justice in the world, according to its own definition (see Afghanistan), especially to protect its allies outside its borders. Military operations cause demographic changes that bring political, economic and financial complexity. These complex structures have weakened the global position of the EU, which has been experiencing ongoing difficulties in speaking with one voice on the world stage. An example of this is the inability of EU states to reach agreement on the matter of Syrian refugees in 2015 and, more recently, the lack of unity among the EU on the issue of sanctions against Russia. The EU decision-making system is based on the unanimity principle, with the consent of all 27 EU member states being required for each decision. This decision-making system shows its limitations in today's complex geopolitical system.

Democratic majority decision-making would give the EU more stability in today's complex world system. When the bloc established relations with Russia after the fall of the Soviet Union, this relationship was, from today's perspective, apparently not in the interest of all partners equally. Some EU countries, including Germany, intensified economic relations with Russia, in areas ranging from technology transfer to manufacturing. EU states have imported raw materials, including oil and gas, from Russia. From a geopolitical perspective, the Black Swan has already appeared. The Russian leadership has, in turn, pursued its geopolitical goals through economic relations with the EU. The West, it appears, exercised a great deal of trust and not only desired fair economic relations but genuinely believed that Russia shared this enthusiasm for fairness. One now wonders what Russia's true motives were in becoming part of the G7[4] back in 1998, although at the time, the EU either did not recognize or at least greatly underestimated the risks involved in economic relations with Russia, especially in energy dependence. Germany relied on cheap gas through the Nord Stream pipeline for industrialized countries and continued to implement strategies to build the Nord Stream 2 pipeline.

In this writer's opinion, the West failed for decades to recognize the dangers of energy dependence, even though Russia seemed to aspire to its former superpower position in the world and continued and even intensified its military operations inside and outside its borders after the fall of the Berlin Wall. The complexity of the global system structure depends on the interplay of economic situations, political systems and military operations of the respective states. In the last few decades, Europe has grown politically and economically, but its military strength has largely been interconnected with NATO. EU unity is a thorn in Russia's side, and Russia has shown the West through its military operations that it is not satisfied with its position in today's global system. The fact is that Russian aggression outside the EU has not, so far, significantly affected Western borders politically or economically. The EU has, after the annexation of Crimea in March 2014, reconsidered its economic relations with Moscow, but has not abandoned its dependence on Russian gas

[4]The population of the G7 countries accounts for about 10% of the world's population and generates about 45% of the world's gross national income.

supplies. The complexity of interstate relations continues to increase, and more and more Black Swans start to appear.

On 24 February 2022, Russia attacked Ukraine, claiming that the attack was due to Russia's need, in its security interest, to protect, demilitarize and de-nazify Ukraine. The West responded with sanctions. The burning question that now remains is, what effect will the sanctions have? In a complex system, this constitutes negative feedback to Russia, namely, that the behaviour of the system is changing, with unclear outcomes. From Ukraine's point of view, Western solidarity is crumbling with weak sanctions and lack of decision on arms delivery. Arms supply can have a positive or negative effect on Western states. One of the EU's goals is to prevent the Russians from encroaching on Western borders. The geographical position of Ukraine holds strategic importance for EU enlargement to the East. On the other hand, the EU and the West have avoided getting directly involved in the war, from a not entirely unrealistic fear that such involvement could also have severe negative repercussions.

Moreover, the Russian attack on Ukraine has had a major impact on demographic changes. By the beginning of September 2022, according to estimates by the UN Refugee Agency (UNHCR), around 12.3 million Ukrainians had fled and crossed the border into neighbouring countries because of the war and attacks by the Russian military. The number of war refugees per day was, in the early days, in the six-digit range and peaked at the beginning of March at up to 200,000 people per day. In addition to internally displaced persons and refugees from Ukraine, civilians have also become victims of the war. According to UN figures, at least 13,917 civilians had been killed or injured by the beginning of May 2022. As of September 2022, forced emigration in Ukraine was still ongoing. Western sanctions have not yet had any major impact on Russia, but Europe itself and, indeed, the rest of the world are feeling the negative effects through inflation and rapidly rising energy prices. With its oil and gas monopoly, Russia has set the West on its heels in terms of energy supply. At the same time, we see food spoiling because of the blockade of grain supplies from Ukraine. We are reminded once again that complexity increases with the number of disciplines involved, such as energy needs, economic action, finance, arms alliances and food transport, not to mention the diversity and characteristics of those disciplines. Globalization has led us to neglect local resources such as agriculture and to instead become dependent on non-local production thanks to macroeconomic and geopolitical constraints. An example of this complexity is the bread shortage in Lebanon due to the Ukraine crisis, with local agriculture having been abandoned in favour of cheap grain imports.

The changes in the geopolitical situation were hardly peaceful after the fall of the Berlin Wall and, later, after 11 September 2001. Europe was at the centre of these changes. As described above, the EU was positioning itself to assume geopolitical power after the collapse of the Soviet Union, but the United States has shown less interest in sharing this power with the EU in the global world. The United States prefers to gain more allies through NATO so that it can increase its military powerbase. Examples of the less-than-peaceful, post-9/11 changes are the failed invasions of Iraq and Afghanistan, the support of proxy wars in the Middle East and the peace blockade between Israelis and Palestinians, when the American embassy was moved from Tel Aviv to Jerusalem. All the strategic decisions of the United States have been purely in its own interests, and the EU will merely play the role of catalyst or supporter function within the geopolitical system. Real EU sovereignty is non-existent within the geopolitical system because of the strategic objectives of the United States.

After the Russian invasion of Ukraine, the Russian leadership gave the United States another reason for wanting to prevent European unity. The fact is that Ukraine alone cannot decide the end of the war. It is becoming increasingly clear that the Ukrainian leadership wants weapons, not just to defend their country but to defeat Russia. The justification for such a claim cannot be easily discerned, and it would largely depend on how great a threat Russia really presents. This time, America is not fighting terrorists or so-called weapons of mass destruction in Iraq to protect its values and its people. Rather, the United States is fighting Russia over Ukraine and supporting a war in the middle of Europe with billions of dollars' worth of weapons. In all likelihood, the European states are going along with that purely because they are seeking protection against Russia. Ultimately, this is a question that cannot be answered without very considerable input from the rest of Europe.

The Unites States is no longer a protective power as we knew it to be in the past and, today, is increasingly perceived by many commentators as using the global community to further its own geopolitical and macroeconomic interests. The Ukraine war can only be ended through EU negotiations if the United States and Ukraine desire this. The sooner it happens, the better, because every minute that the war drags on costs more lives and destroys more infrastructure. That alone should be the goal of the United States, Europe and the global community. Western democracy will not be defended in the global world, neither in Ukraine nor in the Middle East, and certainly not under the banner of solidarity with the United States. Sanctions are not appropriate measures for complex situations; they simply shift geopolitical and macroeconomic strategies from one point of the world to the other. Not to foresee that sanctions on Russia would lead to energy shortages in Europe can only be described as politically naïve.

Theoretically, such a complex geopolitical event should be manageable, but in reality, it begs the question as to what it is truly all about. Basically, it is about geopolitical and macroeconomic power; at the top level it is about business, not mere gifts, so eye-to-eye negotiations will be necessary. The current problem is that the Russians are not negotiating with the EU at eye level, and for this reason the United States should create an interest in peace instead of mobilizing the world community militarily. The Americans have cleared the way to give Ukraine weapons and payment for reconstruction, and the Western states are following this strategy. This writer witnessed how the Americans, the West and the Eastern bloc states propped up the Gulf War in the 1980s with arms deals. This is a geopolitical and macroeconomic strategy of the West, especially the United States, to use money to determine what happens in Iraq, Syria, Afghanistan and, now, Ukraine. Otherwise, one is forced to the following conclusion: if Ukraine needs arms, then it should be able to buy everything it needs and can afford on the global market, from Western suppliers including the United States, UK, France and Germany. Such a transaction would be purely business and would not make any country a war party. Providing Ukraine with free weapons simply makes the provider a party to war. Ultimately, any strengthening of the arms industry is far from being in the interests of humanity. In the current Ukraine situation, more people will die from the supplying of heavy weapons. Ukraine will suffer more casualties, and the destruction will not come to an end in the foreseeable future. We only need to look at the destruction wrought on Iraq, Syria and other countries by war and heavy weapons, regardless of who supplied them to the warring parties. Even if it remains undisputed that Russian leadership is the initial aggressor in Ukraine, it remains a fact that arms deliveries prolong the war and, with it, the suffering and death in that country.

The geographic situation of Ukraine is probably a good example of how the great powers want to implement their geopolitical strategies. From the point of view of macroeconomics, Russia is, among other things, a supplier of raw materials for 500 million Europeans, which influences the economic position of the United States in the global market, especially in recent times with the growing crises with China. The burning question now is whether the EU can ever aspire to an important geopolitical role alongside the United States. It is not only the United States and Russia that are preventing the unity of the EU. The EU should prepare for a new geopolitical power to emerge when China, India and Russia form a community of interests, and at the macroeconomic level, when those BRICS members agree on a common monetary currency against the euro and dollar, then many Black Swans will surely appear.

In Europe, the ongoing problems show the increasing complexity of the global system structure due to, among others, the COVID-19 epidemic, climate change, the war in Ukraine, floods, crop failures, famine and a steadily heating earth's atmosphere. At present, in Europe, we are experiencing the effects of the embargo on Russian oil and gas, including higher energy costs and rising food costs. These are factors that, among others, greatly weaken the EU economically, financially and in terms of its geopolitical role. The question of resilience becomes clear and obvious: who, if anyone, will get through such crises with minimal risk and reverberations? Have governments prepared for such events, and if so, how?

15.2 Globalization

The whole globalization process is closely connected to geopolitics, demographics, technology, macroeconomics, energy and our physical environment. The last of those—in other words, nature—is a major limiting factor in all human activities, even though this fact is often ignored or belittled by today's neo-classical economists. It also creates the potential for conflict, in terms of who owns—or gets to control—the resources that nature provides. Control of natural resources is sometimes exercised—freely in some places—through political give and take, but all too often it is done through the exercise of power and coercion, even resulting in armed conflict. Although our purpose here is not to delve too deeply into the polemics of ownership of natural resources, it is important to bear in mind the link between geography and politics and the political concerns with gaining and losing ownership of resources. In this writer's opinion, access to and control of natural resources is a critical and contentious issue that needs to be thoroughly explored if we are to make the world more resilient.

In the Middle East, oil and gas are the most important natural resources, with major implications for global dynamic system change. The United States, China and Russia exercise control over those resources in different ways and using different strategies. Throughout most of human history, ownership of natural resources was largely ignored. After WWII, the emerging superpowers, namely, the United States and USSR, were developing strategies based on ownership and military control. The future outcome, however, is extremely uncertain, as we have seen from the collapse of the Soviet Union and, more recently, the experiences of the United States in Iraq and Afghanistan and the conflicts in Ukraine, the Middle East, Africa and other parts of the world. The recent emergence of China as a new economic and military superpower makes things even more complex. The question of how a macroeconomic system will likely react to the possession and control of natural resources is perhaps best explained as follows.

There are different ideas and approaches as to how natural resources can be best exploited to serve national and economic interests. Firstly, economic entities work very closely with governments and, through strong lobbying, attempt to influence the strategy of political leaders. Secondly, industry responds to the questions of how natural resources can be used effectively through innovative technologies, and the notion of energy production and management often comes up. What, in fact, does energy management mean in the real world? What types of energy are being used, and through what methods is this energy managed? Does the future of business and finance depend on the availability of energy and its management?

Energy is the core element that links macroeconomics and nature. All types of energy are generated, converted and managed by industry, an activity that enjoys broad political approval and support. Macroeconomics is the winner, and nature becomes the loser, because that resource, which in the case of fossil fuels probably took millions of years to form, is used up within the blink of an eye. This puts the global system in a very precarious position. While macroeconomics is mostly represented by the worlds of politics, economics and industry, who are the real representatives of nature? True defence of our natural environment requires more than well-intentioned protestors and activists who fight with all their heart on various levels. It needs real access to and influence over decision-making at a very high level. At the present time, this critical issue remains mostly tucked away in closed drawers. This creates a very serious imbalance in the global system.

15.3 Economy and Commerce

The fourth industrial revolution is already underway. Although opinions differ on whether it is a true industrial revolution or more of an evolutionary process, what is clear is that what is happening today has never happened before and certainly not at this speed. The first industrial revolution opened the doors to world trade. Industrial areas emerged mainly in Western Europe and, later, in the United States. This built up the rest of the world in small steps and at a slow pace, which was of course fast enough at the time. After the First World War, industrialization slowed down while financial markets and services found their place. The trend was towards money lending, with debt and interest accumulating, and debt deflation due to a reduction in the money supply in the United States in the late 1920s led to the Great Depression of the 1930s. Global industrialization spread after the Second World War. The geographical division was clear, with industrialization and expansion taking place mainly in the Northern and Western Hemisphere, notably Western Europe and North America. Of course, some countries in the South and East also had their share, especially Japan and Australia. The rest of the world, meanwhile, was still waiting for industrialization. The production of goods and direction of world trade were determined by the industrialized economies.

World trade has a rather clearly defined structure. Industrialized countries export finished goods to developing countries and import raw materials from those countries. It is important to note that early on, while the exchange of goods among industrialized countries was very high, it remained low between industrialized and developing countries. This changed in time thanks to a major increase in the prices of oil and gas, two commodities whose distribution became increasingly regulated by the developing countries that produced them, thereby prompting the oil crisis of the early 1970s. Developed countries wanted to export more of their products, but limited and expensive oil and gas supplies presented a big challenge for them. Meanwhile, developing countries lacked the means to increase imports and exports, although they were increasingly important partners for world trade.

Eventually, developed economies became dependent on the OPEC states, who regulated energy prices. This led Western countries to increase their exports to compensate for the higher energy costs, while some OPEC members were heavily dependent on crude oil as an export product. This affected not only global trade but also political positions and bargaining power.

The big change came about through the multinational corporations who, through their expansion of international trade, completely changed the structures of world trade. These companies trade in agricultural products and invest in mining, and they handle all stages of the production of goods from raw harvesting to the finished products on shelves. This structural change became evident in the relocation to, and localization of production facilities in, developing countries.

All these changes have heavily influenced both national economies and international trade. Despite the internationalization of markets, the EU regulates and secures its own domestic markets through, for example, subsidies and financial investments, thus safeguarding the agricultural market and protecting farmers' incomes. The structure of world trade today is constantly changing and becoming more complex. Industrial regions are changing because of globalization, while alternative energy sources are altering the energy supply chain, which is particularly influenced by multinational companies. Foreign trade is volatile and unstable, and this has affected the structure of exports of food, fuel, raw materials, chemicals, processed and finished goods, vehicles, machinery, electrical products and electronics, to name but a few. These changes have had a strong impact on financial markets through government revenues and spending, which is changing the structure of the global system.

15.4 Industry

15.4.1 Information and Communication Technology (ICT)

Computer science developed after World War II with the commissioning of ENIAC[5] computing machines. The first ENIAC digital computer weighed about 50 tons and was financed by the US military in the 1940s. The new system was developed for research and the military, as well as for large companies, for such varied purposes as meteorological forecasting, atomic energy calculations, thermal ignition and other scientific purposes. Military research does not necessarily aim to serve the peace and development of humanity or prosperity of the population, a case in point being the Manhattan Project, which is mentioned here purely in connection with ICT development. Over time, powerful computers were needed but without additional cost, and their physical size had to be reduced. UNIVAC I,[6] the first commercial computer that worked both numerically and alphabetically, was produced in the United States in 1951, followed by the Commodore personal computer in the 1970s, the Dell Turbo PC in the 1980s and, later, a whole range of IBM-compatible computers.

A major driver of computer technology was Siemens and its subsidiaries, from personal computers—Siemens Nixdorf and Fujitsu Siemens PCs—to specialized computers that would serve medical, military and educational needs and various server technologies from the 1950s to the 1990s. The personal computer became increasingly important and enabled professionals to freely program their thoughts, ideas and information. In addition, special applications were developed, which opened new business areas and changed the financial markets. Today, the development of ICT is vast and there is a great deal of research and development, with enormous significance for today's global world. This has led to the fourth industrial revolution, 'Industry 4.0', which aims to respond to the rapidly changing technological and industrial processes and social patterns of the twenty-first century. This leads us back to increased networking and intelligent automation and machine

[5]ENIAC = Electronic Numeric Integrator And Computer

[6]UNIVAC I = Universal Automatic Computer I

learning. The processes are not linear and complex, so it is useful to clarify them through complex systems theories.

ICT has changed industry dramatically over the last few decades. In the beginning, it was just a matter of automating plants, while processes were still overseen by human intelligence. Informatization was a priority for large companies like Siemens, for increasing their technologies and competitiveness. The company used its own resources to further develop informatization and intelligently control its automated products and services through its own programs. Industrial and production machinery, the control and monitoring of conventional power plants and the control systems of nuclear of power plants, among other technological functions, all benefited. Further steps included making processes more intelligent, thus transforming human intelligence into machine intelligence. Simultaneously, AEG and IBM developed their own programs. The computerization of production machines, such as the use of robots with intelligent processes, has increased the amount of data to be processed and thus created new challenges for ICT developers.

From the 1990s to today, ICT system structures have been changing rapidly as the original use has gradually transformed into global use; industry, the military and the other sectors mentioned earlier are, of course, no longer the only users of ICT. Service providers, retail businesses, government bodies, NGOs and individuals have also joined in. Indeed, it is doubtful whether there is any organization, large or small, in the developed and developing world that can do without ICT, with very few exceptions. The amount of data is no longer as manageable as it was in the early days, so modern technology must address limitations and gaps by expanding storage capacity, on the one hand, and by increasing the speed of data processing, which requires faster and faster processors, on the other.

The improvement and development of ICT is not limited to the optimization of processes, and it also focuses on the processing of large amounts of variable data and their combinations, a feature of the age of artificial intelligence and cloud systems for data storage. In the era of the fourth industrial revolution, the focus is on communication from people to people, machine to machine and combinations of both. At the same time, greater security is needed to minimize the risks in modern ICT development, increase the performance and protect the safety of people and machines. In addition to the networking of people via social media, machines are also being networked via the Internet of Things (IoT). The IoT requires intelligent sensor technology that diagnoses and communicates the actual physical and functional state and environment of machines down to the smallest detail. To cope with the amount of variable data and its combinations, machine learning, also known as artificial intelligence (AI), is in demand as a possible solution approach. These demands are not merely limited to hardware development and performance improvement, and the associated software is also more in the focus of developers and enables global participation in the use of technology in all areas of life. For example, the focus on app development is stronger than on any other software, since the ease of use and accessibility of apps allows people to connect to global events and take advantage of potential solutions and benefits. This challenges the broader technological requirements, thereby affecting more and more areas of the global system, as commented on and highlighted by critics.

15.4.2 Mobility and Logistics

Another important area is the creation of resilient transportation and logistics technology for ensuring an ongoing supply chain for goods and services and, of course, the movement of people. Given the current high level of toxic emissions, the ultimate financial cost in terms of GDP and the enormous pressures on the physical infrastructure itself due to overcrowding, it is evident that the current transportation systems and technology are utterly inadequate. A complete overhaul is in order with a shift to new and innovative technology, or even to fewer new systems that are simpler but more resilient. This raises questions around system resilience, such as why we need one-day delivery services from Amazon. Why is logistics among the least-paid professions? Why do we need 24/7 shopping? Why do some supermarkets operate with a three-day limited supply?

Some examples of technological solutions from this author's own experience at Siemens include the Ave high-speed train in Spain (630 Km between two cities in only 2.5 h, at speeds of up to 404 kph) and the Maglev (magnetic levitation) frictionless train in China (known as the Transrapid, capable of 430 kph). In Bangkok, the Skytrain installed by Siemens as a turnkey solution helps massively in relieving traffic on the congestion-plagued streets and has contributed considerably to improving the quality of the city's air. In contrast to cars, the Skytrain—operating 12 meters above street level—is unaffected by traffic jams. In Lille, France, the world's first driverless subway system, also built by Siemens, began operating in 1983. It makes us wonder why it is so important to be driverless, given that a normal metro with a driver would have the same effect, although it might cost more. However, over one million people live in the Lille-Roubaix-Tourcoing regional area, making modern public transportation especially important. Across the UK, London's bus system is among the largest in the world. Around 8000 buses transport roughly six million passengers around the city every workday. Siemens' information systems ensure that each bus can be located, at any given moment, with one-meter accuracy via GPS, thus increasing punctuality. The question has been asked, however: what happens when it gets hacked one day? Or if the GPS fails, possibly permanently after a Kessler event in low earth orbit? Would it be more resilient not to rely on those highly vulnerable hyper-technical systems, and build in some redundancy (more buses and drivers), while only relying on good old-fashioned radio? However, also in London, since February 2003, vehicles from outside entering a 20-square-kilometre zone in the centre of the city are charged a toll. This toll has successfully reduced the volume of traffic in the inner urban areas, and particle emissions have been cut by some 15%. The toll zone was further expanded in February 2007, with the help of Siemens technology.

Across the Atlantic, the New York subway system operates seven days a week around the clock and is used by 6.4 million passengers each day. Without question, the modernization of such a public transportation system is needed. The greatest challenge here, bearing in mind the already-established urban structures and layout, is to improve the current systems and processes and modernize the existing buildings and infrastructures without causing any significant disruption to current operations. An added problem is the danger of flooding, especially given that sea levels are expected to rise significantly by the end of this century, and if the system is not made watertight, the city could lose its whole subway system.

Sustainable, clean, safe, environmentally friendly technology will become an indispensable part of the future. Here, as in other areas, resilience will have to be a built-in feature if we are to ensure that this technology does not fail, with potentially catastrophic results.

15.4.3 Technology and Macroeconomics: The Siemens Case

The process of globalization has been a non-linear one, which greatly depends on the kind and extent of changes in the structure of the global system, and for this reason it is subject to complexity theory. We will focus on the last three decades after the end of the Soviet era in and around 1990. Clearly, one cannot reasonably judge the dynamics of a 500-year-old system by looking at the last 30 years. Hopefully, the Siemens case can help in providing an overview of today's changes, which are not unconnected with the past. For Europe, the turning point was the so-called fall of the Wall. In that time, although the major economic players were in principle eager to invest in new economies and projects, many companies remained extremely cautious and concentrated on long-term (3–5 years) plans—as opposed to short-term (quick-returns opportunities)—to ensure economic sustainability, an important element in increasing their resilience.

In 2011, former Siemens CEO Heinrich von Pierer described it thus [translated from German]: 'Market share in exchange for technology ... China is the rising power and the most powerful economy of the four Asian Tigers of South Korea, Taiwan, Singapore, and Hong Kong. The 21st century, young as it may be, will be a Pacific-Asian century. The old European and Anglo-Saxon powers will have to compete to keep up with the young emerging nations' (von Pierer, 2011).

In the wake of the revolutionary political changes of the 1989–1992 period, it can be safely said that the more substantial changes that followed were of a relatively fast evolutionary nature. These changes, associated with the onset of globalization, were more in the nature of new economic, commercial and financial structures and processes, with more focus by companies on growth, stable cash flow and sustainable value creation for both shareholders and stakeholders over the long term. Such changes could make or break commercial organizations. There were countless opportunities for large companies, provided they could adapt to the new conditions and absorb the changes. However, if they were unprepared, failed to adapt and were sidelined, numerous dangers loomed. To survive in this new world, companies had to make themselves resilient. The most important factor in organizational resilience is the adaptation of the company's structure to new globalization processes, an example of which was the close attention paid to trends in the privatization of state assets[7] during the transition from communism to a market economy in Central and Eastern Europe. Rapid market expansion had created a need for clear, well-defined policies, a necessary part of globalization. BRICS countries and other developing-world economies, with their significantly lower manpower costs, are forcing major Western companies to devise new ways and approaches. Such complex strategic changes have a fundamental impact on the structure of corporate governance and, consequently, on management systems.

15.4.4 Strategic Change

Siemens, as a case in point, did its homework well during the whole period of transformation. I have witnessed first-hand the globalization process and the change in strategy at Siemens for over 25 years. The intention here is to give the reader the benefit of my personal experience of how a company like Siemens has mastered such monumental change and become a resilient company. Indeed, I can safely say that the performance of the company after Fukushima was not only as good as before, but indeed much better.

By 1989, Siemens already had eight different lines of business, effectively making it too large and cumbersome to be managed efficiently, and some drastic reforms were very much in order.[8] The fall of communism and the profound changes that started taking place all over Europe in that period were, we can say, the catalyst that prompted the beginning of that period of change, which would happen over the following three decades, culminating in Vision 2020.[9]

The years 1989 to 2006 saw Siemens facing unprecedented challenges, including dramatic reforms of the corporate organization, the launch of the Ten-Point Program and the compliance crisis. The year 1989 itself was, of course, a year of profound changes, not just for Germany and the world, but for Siemens as well. Although revenues had grown from just under 13 billion euro in 1969 to over 50 billion, there had been very little structural change within the organization during those two decades.

It was now clear that a whole new organizational structure was needed, one that would be much more in line with the company's current operating environment. Major changes included the shift from mechanical devices to electronics and micro-electronics, the growth of international business, a greatly expanded global customer base and ever-increasing competition. A more effective administrative structure was the first step. The eight existing business units were rearranged into 15 new, leaner units, two operating groups with their own legal form and two independent

[7] Buyouts are followed by significant increases in new product development and other aspects of corporate entrepreneurship.

[8] https://new.siemens.com/global/en/company/about/history/company/1989-2006.html

[9] https://press.siemens.com/global/en/pressrelease/siemens-vision-2020

divisions. The senior management team, which up to then had been comprised of more than 30 people, was cut by a third to make it much leaner and more streamlined. That reorganization remained effective until 2006, during which time the groundwork for future changes in management and operations was mostly laid.

Siemens had invested high hopes in computer technology in the late 1980s, and in 1990 it acquired Nixdorf Computer AG, which became Siemens Nixdorf Information Systems (SNI) AG, a wholly owned subsidiary, in 1992. Although SNI became the most successful European computer manufacturer in terms of sales, it failed to live up to expectations as a growth driver and was eventually dissolved as an independent company and fully integrated into Siemens AG. Thanks to a range of factors that led to the business becoming less predictable, including a volatile business environment, short product cycles and dramatic price drops, the personal computer business was transferred to a joint venture with Fujitsu.

15.4.5 Economic Crises and Competitive Advantage

All in all, the 1990s proved to be an economically challenging decade. The economic crisis in Southeast Asia, delivery delays in rail transport equipment, the repercussions from the misjudgement of the mobile phone market and the collapse of the semiconductor market all affected the price of Siemens stock, which lagged significantly behind the DAX exchange. The situation made extensive reform unavoidable.

The Ten-Point Program announced by CEO Heinrich von Pierer in 1998 represented an important turning point in Siemens's history. Driven by the motto, 'Buy, cooperate, sell or close', it led to drastic changes within the company. In effect, the company's portfolio retained only those activities where Siemens was first or second in the global market. The expanded corporate program made added value the benchmark measure of performance, and the company's accounting system was changed to the US GAAP[10] standard, mainly in preparation for listing on the New York Stock Exchange, one of the key goals of the program. However, the foray into the United States turned out to be not worth the expense and effort involved, since investors were doing the bulk of their trading in Germany and through online trading platforms, and ultimately, there was hardly any effect on the company's global business. Overall, the Ten-Point Program turned out to be hugely successful. The price of Siemens stock soared. Revenues and profits improved substantially, and an overall positive economic value added (EVA) was achieved 1 year ahead of schedule.

[10] US Generally Accepted Accounting Principles

15.4.6 Megatrends of the Day

From 2005 on, Siemens focused primarily on the three major sectors of energy, plus infrastructure and healthcare, as being the most profitable. When Klaus Kleinfeld took over as CEO, he decided to focus the company's attention on the megatrends of the day: urbanization, population growth and demographic changes. These trends were reflected in the company's core business areas—energy and the environment, automation and infrastructure, and healthcare—and in its acquisitions during that time. Peter Loescher maintained this focus on megatrends when he restructured the company into the sectors of industry, energy and healthcare in 2007 and, later, infrastructure and cities.

15.4.7 Surviving Crises

In the mid–late 2000s, Siemens entered one of the most dangerous phases in its entire history: the compliance crisis. When a combination of lack of transparency, lack of clarity regarding responsibility, and the manipulation of both suppliers and customers, not to mention downright criminal acts in some cases, all came to light in 2006, the company was thrust into a major public scandal that could endanger its very existence. Fast action was required, and the company did not hesitate in taking it. As well as the replacement of some top managers, compliance became a major priority. Both the CEO and the chairman of the Supervisory Board pushed for a thorough and deep-reaching investigation, with strong and immediate cooperation with the authorities—which ultimately had the effect of keeping the penalties imposed within controllable limits. A code of conduct that would be in full compliance with the law was established, which was declared a benchmark for business in 2011.

By 2007, after 17 eventful, turbulent years—a period characterized not just by challenges and crises but also by the successful management of these obstacles—Siemens was able to look back with pride at having survived and indeed thrived, with the immense benefit of lessons learned. There were obviously a few regrets too, but the company had, in the main, managed to survive a series of potentially devastating events both internally and externally and to vanquish the obstacles and threats it had faced, emerging from the crisis stronger and more resilient.

15.4.8 Environment Portfolio

In 2008, the company presented its environment portfolio. This included products, systems, solutions and services for the purpose of using renewable energy, enhancing energy efficiency and environmental protection through technology. President and CEO Peter Loescher saw this as a gigantic opportunity for a company that was already a leading green infrastructure giant, whose experience, technical expertise and financial soundness made it ideal for advancing this Green Revolution. His vision proved correct, and by 2014, revenues had reached 29.9 billion euros, and CO_2 reduction was at 317 million tons. Two years later, this had risen to 36 billion euros and 521 million tons, respectively. This course of sustainable corporate management has been maintained consistently and integrated into two more corporate strategy programs: Fit42010 and Vision 2020. This commitment to the environment has proved beneficial in business terms also, and as President and CEO Joe Kaeser observed in 2015, 'Cutting our CO_2 emissions is not only an expression of our sense of responsibility; it is also good business'.[11]

The 2005 change in Siemens's focus to the megatrends of urbanization, and to demographic and climate change, was incorporated into its organizational structure three years later. The 10 groups were replaced by three sectors—industry, energy and healthcare—and 15 divisions, and the regions were combined into clusters. There were also two cross-sector business lines, Siemens IT Solutions and Services, and Financial Services, and a further sector—infrastructure and cities—was added in 2011. The new structure, however, fell short of expectations, and in late 2014, the sectors and clusters were broken up. The number of divisions was reduced from 16 to 10, and a healthcare business unit was established.

15.4.9 Organizational Change

In July 2013, a new long-term plan for the company was launched. Vision 2020 incorporated a major shift in focus to the growth fields of electrification, automation and digitalization. The former sector structure would go and, as mentioned above, the number of divisions would be reduced from 16 to 10, plus healthcare. It was projected that by 2020, among other benefits, costs would be reduced by a billion euros, underperforming businesses would be revived, and customer satisfaction would improve significantly. Capital efficiency was anticipated to be 15–20%, and employee participation in the company's success was to be increased by at least 50%. Underlying these measures was an 'ownership culture' designed to incentivize each employee to do his best, thus contributing to Siemens' long-term success. In effect, goals were being set that could serve as both a compass and a benchmark on the way to 2020.

One of the Vision 2020 objectives was for Siemens to grow in attractive markets with a solid-looking future. The company acquired Rolls-Royce's aero-derivative gas turbines and compressors business for almost a billion euro in 2014, thus strengthening its position in the growing oil-and-gas industry and distributed power generation. In 2015, the world's leading manufacturer of compressors, steam and gas turbines and engines, US Company Dresser-Rand, was acquired for almost eight billion dollars. These two additions to Siemens's own portfolio reinforced the company's ability to provide complete solutions and services all along the value chain in energy. The year 2016 was one of Siemens's strongest

[11] https://press.siemens.com/global/en/pressrelease/siemens-vision-2020

fiscal years—new orders, sales revenues and profits were up substantially, with further gains the following year.

15.4.10 Value Creation

The goals of Vision 2020 had already been almost fully achieved by 2017, and CEO Joe Kaeser at that point initiated the next stage in the organization's transformation, Vision 2020+. This is expected to bring about long-term value creation and stronger profitability, within a more streamlined corporate structure. The Vision 2020+ strategy is designed to give Siemens' individual business branches significantly more entrepreneurial freedom while retaining the strong Siemens brand. The year 2018 saw an optimized corporate structure, comprising three operating companies and three strategic companies, incorporating the former divisions and business units. Among those, Gas and Power covers the entire energy business, Smart Infrastructures handles all of Siemens' infrastructure solutions, and Digital Industries handles industrial digitalization. These new arrangements are accompanied by three strategic companies: Siemens Healthineers, Siemens Gamesa Renewable Energy and Siemens Mobility.

Joe Kaeser firmly believes that the key factor in business survival is the ability to adapt—in other words, resilience—and not size: 'It would be irresponsible to rest on our laurels now. It won't be the biggest companies that survive, but the most adaptable. That's why we'll . . . give our business considerably more entrepreneurial responsibility than before'.[12]

Today, after some further changes and realignments, Siemens AG, Siemens Energy and Siemens Healthineers are three separately managed companies forming a powerful ecosystem under one brand: three different companies focused on three different sectors but united under the Siemens banner. All three seem poised for industry leadership in terms of indicators such as market share, growth and sustainable profitability—a goal that would have been hard to reach in the old days and ways.

From this short history, we can see that by taking the right measures at the right time to cope with unexpected changes, the resilience of the company was defined.

15.4.11 Mergers and Acquisitions

Big companies normally seek to become stronger through mergers and acquisitions; in doing so, they acquire or merge with companies with the best-placed market positions. It is questionable, however, whether many acquisitions have a real effect on successful growth. Further growth is sought through the extension of solution, product and service portfolios that can ensure variety in the supply chain, market

[12] https://new.siemens.com/global/en/company/about/history/company/2007-2018.html

position and market share and even through price regulation, which can be seen as a long-term strategy for creating resilience in times of crisis and adverse events. As the BSI Guide on Organizational Resilience points out, resilience as a strategic objective is intended to help an organization not only to survive but to prosper, and its connection to strategic planning is emphasized (BSI, 2014). Conglomerates tend to have multi-business portfolios, and M&A is a part of their long-term strategy, with goals such as improving a weak technology portfolio. It is through M&A that they invest in future business portfolios and fast-growing markets and business sectors. An M&A strategy is a ticket for market (re)entry as well as for international business, which can ensure business continuity, especially when, for example, business in the domestic market is limited possibly because of customer relationships or insufficient market reputation. The competitive edge of other operators in the domestic market can be difficult to replicate, and expansion into other markets is often necessary for ensuring economic stability.

References

BSI. (2014). *Guidance on organizational resilience, in BS 65000:2014* (p. 16). © The British Standards Institution.

von Pierer, H. (2011). *Gipfel-Stürme: die Autobiographie*. Econ.

So, in a Nutshell, What is Enterprise Resilience? 16

Knowledge of complexity is an important prerequisite for building a resilient enterprise. In this book, we have gained some valuable insights into complexity and its governance, gleaned from both academic and practical knowledge and research. Coping and dealing with complexity is required at all levels: strategically, from top to bottom, and operationally, from the bottom up.

Taken together, this gives a holistic view, using the following factors, which can also be used as an index for the assessment of enterprise resilience in practice. This framework for assessing organizational resilience factors comes at a critical time in our history, when COVID-19, the Ukraine war and the energy crisis are hot topics that lie at the heart of European life. In a time of immense economic disruption, only resilient organizations will thrive—or even manage to survive—in the long term. It is hoped that this book and the tools we have created can provide guidance to business leaders on how to assess their organizations for the resilience factors listed.

The most important strategic factors are clustered into seven sub-categories: processes, organization, environment, technology, finance, resources and leadership. This can help to assess the characteristics of effective emergent strategic thinking and decision-making and clarifies further aspects of enterprise resilience. The powerful resilience factors are clustered into nine sub-categories: organization, technology, people, process, information, supply chain, operations, environment and leadership. This enables leaders to gain a better understanding of the characteristics of resilience, and it makes clearer their relationship with further aspects of enterprise resilience. The presented risk factors can be considered as important risk indicators, in nine clusters: compliance, environmental and social, financial, information technology, information and communication, operational risks, process, strategic and technological.

How these factors come about, along with their interrelationships and clusters, has been described in detail in this book.

Strategic thinking and decision-making are the main objectives of enterprise resilience, in economic, political and social terms, from both the top-down and bottom-up perspectives. At the top level—in a commercial enterprise, this

K. Dindarian, *Embracing the Black Swan*, Future of Business and Finance,
https://doi.org/10.1007/978-3-031-29344-3_16

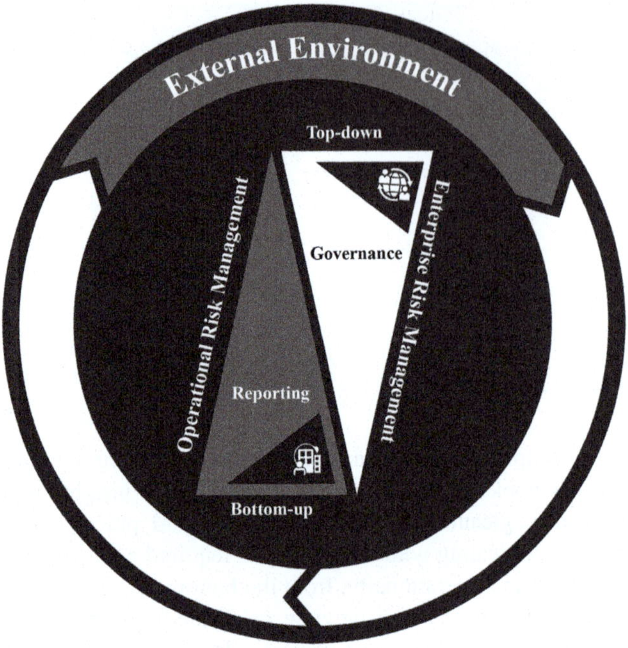

Fig. 16.1 ERM: top-down -v- bottom-up

means senior management—strategic thinking and decision-making are supported by most globally accepted ERM processes, which respond to the relevant authorities and ensure that stakeholders' expectations are met. On the other hand, from the bottom-up perspective, there are various interests to be considered, such as social environment, the general population of a country in its various demographic forms, and the commercial/economic sector. Among those in the last-mentioned interest group are operational divisions, together with a range of groups, teams and individuals. Both the top-down and bottom-up approaches must be aligned for building enterprise resilience. Figure 16.1 presents a simple illustration of that alignment.

The identification of risks at senior corporate level is an important part of ERM, along with risk mitigation. For this reason, top management must be able to influence the ERM process. Organizations must accept the consequences for every decision that is made, whatever the prevailing economic or political conditions. Because of environmental changes arising from recent crises, organizations are being forced to change from centralized to decentralized decision-making structures, which means devising new processes, procedures and ways of cooperation. The capacity for versatile responses to emergencies requires the adoption of a decentralized, team-based approach with, ideally, built-in networking abilities.

In order to succeed, an organization needs rules and practices—namely, governance, which has several communicative functions. These include the development of a comprehensive communication strategy, the provision of messages concerning the main topics of concern to the company and the management of the various incidents and events related to it. This, in turn, involves a variety of actions and procedures, including the day-to-day running of the organization, using a combination of specific information and structure-control methods. The mechanisms for acquiring and filtering such information must be designed to ensure it is comprehensive, precise and timely. Ideally, good information leads to good governance. Conversely, good governance leads to good communication, by ensuring the transparency of consequences and procedures so as to create added value for those working in the field of communication.

Enterprise resilience is about dealing with an environment that is broad and complex, which can change due to unforeseen forces and unexpected events, giving rise to uncertainty and emerging risks. Such forces and events are caused by an interplay of man and nature, working in a continual cycle of cause and effect. Geopolitics and macroeconomics are ever-changing, in the process creating a whole new order. From this constant flux, we get to witness an environment in a perennial state of transformation. This is what creates the complexity of which we speak, and which we must understand in depth if we are to make our enterprise resilient to uncertain outcomes and events that can turn out to be catastrophic in their effects.

An understanding of—and ability to cope with—complexity is essential for developing resilience. We can see this in practice within enterprises, not just business organizations but in social groups, communities, political entities and macroeconomic systems and, indeed, in nature itself.

In Part Three of this book, we have examined and clarified some important complexity factors of geopolitics and their relationship to macroeconomics. The purpose of this is to open the door to making our world more resilient by taking these important factors into account in strategic thinking and decision-making.

16.1 Demographic Change

The growing world population and demographic change are a part of human development that cannot be eliminated using populist measures. Decision-makers should be aware that the complexity of demographic change should not be underestimated, and any measures taken should be up to dealing with this complexity. On the one hand, local changes should be taken into consideration, while on the other, the impact of local changes on the other related areas should be considered, and vice versa. In African and other developing countries, local conditions have been strongly influenced by geopolitical objectives in both economic and military terms, and it is also important to mention ideological and cultural influences as further elements of local change.

The growing world population and demographic changes should not be seen as a problem, but rather as both a challenge and an opportunity. It is advisable, therefore, not to confine our thinking to silos. The real question is not so much about how to secure the Italian, Greek, Mexican and other borders against migration and demographic movement, but how to cope with local changes and deal with their impact on the whole demographic system. To achieve balance in such complex systems, it is necessary to compensate for negative impacts. Instead of costly and politically sensitive plans to secure borders, the problem might better be considered holistically and solutions found through the processes of complex systems that would make our world much more resilient.

In a world of rapidly changing demographics, whole systems will need to be re-evaluated. Key elements will include safety and security, water and food, healthcare, mobility and logistics, ITC, digitalization, education, energy (electric power generation, transmission and distribution), economic and financial solutions and rapidly developing technology. Linked to these, infrastructure for more and better living and working spaces is becoming an increasingly critical issue. Developing, expanding and protecting all of these will become a matter of resilience.

16.2 Natural Resources

There are no agreed measures for how to use natural resources, which ones to use and in what amount. This factor is a highly fragile and sensitive issue that opens the door for Black Swans. It is a matter that must certainly be addressed, but perhaps from a different mindset.

First of all, a whole rethinking of the concept of gross domestic product (GDP) is in order. In the Gulf region, oil and gas producers export their products worldwide without any measures or consequences. A majority of the workforce in those countries are foreign workers from poor countries with very low GDP, a very substantial proportion of whose earnings are repatriated, thereby increasing substantially the real amount of money in circulation in their home economies. While a large-scale reduction in the use of oil and gas would significantly affect those economies, not to mention those of the producing countries, the fact remains that the current enormous consumption of fossil fuels must be drastically curtailed. The economic situation—the real losses in GDP—of those economies will have to be borne in mind by the developed West when planning for the post-fossil-fuel world. It is interesting to note that the main Gulf economies have already started to diversify. Saudi Arabia, for example, has invested massively in alternative energy, especially solar, and it is also developing its tourism, manufacturing and agricultural sectors. Similarly, Qatar is working hard at developing tourism, especially sporting tourism. The disproportionate use of natural resources is a very important factor for the resilience of the global system, which is not measured by GPD alone. Decision-makers have the task of not only addressing this whole issue, perhaps through NGOs, but also defining and implementing new measures within the structures of the global world system.

Secondly, a rethinking of the global political position and ideological behaviour of countries is called for. Industrialized countries largely rely on poorer countries for raw materials, and different parties are left in vulnerable positions. Governments, business leaders and consumers in industrial nations worry about availability and supply of various commodities, while an ongoing concern for producers in the developing world is continuity of market demand and possibly the effects of natural disasters such as drought, typhoons or floods on supply. A greater focus on signing long-term commodity agreements would ensure continuity of supply for industry, price stability for consumers globally and more stable revenue sources for the producing countries. This would, of course, require a more unified approach and a greater spirit of cooperation globally, and much would depend on countries' political positions and ideological attitudes.

Another area that might usefully be examined more closely is the true efficacy of economic sanctions. For example, how well the current Western sanctions against Russia are working in terms of benefiting Ukraine or the Western world in general is a question that merits greater consideration. Already, there is much to suggest that those sanctions have already resulted in an imbalance in the availability and use of current energy sources.

16.3 Energy

Energy sources and supply lie at the centre of all resilience factors and will remain so. This most critical factor has never been brought to the forefront of the global value system because of various geopolitical agendas that were not always obvious or open. Energy sources and supply have a direct bearing on prosperity in industrialized countries, and measures for securing this important resilience factor will assume even more critical importance as energy demand, which has been rising exponentially since the first industrial revolution, will continue to do so as we enter the fourth.

Unavoidable changes are happening as fossil fuels approach their limits of availability. An equally serious issue is that of sustainability, as the full impacts of environmental damage and global climate change become starker each day. It is for this reason that although substantial coal reserves remain, the phase out of coal is an already-decided issue in Western industrialized countries. Alternative energy sources are being sought as a matter of urgency to replace existing ones. The big question facing mankind now is: replace with what?

We have seen the limitations that currently exist with renewable energy, and while those will be overcome in time, that may not be soon enough. Important factors coming into play in this equation include technology, funding for investment in new energy production, the ideological and political positions of various countries and trading blocs, and various political and economic interests. Although a significant amount of the energy needs of industrialized countries are still met by nuclear reactors, many Western countries have already taken the political decision to abandon nuclear energy, despite uranium reserves being far from depleted. For the future, it does seem that few options remain but to invest in alternative, renewable energy sources (such as wind and solar power or biomass gasification), which in many cases will require ideological change and political will. It may also, until certain gaps have been filled, require some imaginative thinking on the part of business and political leaders and even an increased level of patience or hardship on the part of the consumer while fossil fuels become exponentially more expensive. Developing a mentality of renewable energy use and reduced consumption is one critical task now facing us. One example of a different approach might be the development and use of hydro technology for passenger and freight transport. Current initiatives for reducing urban traffic are to be commended, although there is scope for much more to be done in this area.

16.4 Water and Food

Food and clean, fresh water are critical for all life on earth, and their availability is a matter of enormous relevance in geopolitical and macroeconomic terms. Food issues needing to be resolved include disproportionate land use for agricultural production, a diminishing agrarian labour force and rural depopulation, pollution and preparedness for natural disasters. These issues will require better logistics and distribution, more focused management, the improvement of living conditions in rural areas, the design of effective crisis response systems for dealing with natural (and even man-made) disasters, investment in technology for production, transport and storage, and more imaginative approaches to storage and land use.

Drinking water is also facing challenges, as clean potable water supplies in large cities come under increasing pressure. Investment in water distribution, cleaning and storage technology and facilities will become crucial for resilience in this regard.

16.5 The World of Work

Human migration is an inevitable feature of life on this planet, and it is a factor that will need to be addressed urgently on many levels if future crises are to be avoided. The relationship must be re-examined between different sectors, namely, industry, agriculture, fishing and mining, services and logistics. Not only will proper urban planning be critical if people are to be housed and taken care of in a dignified and healthy way, but so will employee protection legislation in the areas of health-and-safety and working conditions, new work systems and structures, and new approaches to preventative healthcare. The recent moves towards hybrid onsite-remote working and greater investment in health education and illness prevention are welcome developments in this regard.

Perhaps the greatest single problem facing us, however, is the enormous income disparity not just within countries and regions but globally. A case in point is the number of workers from South Asian countries such as Nepal and Bangladesh currently employed in the Gulf States. The controversy surrounding the recent FIFA World Cup tournament in Qatar has highlighted this income disparity, along with health-and-safety issues and the availability of support services for injured workers and their families. Despite the high net income in those economies and their high nominal GDP, wages for unskilled and semi-skilled workers remain notoriously low, and working conditions are difficult (employees working in temperatures of up to 45°C often have only 90 days' home leave every 3 years and work six- or even seven-day weeks). Health-and-safety compliance is poor, and protection for workers injured in industrial accidents and support for their families is said to be significantly lacking. These issues have been highlighted by several NGOs and various media, and they must be addressed in the short term—among many other issues—if we are to see real global economic progress. The Gulf States are not the only ones at fault in this regard by any means, but the problem in that region is exacerbated by the fact that the ratio of workers to locals is extremely high, with up to 90% of Qatar's resident population being made up of foreign employees. Employers, especially small employers (many of the worst-treated employees are domestic staff), cannot be relied upon to bring about any significant changes, and the responsibility in this regard falls upon governments.

16.6 Education

Communication systems are important for the exchange of information, but this only takes place in industrialized countries, where the means of communication are technologically advanced, and even the most traditional means of communication are in a transformational state of digitalization. Newspapers, telephony and television in developed countries are being digitized at great expense. The uneven pace of digitalization and the money being spent on it are not sufficient, however, so delays are inevitable. In many developing countries, this transition will take much longer. For education to be highly effective and on a global level, there will have to be a rethink in terms of prioritizing funding for not just education programs, but the digitalization of education to ensure that populations and workforces are trained to operate at the highest levels of modern communication.

Teacher ratio is another area that merits serious attention. Education depends heavily on the proportion of teachers in the total population, which is extremely low in many countries, especially in developing countries. The big challenge is to equalize the level of education of the total population worldwide, and substantial investment must be made for this to happen. Countries allocate inadequate budgets for education. Education is a core issue that greatly influences changes in the structure of global system dynamics.

16.7 Economics and Commerce

Economics and commerce play a multifaceted role within the realms of geopolitics and macroeconomics. There are no geopolitics without economic interests and no macroeconomics without commercial influence. Economics is a powerful lever for political leaders and decision-makers within the global system. Living standards and related quality of life will remain the most important economic index. The implementation of any innovation will always depend on economic power, industrial know-how and access to technology, to name but a few. The future of any successful economy is linked to how it can implement and integrate digitalization in any industrial area, including ICT, IoT, AI, blockchain and, now, metaverse technology. The critical areas for attention are personal security, people's EHS and digital security (including cybersecurity), along with access to important information, environment, ease of operation in everyday activities and supply chain.

16.8 Financial Markets

The area of finance is highly relevant, and it lies at the heart of enterprise resilience. In this book, we have discussed the financial considerations within the relevant areas, and it is worth reminding the reader that the complexity of the financial markets needs further and ongoing research from both the academic and practitioner points of view. There are, however, many critical areas related to enterprise resilience that are important for evaluating risk, sustainability and resilience.

- How does our current money system work (debt-based fiat money, fractional reserve banking, central banks), and who controls the money supply?
- Boom and bust cycles—what are their causes? Are they accidents, or inherent to the current financial/economic system?
- How is finance linked to the economy? Who leads, and who follows?
- How big is the financial economy compared to the real one? Is this a risk factor?
- Social impacts on the current finance system: how is the current finance system influenced by social systems?
- Can a static (i.e. non-growth) economy still be made sustainable within the current financial system?

16.9 World Politics

Taking Europe as a microcosm of the global system and its complexity, ongoing problems include a COVID-19 epidemic that has not fully gone away, the war in Ukraine, the visible effects of climate change including both flooding and drought, and the all-encompassing effects of the embargo on Russian oil and gas, namely, higher energy costs and their spin-offs, which includes rising food and transport prices. This leaves us with the burning question, who—if anyone—will get through such crises relatively unscathed? Have governments prepared for such events, and if so, how?

All the factors presented throughout this book have a causal relationship with each other. It is quite clear that the only long-term answer is to build a system for measuring the issues facing us today and that will continue to do so tomorrow, and through which we might recognize the opportunities arising from them.

Our approach to the assessment of resilience through the theoretical lens of complexity is a guideline for coping with the many facets of this complexity and creating value for all the stakeholders, be they business owners, governments or us, the public at large.

It is often said that half the battle in solving a problem is in recognizing that it exists. While this book has, hopefully, given you, dear reader, an insight into how future problems that threaten your business, organization or community might be resolved or, better still, avoided, we sincerely hope that at the very least it has given you the tools to recognize those problems before they affect you.

The manufacturer's authorised representative in the EU is Springer
Nature Customer Service Centre GmbH, Europaplatz 3, 69115 Heidelberg,
Germany. If you have any concerns regarding our products, please
contact ProductSafety@springernature.com

Printed and bound by CPI Group (UK) Ltd, Croydon, CR0 4YY
01/10/2026
02225853-0004